Bioethics

When the Challenges of Life Become Too Difficult

Gareth Jones

Bioethics

When the Challenges of Life Become Too Difficult

Gareth Jones

ATF Press
Adelaide

First published 2007

ISBN 978 1 920691 79 0

ATF Press
An imprint of the Australasian Theological Forum Ltd
P O Box 504
Hindmarsh
SA 5007
ABN 90 116 359 963
www.atfpress.com

Contents

Section 2 Beginning of Life Issues

Section 3 Coping with Life

Acknowledgements

In writing a book that attempts to cover a large amount of ground, it is inevitable that I make use of material that has appeared in other books of mine. While the material has been thoroughly integrated into this new text, some of what I have written previously will be recognisable. The major sources containing some of the material are:

Valuing People (Carlisle: Paternoster Press, 1999), parts of chapters 2, 3, 6, 8, and 12.

Manufacturing Humans (Leicester: Inter-Varsity Press, 1984), part of chapter 7.

Designers of the Future (Oxford: Monarch, 2005), part of chapter 3.

Human Cloning (Tauranga: AFFIRM Publications, 2004), part of chapter 9.

'Why should cloning and stem cells be on interest to theologians?' in *Stem Cell Research and Cloning*, edited by Gareth Jones and Mary Byrne (Adelaide: ATF Press, 2004), 73–94, part of chapter 10.

'Genetic prospects: Finding a balance between choice and acceptance', *Perspectives on Science and Christian Faith* 57/3 (2005): 202–10, part of chapter 11.

Preface

My aim in this book has been to give an overview of a range of issues that are currently under discussion within bioethics. They are the sort of issues that frequently make the headlines, sometimes helpfully and sometimes not so helpfully. They are issues from which no thoughtful person can escape, since they challenge us at a number of levels: personally, since they affect the way in which ordinary people react to difficult situations, and conceptually, since they raise fundamental questions at the interface of religion, science, and society.

Modern medicine has two sides, the one we encounter in our everyday lives and the one that belongs within the research environment. It brings immense hope, but never far removed from the hope are negative consequences of many descriptions. Quite simply, we are in new territory, and new territory always has to be explored. What is so unusual about this exploration is that the explorers are not just scientists and clinicians, but people like you and me. The extraordinary dimension of modern medicine is the manner in which it influences the lives of ordinary people in an intimate and almost immediate way. This is what sets modern medicine apart, and what bestows upon it such power to bring both hope and peril at the same time.

What is the nature of these two opposites? There is the improvement in the quality of our lives, regardless of how quality is measured. Along with this have gone greatly increased standards of living, and fundamental changes to our expectation of what life has to offer. While these are improvements to our biological and physical condition, they have consequences well beyond the biological and physical, in that they raise far-reaching theological and social queries. If humans can so profoundly affect the sort of lives we live, what room is left for God? Has the human dimension so expanded that there is little room left for a divine dimension? Has the balance between the two been so upset that any vestige of equilibrium between science and faith has been irremediably destroyed?

These predicaments confront everyone, and yet they have especial poignancy for those with a religious view of human and personal existence. For them the challenges acquire an eternal dimension, in that medical science assumes roles formerly regarded as the sole province of God. The impression is readily conveyed that God's interest in the well-being of individuals and whole communities has been supplanted by the control over human welfare now residing in the hands of an all-conquering medical elite. In its extreme manifestation one can question whether there is any need for God at all?

This is no mere theoretical discussion since not one of us is immune to the tentacles of the medical enterprise. After all, how many of us exist without taking some pill or other? And yet we probably don't think that pills have theological significance. Perhaps that is a serious underestimation of how our lives have been changed by even the most innocuous of pills. The point I am making is that a book like this is aimed at a broad readership—at everyone who takes pills from time to time! This is not an academic tome.

For a start, I think it is important to give some idea of where I am coming from. What are my biases and perspectives, because I obviously have them? Not only that, they provide an important backdrop to what I have to say. I am an anatomist, with interests in neurobiology, the human body, and bioethics, and I approach all these within a Christian framework. I also function within the domain of the health sciences, and so am deeply influenced by possibilities for developing therapies, and for finding ways in which the health of patients can be improved.

This brief introduction will set alarm bells ringing for some people, and these will be on two fronts. The first front is that, alongside any commitment to a Christian framework, I have alluded to the seriousness with which I take the contributions of science. For some this is a contradiction in terms. Will not the tenor of the scientific ethos weaken my dependence upon the biblical revelation or Christian tradition? This is a concern which surfaces repeatedly in areas regarded as impinging directly on the human person—anything that makes us the sort of people we are.

The second front that leads to concerns is the ever-increasing power of biotechnology, and especially medical technology. For some commentators, the replacement of organs, the use of stem cells to repair tissues, the desire for healthier children, the human genome project, and attempts at increasing the life-span, are all illustrations of hubris. They are as readily associated with illicit enhancement and eugenics as they are with legitimate therapy.

I take both concerns very seriously. Whether I like it or not, I am walking a tightrope, but if I am to be faithful to the different facets of my calling, I have no option. A tightrope it is, and I hope you will walk it with me.

I write as someone brought up in a Protestant tradition, and this will be reflected in my stance at a number of points. Nevertheless, my hope is that what I write will prove helpful to those coming at these issues from other Christian traditions, as well as from non-Christian religious traditions, let alone from non-religious perspectives. What is important is the integrity of the arguments put forward and the context within which these are addressed.

My aim is to be very practical. I will not shirk difficult or contentious issues. However, I am not aiming to cover every topic; this is not a text book. For instance, I do not deal with what may be regarded as bread-and-butter issues, like abortion and euthanasia. I consider these are covered very adequately in a host of books and articles. The pros and cons have been laid out endlessly, and important as these are, they do not bring us face-to-face with the cutting-edge questions I have in mind.

I have written extensively on many of these topics previously and I have used snippets of material from previous books (see Acknowledgements). However, this book is written for a wider audience than any of my previous books, and a wider range of topics is covered here. I have also taken the opportunity to ensure that it reflects current thinking and data.

This book is based on a block course of lectures given at Carey Baptist College in Auckland in the latter part of 2005. I am grateful to Paul Windsor, the Principal of the College, for the invitation to give these lectures, and to Myk Habets for his oversight of the course. I am especially grateful for Alicia Elder, whose work in helping put together the original lectures and then in adapting them for book form has been invaluable. She has kept me informed of the latest ideas and data, and has ensured that they are put into the context of my own thoughts. I would also like to thank Maja Whitaker for her oversight of the final stages of the writing and for her helpful critiques throughout. Without these two contributions there is no way the book would have seen the light of day in the midst of my university responsibilities.

Gareth Jones
Dunedin
February 2007

Section 1

Confronting the Big Questions

1

What Should We Do?

There was a time when the practice of medicine was considered to be straight forward. Medicine was widely regarded as a caring profession, in which doctors invariably did good. Those entering medicine as a profession did so in order to help others, to cure where possible and always to care and protect. Doubts were rarely, if ever, expressed about their motives; they would be doing good, and they would be serving others. Little was ever heard of medical ethics; it was obvious what was the right thing to do. There were discussions about medical etiquette, but those principally concerned how one was to act in relation to others members of the medical profession. Undergirding everything was the Hippocratic Oath, with its protection of human life, and its paternalistic ethos. The doctor knew best, but by the same token the doctor always acted in the interests of the patient. Little wonder that the medical profession was held in extremely high regard by most members of the public.

In many regards whatever was legal was also ethical. To act lawfully was to act ethically; to abide by the standards of the medical profession was to act ethically. There was little need to think about ethical matters. All this began to break down with the passing of more liberal abortion regulations in the 1960s and 1970s. With these the close association between what was legal and what was ethical began to crumble, since what was legal was considered by many to be unethical. No longer could the easy alliance between the two continue. Many were forced to think ethically and to question whether everything that the medical profession allowed was, by definition, ethical.

At the same time as this development was occurring, advances in the scientific basis of medicine were also underway. Consequently, medicine itself was being transformed from within by massive shifts in its biological substructure. As these became evident in genetics, neuroscience, reproduction, developmental biology, and public health, the ability of medicine to control human beings in previously unimaginable ways began to surface. The power of medicine to do harm became a possibility, something previously undreamt of. Its power to do good now had to be seen alongside this far less desirable power, and choices had to be made. Medicine began to be seen as an ambiguous venture. No longer could its practitioners act as though everything was clear-cut; it was not. Enter bioethics.

The difference between medical ethics and bioethics is not particularly important, and different authorities will give different definitions. While medical ethics traditionally dealt with ethical decision-making in clinical medicine, bioethics includes within its scope ethical questions relating to the basic biomedical sciences and research. Since these frequently have considerable implications for clinical medicine, and since this is where the rapid developments have taken place, it is bioethics in this broader sense where we encounter much of the cutting-edge and most contentious ethical decision-making.

It is hardly surprising that Christians have been caught up in this maelstrom. They, no more than anyone else, can escape the implications of the changing face of medicine. They have to produce ethical responses across a very wide front, and in some cases they are finding this enormously demanding. The old certainties have gone. The assumptions on which traditional medicine was based have undergone radical revision, in part due to changing moral standards across societies; in part due to the changing scientific basis of medicine. This is a major challenge, demanding both moral and scientific expertise. The following case studies give some idea of the nature of these challenges.

1.1 Case studies

Think about the following case studies, and ask what it is about each of them that presents us with challenges and queries.

> ***Case 1***: Stephanie and Joe go out of their way to help those around them. A couple of years ago Stephanie gave birth to a premature baby at twenty-four weeks' gestation. Enormous efforts were made in a specialist unit to save the baby's life. These were successful, and four months later the baby came home to much rejoicing. The cost of nine hundred thousand dollars did not concern them since they were so delighted with

their child. Recently, they have become involved in the running of a nursing home for geriatrics, and are appalled by the costs involved in maintaining some of the patients with multiple catastrophic illnesses. They cannot justify these costs, and feel that less 'heroic' treatment should be made available to many of these patients.

Challenges: Putting those who are close to you and with whom you have warm feelings of commitment, ahead of those who are far from you and for whom you have no personal responsibility; inconsistency in ethical standards and expectations; resource issues.

Case 2: A surgeon operates on a frail elderly patient, John, to repair an aortic aneurysm. A few days later it is necessary to operate for the second time as adhesions have formed. Following this John is placed in intensive care, since he is very fragile (or in spite of being very fragile). The patient's family want no further treatment because they feel that what is being done to John is simply 'heroic' and will never benefit him. In spite of this, the surgeon undertakes a third operation for further adhesions. John dies shortly after the surgery.

Challenges: Ethical uncertainty regarding what is in the best interest of the patient; conflict between patient's family and medical profession; definition of what constitutes heroic treatment.

Case 3: Patricia is thirty and is on renal dialysis; she needs a kidney transplant and is on a waiting list. Apart from her kidney problems she has no other major health problems. She is married with a young son. Mary is seventy and is also on dialysis. She too is reasonably healthy apart from her kidney problems, and she too would like a kidney transplant. Discussion is taking place about the justification of this and whether she should be put on a waiting list, the doubt surrounding this stems from her age. Katherine is eighty and is in similar circumstances, suffering from kidney failure. She has just been put on dialysis but there is considerable discussion about whether this is justified, since she has moderate dementia and various heart problems, and she also

finds it difficult to understand what is going on. Under no circumstances would anyone contemplate a kidney transplant.
Challenges: The issue of whether age and family circumstances are relevant in determining what treatment can be justified; the use of expensive resources for older people; whether dementia should be taken into account when expensive and demanding treatment procedures are being contemplated.

Case 4: Miriam is in a persistent vegetative state (PVS). It is now seven months since the car accident that resulted in severe damage to the higher centres of her brain. Since the accident she has been sustained by excellent nursing, by artificial feeding, and by treating infections as they arise. In normal clinical terms the chances of recovery to any sort of meaningful human existence are nil. She could continue in this state for many years. There is ethical ambivalence on the merits of continuing to keep her alive in the knowledge that she will never again manifest any of the marks of human personhood. The medical and nursing staff want all forms of artificial assistance discontinued; her parents wish it to be continued indefinitely.
Challenges: The status (ethical and theological) of those in a PVS; whether there is a maximum length of time those in a PVS are to be maintained 'alive'; the resources expended in this maintenance; the role of human control in medical care.

Case 5: Gavin was born with Down syndrome and oesophageal atresia. His parents refuse to consent to the surgical procedure necessary to correct the abnormality of the oesophagus, even though it is a straightforward operation. The obstetrician supports the parents in their decision, while the paediatrician disagrees. The ensuing conflict goes to court, the outcome of which is refusal to order the surgery necessary to correct the oesophageal malformation. As a result, Gavin, who was unable to feed, died five days after birth.
Challenges: Clinical conflict between different medical specialities; the relevance or otherwise of a condition such as Down syndrome in correcting congenital defects that would be routinely corrected under other circumstances; our views on disability.

Case 6: Four young couples (Allan, Brown, Cardrew and Davies) were recently married, and not one of them wishes to conceive. Couple Allan decides to use the rhythm method, thereby hoping to prevent the birth of a child. Couple Brown has intercourse; an oral contraceptive is being used, fertilisation does not occur, and no child results. Couple Cardrew has intercourse. Since the wife is using an intrauterine contraceptive device, fertilisation does occur, but the embryo is prevented from implanting; no child results. Couple Davies has intercourse. No contraceptive is being employed since they think they are infertile and have no reason to expect to conceive. However, on this occasion fertilisation occurs. A child is not wanted on account of the wife's serious and chronic ill-health, and so a first trimester abortion is carried out; no child results.
Challenges: The legitimacy or otherwise of using some form of artificial contraceptive; the significance of fertilisation; the legitimacy of abortion on account of serious health concerns.

Case 7: Five young married couples want to conceive. The partners of couple McDonald know they will be successful within two to three months. Couple McGregor is also fertile but there are certain sexual problems requiring counselling. With help, they overcome these problems and are able to conceive. In the case of couple McIntosh the male partner has an infertility problem. However, the use of artificial insemination by the husband helps to circumvent this problem, and fertilisation occurs. With couple McMillan there is again an infertility problem, this time on the female side. This is solved by microsurgery on her uterine tubes, and fertilisation subsequently occurs. A similar problem exists with couple McLeod; surgery is unsuccessful in this instance, but fertilisation is brought about using *in vitro* fertilisation (IVF).
Challenges: The ethical significance of different types of assistance to conceive; the intrusion of artificial elements into the reproductive process; overcoming fertility problems by manipulating embryos.

Case 8: 'Surplus' embryos have been produced as a result of Couple McLeod's IVF procedures. Of the ten embryos produced, three have been used in a first IVF cycle, but two of these were found to be unsuitable to be implanted; one was placed in the woman's uterus, and a baby is born. The other seven embryos are frozen and two years later, another four are used; on this occasion, one again survives, and a second baby is born. The remaining three frozen embryos are not required by this couple, and are destroyed (by thawing) after a further five years.
Challenges: The ethical significance of *in vitro* embryos; the legitimacy of destroying surplus embryos (those not required by the originating couple); what to do with surplus embryos; whether surplus embryos should be produced in the first place.

1.2 Learning to make decisions

These cases present us with a range of the bioethical dilemmas encountered almost daily in medical practice. They are all relatively normal, and yet in their different ways each of them challenges many of our ethical systems. They also raise theological questions that Christians have to come to terms with. But how are they to do this? What principles do they have to guide them, since most of the cases I have alluded to are modern developments? Our forebears did not have to answer these questions or confront them in the clinic or home. This does not mean that Christians have no resources for confronting them, but they first have to work out what they are.

It is also clear that all of us are involved with such bioethical questions. Most of the people here are ordinary people. They are not theologians or bioethicists. They are people going about their ordinary activities; they want to do all the usual things all of us enjoy. But they have been stopped in their tracks. Something has gone wrong, someone is ill, or the wife does not become pregnant when a couple hopes she will. And modern technology may be able to help. Should it be used? Will it be of benefit? Or will it be a hindrance? Or perhaps it will force us into a corner, contemplating undergoing procedures we are unhappy with? The trouble is most of us have never thought about these possibilities, and so are unprepared when we face them. After all, they are difficult to understand if we lack the scientific, ethical or theological know-how. What are we to do?

One thing is certain. There are no simple answers to what are generally complex questions. We cannot look up a rule-book and emerge with a definitive answer. This does not mean we have no guidance, but it does mean we have to work hard to find what may be the best way forward in any particular situation. Sometimes this will bring with it hardship and make considerable demands upon individuals, families, and communities. We may also find that different people with similar beliefs and lifestyles will make different decisions in similar situations, resulting in conflict and unease. People in faith communities may accuse each other of being unfaithful or of having made unworthy decisions. This is because we are so used to thinking and acting in similar ways. However, the difficult types of cases explored above introduce a fresh dimension to decision-making, where there are no generally accepted guidelines within the community. We all have to learn to live in new ways, assisting each other and supporting each other, even when we are not entirely happy with the direction others are taking. In other words, the ethical issues we are having to address have pastoral dimensions that may be as important as anything else. We will find that in considering bioethical quandaries we can never get far away from the real people involved.

And then there is another dimension. We live in pluralist societies so that whatever tensions may arise within relatively homogeneous faith communities are dwarfed by the tensions that arise when those with markedly different value systems and world views come close to each other. The society we live in is, quite simply, complicated. There is no universal consensus, no general understanding. A pluralist society demands that its members are accepting and non-judgmental, deriding any who think that they know the one 'right' way. Such a society forces the masses along the path that is considered acceptable to the majority, ignoring the cries of those of differing persuasions. It is expected that some will disagree, and yet it is considered untenable that those who do should have any sway over the common consensus. How are Christians to act in such a society when they are often in the minority? How are they to attempt to influence the directions of the society in the bioethical arena?

Whatever answers we come up with, it is pertinent to remember that all, no matter what their persuasions may be, are struggling with the same issues. While Christians have no assured answers on many of the very recent developments in biomedicine, neither does anyone else. Views within a pluralist society extend from the rampantly secular to remarkably traditional. Some are expressed with amazing assurance; others with timidity. It is in this melting pot that we all find ourselves, and it is here that we have to begin to work through not only what we think in these areas but how we best interact with those of myriad persuasions.

This is the contemporary world, but where have ethics and bioethics come from?

1.3 Delving into ethics

We might be forgiven for thinking that the study of ethics is a recent one, but that would be very far from the truth. In fact, the study of ethics has a long history stemming in fact from the Greeks. It was in the fourth century BC that Socrates asked the question: 'What sort of person ought one to be?' In doing this he was relating ethics to personal morality and character.[1]

The subject of ethics is the critical scrutiny of moral thought and practice. Although most people consider it is wrong to kill, the task of ethics is to enquire why this should be the case. Why is it wrong to kill? Is it always wrong to kill? Are there some circumstances under which it is justifiable to kill (or it may actually be moral to kill), and if so what are those circumstances? In asking these sorts of questions, the ethicist moves beyond mere moral intuition, opening up the possibility of dialogue and debate. This is why opposition to new developments based on a 'yuk' factor are not generally considered to constitute serious ethical analysis. This does not mean that intuition is of no value. What it does mean is that the initial opposition has to be supported by other arguments if it is to be open to fruitful debate.

---

1. In this section I am indebted to the discussion found in chapter 1 of A Campbell, G Gillett and G Jones, *Medical Ethics,* fourth edition (Melbourne: Oxford University Press, 2005).

Plato answered the question 'What sort of person ought one to be?' by stating that a good person was one who was guided by the 'form' of the good. This was a divine and eternal reality only imperfectly seen in everyday human existence but supremely disclosed by the calm contemplations of wise men. Interesting as this was, we realise that we have to get beyond mere thinking and intellectual answers. For us, theory has to be put into practice, since great thoughts do not necessarily lead to good deeds. If morality means anything, it has to influence the way in which we behave, and hence has to mould our attitudes, and the manner in which we relate to one another. This is why this chapter has as its heading: 'What should we do?' rather than 'What should we think?'. Doing incorporates thinking, but also goes beyond it to action. 'How should we live?' would have been an equally apt title.

The next Greek thinker of relevance to ethics is Aristotle, who offered a more pragmatic analysis than Plato. For Aristotle, 'forms' were modes of being found in the creatures around us, and the form of human excellence was that which best suited rational social animals (or mortal beings). And so, the qualities that make us human are shown in our thinking, our associations with each other, and our functions as members of the natural order. Aquinas took Aristotle's views and translated them into a Christian context. For Aquinas and others, this concept of the ideal of human function as the way we are meant to be was seen as representing the design of the Creator. Like the Aristotelian tradition, this allows us to examine what counts as human excellence or well-being in an attempt to discover how we should act. In fact, Aristotle and another great Greek thinker, Hippocrates, began with observations of the actual world in which they lived, rather than beginning with theories about life and the universe. Hippocrates has become famous for the medical oath named after him, the Hippocratic Oath, dating from around 400 BC. This is the earliest document in existence that discusses ethical issues to do with medical care.

Perhaps the next highly significant figure in the development of ethics was the eighteenth-century philosopher, David Hume. For Hume the form that constitutes right living is exemplified by decent, clear-thinking eighteenth-century gentlemen (like himself). People like this acted on the basis of their moral sentiments, the sentiments of decent people, which were essentially a matter of emotion. This idea leads in medical ethics to the image of decent, kind medical persons with sound opinions. On this basis, doctors do what they feel is best for their patients. The problem is that the basis for our assessments can vary from sensitive and informed consideration for another person's feelings to 'paternalism', a rather arrogant assumption that one knows best.

Paternalistic doctors make decisions for others on the basis of their own values, which others may not share. The onus is on the doctor with little responsibility given to the patient. It is an asymmetrical relationship, with the doctor having all the knowledge and the patient none. Such a relationship worked for very many years when doctors belonged to one of the few highly trained professions, in contrast to so many of their patients who were unskilled and even illiterate. However, even then there were potential problems. What if the doctor was wrong? Patients would suffer without having any come back whatsoever. The trouble is that this type of doctor-patient relationship leaves little if any room for the patient's wishes, since the patient would not be adequately informed about the risks and benefits of any course of action being contemplated. A paternalistic approach like this ignores proper ethical constraints on medical practice because it equates the right decision with what the doctor feels to be right for the patient. But it is the patient's interests that are paramount in the practice of medicine. It is this realisation that has led to a move away from paternalism.

A name that comes up repeatedly in bioethics is that of Immanuel Kant; the focus of his ethical system being on rights and duties. Rights have come to the forefront today, as any cursory glance at newspapers or TV will demonstrate. We hear much about my right to free speech, my right to a certain standard of living, my right to have a child, etc. But where do rights originate? How can they be justified? And what happens when rights and duties come into conflict?

What then about the consequences of actions? How might these be considered in medical ethics? Questions such as these form the basis of a utilitarian approach that rests on the premise that the right thing to do is to create the greatest good for the greatest number. This approach focuses not on our actions and how they accord with our conceptions of duty, but on the consequences of those actions. This system generates an obligation to do our best to increase happiness and diminish suffering so as to secure net overall benefit for everybody concerned. This is a very congenial aim for most health care workers, who tend to see their profession as involved in benefiting humankind in ways to do with health. Nevertheless, there are problems, since it is not always possible to know what the net benefits might be. Additionally, it is notoriously difficult to compare different outcomes in health care, for instance, someone requiring long-term mental health care support against someone requiring a varicose vein operation. Not only this, but some actions that increase the net happiness of a majority may be attained at the expense of the minority. For example, if society insisted that all foetuses with Down syndrome be aborted in order to decrease health care costs, regardless of the views of these particular parents.

These problems do not mean that we should never take the consequences of decisions into account in medical care (or in anything else for that matter). We invariably do so, but this is not the same as espousing consequentialism. Means and ends are inseparable. To achieve a particular end, actions have to be performed in certain ways, and this entails that they are carried out with certain attitudes. Once the latter are brought into the picture, we enter the domain of what is termed virtue ethics. Ethical conduct must take account of the character of the person concerned. What sought of person is the doctor or health care professional?

According to virtue theory, character is central to moral concern, and the model of moral conduct is someone who shows virtues, such as kindness, honesty, compassion, and respect for others. Of course these have to be worked out to see what they mean in practice, and once again there will be no sure-fire answers. But what we have here is a realisation that the way in which we interact with others, seeking the good of others and taking their feelings and goals into the equation, are fundamental components of good medical practice.

It in this context that we can refer to the Hippocratic Oath, with its stress on the duties belonging to a special group, and its basis for the notion of professional integrity. The basis of the Oath is that the ethical analysis of a problem in medicine must be to ask whether the individuals concerned have acted in accordance with adequate standards of health care practice. From this it follows that one ought to act in the 'best interests' of patients, seeking to determine what the welfare of the patient requires to be done. This will take note of what the patient wants as well as what good medical practice points to.

Underlying all that has just been stated is the crucial importance of respect for persons. Patients have their own opinions and aims in life, which require them to act intelligently in most of the things they do. But in order to act intelligently, patients must (a) be given information, and (b) be allowed to make up their own minds. It is incumbent, therefore, on the professional to inform his or her patients about their disease and its management, and to allow them to make the significant choices required where the disease affects the course of life. This leads to a model of cooperative partnership between doctor and patient, with note being taken of the patient's values and the doctor's expertise.

Some talk about a 'worthwhile life'. Patients are not simply bodies but whole people, who generally aim for an acceptable quality of life. Unfortunately, reference to quality of life immediately raises the spectre of relegating some people to substandard and unacceptable categories. Quality of life does not mean that we deny treatment to human beings who are less fit than their fellows; nor that we apportion health care on the basis of merit. This concept of a life worth living merely implies that human beings can quite reasonably decide that certain kinds of life and the prolongation of life are of no benefit to themselves or anyone else. The admission that such a judgment is possible does not mean that we must take certain actions, such as mercy killing, in those circumstances. But it does mean that sometimes a patient's evaluation of outcomes will lead to a reasonable decision not to undertake certain kinds of treatment, even those considered by some doctors to be 'life-saving'.

1.4 Underlying ethical principles

Against this background we find that ethical analysis of medical issues is currently dominated by a small number of broad principles. These were articulated first by two bioethicists, Beauchamp and Childress. These principles do not aim to provide ultimate guidance in medical practice, but they do provide general directions in areas of uncertainty. They should not be regarded as rules as such, but are general maps to point the way in the broadest of terms.

The first principle is that of *non-maleficence/beneficence*. The negative side of this principle is the aim of not causing harm to patients. Under no circumstances should a treatment *knowingly* do harm. The positive side of the equation is provided by the drive to bring about substantial benefit. In other words, the treatment should aim at proving worthwhile to the patient. While this may sound obvious common sense, it is not difficult to imagine situations where it can easily be overlooked. For instance, the insertion of a naso-gastric tube into a dying patient may in no way be in the interests of the patient. If there is no possible benefit to the patient, such a procedure cannot be ethically justified.

The next principle is that of *autonomy*, something I have already touched upon. This looks to the centrality of the patient's status as a person, with the power to decide and act in his or her own best interests. Even when the doctor and allied health carers think that a certain course of action is in the patient's best interests from a professional standpoint, they still have to recognise that patient's autonomy. This principle comes to the fore when the patient is incompetent. In this case, the question to be asked is, what would the patient have wanted had they been in a position to do so? The aim all along should be, as far as possible, to treat patients as responsible people, since this is the crux of the healthy doctor-patient relationship.

Another principle of considerable importance is that of *justice*. The goal here is that of fairness, according to which people with equal needs are treated, as far as possible, in the same manner. There are, of course, limits to what can be achieved, especially within health care systems where resources are inadequate to treat everyone who ideally should be treated. Choices have to be made between individual patients or groups of patients. Nevertheless, the thrust of a just health care system is that everyone is provided with basic care based upon needs and not some other arbitrary criteria.

These principles have a major contribution to make to medical ethics and bioethics. They all have a part to play in any ethically-based health care system, and we all use them to varying degrees. However, they do not provide some easy way forward. They certainly do not take away from us the task of grappling with horrendously difficult issues, where apparent conflict between principles is integral to decision-making. It is also important to realise that none of us uses just one approach at the expense of all others. For example, no one uses only a rules-based approach or only a consequentialist approach. We make use of different approaches, taking from one and another as the situations demand.

Where do specific Christian principles enter the picture? How do they fit alongside the principles and approaches I have just been considering? In order to answer these questions we shall look at the role of Christian theology in the next chapter.

2

The Role of Christian Theology

It is not just in matters relating to the bioethics realm that Christians fail to agree; there is no common consensus in Christian theology. However, my concern is solely with bioethical issues. As we saw in the case studies in the previous chapter, the complexity of the issues facing us is such that we will have to use all the resources at our disposal to be able to provide adequate answers to any of them. It also became evident in that chapter that Christians are not functioning in isolation of the rest of the world. We are all in this together, and the same issues can affect all of us. There are no approaches that only Christians can use. But having stated this, we should not go to the other extreme and think that Christians have no contribution to make. Christians bring certain emphases to bioethics, and it is these we shall be searching for in this chapter.

Those from different Christian traditions bring their respective contributions to bioethical debate. I readily acknowledge this. However, rather than attempting to see what a range of major traditions might bring to the table, I shall confine myself to what I think I can bring from my own background—that of a scientist who speaks from a Protestant background with an emphasis upon what we can learn from the biblical writers. I do not wish to be more specific than this since I do not think it will prove helpful in the task before us. My emphasis will be on the value we bestow upon human beings, since this is central to the task of bioethics.

2.1 Theological themes and human value

2.1.1 Created in God's image

One biblical theme is crucial: human beings are made in the image and likeness of God. This was expressed vividly by John Calvin when he wrote that: 'God looks upon himself . . . and beholds himself in men [people] as in a mirror'. This suggests that, as God looks on people, he recognises that they are icons (images) of himself. In people God finds his own perfections and characteristics mirrored back to himself. Consequently, when we see another human being we see another creature who delights God by mirroring him. In the same way we also mirror each other.

People are like God, in that we relate to the world, to other people, and to God. We make choices and act upon them; we have values and value systems; we are aware of ourselves and of others; and we are held responsible for our actions. We are aware of God and are capable of responding freely to his call. Therefore, it is clear that all of us have some of the relational features of a personal God.

This principle is foundational to an understanding of people, and as we delve deeper, we find within it a number of more specific themes. The first of these is that, like God, we are capable of understanding: the more we understand, the more like God we become. This is a pivotal mark of human existence, and all of us have something of this capacity, either actual or potential.

The second theme is that of control. God has placed humans in control of themselves and their world, and this in turn is control of God's world. From this stems yet another theme, responsibility for other people, for human welfare in general, and for all facets of the environment. Responsibility is essential if the control bestowed upon us is to be harnessed for good ends. Such responsibility, far from depicting humans as rebellious creatures, emanates from our creation in the likeness of God; it is built into what 'being human' is all about. In other words, to 'be human' is to act responsibly, it is to take decisions, to forge new paths, to be creative, and to seek new solutions to old problems.

A final theme is one of our dependence upon each other within the human community. Whenever we are confronted by other human beings, we are in the presence of images of God who make claims on us. We are dependent upon them, and they upon us, because of our likeness to each other, and our mutual likeness to God. It is this interdependence that should constitute the basis of our response to other humans, rather than any 'rights' they (or we) may possess. In other words, justice, equity and fair dealing stem from our joint mirroring of God; we are to value others because of what both they and we are in the sight of God, and because we depend upon each other within the human community.

2.1.2 Christ's redemption

Our creation in God's image is an important place to begin, but it is only a beginning. It assumes even greater significance when seen against the background of the Son of God assuming human identity, and becoming human like us. In Jesus we see God incarnate, God in truly human form—real God and real man. In becoming a human being, God brought about the redemption of lost humanity, but that was not all. This very act also bestowed unequalled value upon the human race. In identifying himself with the human race, Jesus, the God-man, acknowledged the value of all human beings. In other words, God's concern for mankind was so great that Jesus Christ, his Son, became a vulnerable human and then gave his life on behalf of human beings. Although this remarkable self-giving is generally stressed from the viewpoint of salvation, it also has profound implications for the ways we view each other, we are all of immense value from God's perspective, a value that should be reflected in our ethical systems.

Both the creation and redemption of mankind demonstrate that human life is precious to God. We are accountable to God for our own lives and, where we are responsible for other human lives, we are accountable to God for those lives. Consequently, when people are undervalued, we fail to take seriously the work of God, negating the incarnation and Christ's commitment to humanity in becoming one with God's creation. We adopt values diametrically opposed to those of Christ for whom human life was worthy of his own life.

2.1.3 Dignity of people

From this it follows that everyone has an intrinsic dignity, resting not on what they can accomplish in material, social or spiritual terms, but on the basis of God's love. Consequently, human dignity is based primarily on what individuals are in the sight of God and never on what they can or cannot do for society, for mankind, or even for God. Those who are of no functional value to society still retain a dignity, since they remain important in the sight and purposes of God. It is in this light that we who come into contact with them are to deal with them.

From here it is but a short step to the notion of servanthood, by which we give ourselves for others, serving them in a self-sacrificial way, and putting their interests before our own. Such a lifestyle finds its warrant in the worth of others, and in the claims others make upon us because they are so like us and because they are of such value in the sight of God. These 'others' are not simply our friends and those who will repay us fully for our concern, but include our enemies—those who have little interest in our welfare, and perhaps would even do us harm if given the chance.

If individuals have a dignity bestowed upon them by God, they are never to be valued simply because of their worth to another individual, an organisation, or society. To treat people in this way is to treat them as nothing more than means to an end, and therefore as the property of another. Attitudes of this kind deny to individuals a worth and dignity of their own.

Other human beings are one with us in the human endeavour, they are like us, and we all have significance in God's sight. In this sense human dignity is indiscriminate, pointing towards a flowering of human abilities that should be encouraged and developed wherever and whenever possible, since it reflects what God wants for people.

2.1.4 Namelessness

The flip side of human dignity is what I shall call human namelessness. As I contemplate bestowing dignity upon human beings, what impresses me is that a central element in practice is the recognition that people have names. They are individuals to whom we can relate in ways that are meaningful for both them and us. By contrast, lack of dignity is evident when people are treated as though they have no names; they are anonymous; they have become nameless.

We all know what happens when there are vast tragedies and thousands are killed or slaughtered. There is no way that even those close to the scene can respond to situations like this in other than an impersonal fashion. The deaths become little more than statistics; the people are nameless. Some of course will mourn the loss of real people, but the human sense of mourning is quickly overtaken by the brutal statistical nature of the event. These people, whoever they may have been, are not seen as those who had individual relationships to God; they lose their worth and dignity as the sheer magnitude of the occasion overtakes everything else.

People become nameless when no one cares about them. They may have potential worth, and yet are treated as cogs in a wheel. This transformation into namelessness occurs, as I have just indicated, in tragedies of huge magnitude, and yet is also found in families, societies, hospitals, and work situations. Namelessness is also a frequent accompaniment of illness. As dignity is lost through illness, especially when the illness is debilitating and catastrophic, enormous effort is required to maintain a feel for the individual as a person. Unfortunately, this condition can be precipitated by impersonal health care systems, as a result of which the situation becomes even worse. How can someone 'be someone' when they appear to have lost their status within society? Relationships break down for the nameless ones, since relationships with a nameless individual cease to be meaningful. In other words, the nameless are also 'relation-less', and this is the antithesis of any Christian understanding of the human condition.

We need to recognise the ease with which namelessness can occur within impersonal institutions that so readily depersonalise people by the ways in which performance, redundancy or illness are tackled. The task of advocating systems that insist on giving people names, and that recognise and empathise with people in their suffering and struggles, is an important one.

2.1.5 Relevance of human suffering

When considering human suffering, we generally limit our thinking to the suffering of human beings. Obvious as this sounds, and eminently sensible as it may appear, it has immense limitations. A Christian perspective broadens the whole approach by arguing that God's suffering and human suffering are inextricably linked. The suffering of a human being has direct implications for God, since it is one of God's images that is being hurt. In a sense, therefore, God is himself violated when a human being is destroyed or injured. And so, when one person injures another, God himself is wounded.

It is against the background of this close linkage between human and divine suffering, that we can conclude that illness and injustice bring sorrow to God. If this is so, the relief of illness and the pursuit of justice are important means of helping relieve not only human suffering, but also, in some way, God's suffering. This is why the suffering of others should be of immense concern to us. All attempts at relieving suffering are responses to the vulnerability of God's love for people, who are his images. Not surprisingly, they are to be given high priority by the followers of Christ.

The repercussions are immense. Everyone is to be viewed within the context of a suffering world, from the immediacy of the human suffering which implicates all of us, to the suffering of the creator and redeemer who loved humans so much that he became one with humanity. That act demonstrates that God is not immune to the plight of humanity, and this in turn shows how much we ourselves should value humanity.

2.1.6 Misuse of human responsibility

Although human beings are capable of understanding, control, and enormous responsibility, we are prone to debasing our understanding, to exercising control selfishly, and to acting irresponsibly. The ease with which we misuse our many abilities lies at the heart of our problems, giving rise as it does to strife, enmity, selfish excesses, inequality, and injustice.

It is this misuse of responsibility that leads in part to the existence of conflicting moral claims, since there are some situations in which we cannot act in ways that are wholly good and totally free from guilt. We need to beware, therefore, of establishing idealistic standards, and judging everyone by those standards. Much as we may desire such standards, and the absolute goodness they depict, the reality is that neither others nor we ourselves live by absolute standards. We frequently fall short. As a result, we often need to work with a hierarchy of moral claims, according to which we evaluate lesser evils and greater goods. To acknowledge this is not to denigrate human value or attempts at upholding human dignity; neither is it a means of introducing situationalism and relativism into ethical discussion. It is simply an acknowledgement of the world in which we find ourselves—a broken world, where the images of God are in rebellion against God's authority.

2.1.7 Humility

As we realise the immensity of our dependence upon God, we realise the need for humility. We recognise that we are not our own, but belong to God to be used according to his purposes. Allen

Verhey has argued that humility in this sense reckons with the brokenness of the world and accepts that there are events beyond our comprehension. We have to live with the brokenness and tragedy of the world in hope and faith and love.

We are learning to accept the brokenness and tragedy of the world—our world, our lives, our families, our hopes, and our dreams. The world lets us down, and the temptation is to cry out against God and all that can make sense of the catastrophes. The way of humility and heroism is to acknowledge the brokenness and tragedy, to stare at it, and through it see the suffering of God, suffering that touches us and that can bring healing. What we see is the relevance of God for those enmeshed in hurt and deprivation. We come to see that God sometimes interrupts lives and hopes, but that even these interruptions have to be faced up to in the spirit of Christ. We come to see God's presence in places neither we or others would ever have chosen, and in circumstances that repel us.

2.1.8 Who is my neighbour?

Are we inconsistent in the value we place on human lives? We may accept that some lives actually are worth more than others. For instance, a healthy thirty-year-old is worth more than a seventy-year-old with advanced Alzheimer's disease, or a healthy three-year-old in the United Kingdom is worth more than a severely malnourished three-year-old in the Sudan. Alternatively, we may not accept this: all human lives have the same value, but we fail to live up to this standard in practice. We should care as much for the seventy-year-old with Alzheimer's as for the healthy thirty-year-old, and this implies we should direct as many resources to the one as the other. And we should care as much for a starving child in a region with endemic poverty and starvation as for a healthy child in an affluent suburb in our own country. In practice the latter rarely occurs, and there are pressures against the equal distribution of resources in the former.

What do we do about the chronically ill, the retarded, the demented, the unemployed, those with social problems, the under-class of society? What value is to be ascribed to all these? As far as they are one with us in the human endeavour, they are to be valued as others value us and as we value others. There is to be no discrimination. Does this lack of discrimination continue to apply when there are not sufficient resources to go around, when hard moral choices have to be made between one group and another, or even one individual and another? Can we continue to act on the presumption that all are always to be valued at precisely the same level?

From a Christian perspective, no group is to be stigmatised as valueless, or even as of only limited value. Every group is of value, and is therefore to be assisted in whatever way we would assist a privileged member of society. Every effort is to be made to put this anti-discriminatory ethic into practice, and to render it public policy. Nevertheless, a point may come where invidious choices have to be made, and where all courses of action will involve loss and suffering. Perhaps we have then to seek the lesser of the two evils. But if we do this, human dignity will be sacrificed whichever course is followed. At this point of unavoidable tension, we may well find that, in practice, the value being ascribed to some human beings is being downgraded. Perhaps there actually are limits to the protection we can give to the value of some human beings in situations of unavoidable conflict. However, any course of action that downgrades human value is never the desirable course, it reflects the plight of humans in a suffering world.

In attempting to unravel these issues, we have obligations to take seriously the dignity and value of all human beings. That is the furthest we can go. We have enormous responsibility to help a person if nothing obstructs us from doing so. If we are in a position to help we must do so, we are duty bound. For example, an elderly couple living next door will on occasion need practical help and perhaps emotional support, and we should help them accordingly. People with whom we have direct contact are our near neighbour(s); this may include our family, friends, church, neighbourhood, work situation, and (within limits) our community. Our near neighbours are the people to whom we have considerable responsibility.

At the other end of the spectrum is a person far from us, in a situation over which we have no control. Here our responsibility may be negligible. Consider an elderly couple living in a nursing home in another country. We know they exist only because we are aware that elderly people do live in nursing homes in other countries. These are people with whom we have no direct contact at all, those in other countries, in other communities. I know about these through the media but our knowledge of them is limited to them as a group and not as individuals. These are our far neighbour(s) and our responsibility to them is very limited indeed.

In the middle of the spectrum there is the responsibility we have towards those we know but with whom we have no direct contact; our control of their well being has been markedly reduced. We can think of elderly parents living in another city; we are unable to help them on a daily basis and we should not be expected to do so (although we may be able to provide considerable indirect support). People whom we know and care for, but who are geographically removed from us are our personal neighbour(s). We do have a responsibility to them, even though it may be largely exercised at a distance.

This is a parochial view and yet a practical one. There is a tension here, but it should be a productive tension. It is a way out of the paralysis of feeling that I am responsible for everyone, but knowing that in practice this is impossible. Our responsibility first and foremost is for our near neighbours, those whom we can truly help. If we fail here, we fail totally as human beings. If we succeed here, we enlarge the scope of our neighbourliness.

2.2 Interpreting the theological themes

These themes open up new dimensions for an understanding of our relationship to our fellow humans, and underscore the high priority to be placed on efforts to improve the welfare of those around us. We are to see others as those who are imaged after God, as those to whom we are to commit ourselves as fellow images of God, and as those who are one with us in the suffering of a world at enmity within itself and also with God's designs. We are to see people as individuals who merit our concern because they merit God's concern. The next step is to draw out from these themes more specific conclusions regarding human value.

The first of these is that human life is on loan from God; it is a gift from God. Our own lives, as well as the lives of others, should never be viewed as having only biological value. Life belongs to God, even more than it belongs to us. And so, whenever we consider the value of a human life, we have to bear in mind its relation to

God. In assessing how to deal with difficult ethical questions in the realm of bioethics, we need to recognise that human life is life-derived-from God, not life-in-isolation-of God.

A second conclusion is that, as we emphasise the wholeness of human beings, their biological-spiritual unity has to be treated with seriousness. Individuality is lost when there is no scope for growth and fulfilment as a being in one's own right. It is less than Christian to live as though all that matters is the existence of human life regardless of its quality. Such an attitude leads to mediocrity in our own lives and to a gross neglect of the welfare and aspirations of others. The mere existence of human life in its barest essentials is hardly sufficient. This applies through all stages of human existence from the earliest beginnings of human life in the uterus to the end of human existence in extreme old age. A corollary of this is that, although human value may be severely jeopardised in extreme situations (as in very severe brain damage), there is generally never any time when human life has no value at all.

A third element is that the quality of an individual's life is important. It is unfortunate that the term 'quality of life' has, in the eyes of some, become confined to the biological or medical quality of life. This is sad, since it reduces human existence to physical dimensions alone; this is a complete antithesis of the biblical picture of human life. The goal for the lives of individual human beings is an adequate physical existence, and a satisfactory day-to-day experience of family and social obligations, work, recreation, moral responsibility, and a whole range of challenges and expectations. It also incorporates spiritual experience, the service of God and one's fellow human beings, and interaction with other humans in love, forgiveness and hope.

A fourth observation is that the undervaluing of human life takes many forms. It stems from the widespread destruction of foetal life for superficial reasons. But it may also be the result of the irresponsible creation of new life, from pregnant women smoking or drinking alcohol, from unjust social or commercial practices, from an inequitable distribution of resources within our society or between societies, or from gross inequality of opportunities within a society

Tragically, human life is easily wasted, and all instances are an implicit denial that human life is precious to God. Wastage of human life is everywhere, as millions of people are killed in wars, automobile accidents, earthquakes and famines, by other people in homicides or by themselves in suicides, and by unhealthy lifestyles. Malnutrition has killed countless human beings, as have epidemics of infectious diseases, while the loss of prenatal human life through spontaneous and induced abortion should be of deep moral concern. The widespread loss of human life in these ways leads to a debasement of human existence, which is seen as being readily expended and of little value. This, in turn, engenders a callous attitude towards human life. So much of this wastage is preventable, but we have learnt to live with it and accept it as a normal part of human life. Automobile fatalities are accepted with little questioning of their futility, but they as much as any of the other forms of pointless human wastage question the value humans place on each other.

In the fifth place, choices sometimes have to be made between one human life and another, or one group of humans has to be favoured above another group. Any such choices are invidious, and social and economic systems should not precipitate these dilemmas with their overtones of injustice, exploitation and despair. There is no escape from ethical ambiguity, moral imperfection and errors of judgment.

2.3 Where does the Bible enter the picture?

One approach is to use the Bible as a source of moral rules. According to this, moral dilemmas can be assessed by discovering an appropriate moral rule, such as the rule against killing, or the rule against committing adultery. Such rules are absolute. However, problems arise when these rules come into conflict. How do we judge whether rule A is more significant than rule B? And what are we to do in morally perplexing situations for which there is no specific guiding rule?

A second approach is to recognise in the Bible sets of moral principles. An example of such a principle is the dignity and worth of every individual before God. According to this approach, these principles are applicable for all times. What we have to do is to seek to understand their meaning and relevance, and then apply them to the specific problems confronting us. We are to use our judgment, discernment and intelligence, and then in faith make decisions in the concrete circumstances of which we are a part.

A third approach stresses the response in faith, which the believer is to make to the living presence of God. What is important here is the person's own relationship to God, and the way in which he or she puts this into practice. With this approach, rules or principles assume secondary importance. The chief concern is with what God is doing now, and therefore with the manner in which he wants us to respond and live, rather than with commands or directives he has given in the past.

My own approach is to acknowledge that the biblical writers do, indeed, lay down certain basic rules, such as those in the Ten Commandments. But these in their stark simplicity will not provide specific direction in many contemporary situations. They need to be fleshed out by more specific moral values. Once we have some idea of what might be the relevant biblical principles for a particular situation, we have to apply them, realising that we will also be dependent upon some of the general principles we met in chapter 1. Christians need to convey to others the life of the risen Christ, and never a harsh unyielding legalism. They are to be firm, and are not to yield on their standards, but running through their stance must be a deep concern for human life in all its wholeness and completeness.

2.4 Revisiting ethical guidelines

In the most general of terms one can say that the specific conflict encountered in medical dilemmas is a manifestation of a more fundamental conflict, that between absolute principles and consequentialist principles (see chapter 1). Absolute principles emphasise the inherent rightness or wrongness of actions, whereas consequentialist principles stress the consequences of actions. The difference can be illustrated by the following:

> An absolutist may say that, since killing innocent people is always wrong, it is better to refrain from killing one innocent person even if the end-result is the unintended death of three other innocent people. This is preferable to being guilty of the death of the one person. In contrast, a consequentialist may contend that one's aim should be to save the three at the expense of the one.

Consider the sanctity of human life. An absolutist may argue that we are obliged to try and save every single life no matter what the consequences, whether economic or affecting the welfare of other patients. On the other hand, a consequentialist may advocate the destruction of handicapped people, considering this to be in the best interests of society as a whole. I have no wish to defend either extreme position, since each leads to the neglect of patients: other patients in the case of the absolutist position, and handicapped patients in the case of the consequentialist.

In practice, the two principles co-exist within society, and most, if not all, medical practitioners (including Christians) utilise the two principles. This is simply because each approach has advantages and disadvantages. Consequentialism is realistic, it assumes responsibility for the effects of human actions, and it aims to reduce the lot of human suffering. On the other hand, actions cannot be evaluated solely in terms of their consequences, and this approach may put at risk unpopular minorities within society. For its part, absolutism is valuable because rules provide crucial signposts for ethical decision-making, and some rules may protect exceedingly basic values, such as human dignity. Nonetheless, rule-centred approaches also have limitations: they may obscure fundamental principles underlying the rules, some rules are relative, and on occasion fundamental moral rules come into conflict with one another.

Many seek to find a middle path, balancing the two approaches. It is possible to show very great respect for widely-held rules, but at the same time be prepared to deviate from them when confronted by exceedingly difficult circumstances and undesirable consequences. We frequently live with conflict between principles such as these, and we experience the tension that inevitably exists between the two. Distinctions have to be made between first-order and second-order principles.

The first-order principles are all-embracing values like justice and love. They are unequivocal and cover every conceivable human situation.

The second-order principles are more specific and include values such as:

- Doing good and not doing harm.
- Respecting people rather than using them.
- Respecting the autonomy of people.
- Preserving life.
- Telling the truth.
- Seeking not to harm innocent people.
- Ensuring that a professional relationship is never exploitative.

A little thought will show that none of these values are straightforward: they all enshrine moral ambiguities. For instance, with regard to preserving human life, existing ethical codes stress the doctor's obligation to respect life, rather than to preserve it at all costs. However, if there is no obligation to preserve life at all costs, a distinction may have to be made between actively killing a patient and letting that patient die, or in different circumstances one person may be allowed to die or be killed indirectly in order to save the life of another person. There is no escape from decision-making, either for those who accept that human life cannot always be preserved, or for those who think otherwise. Moral ambiguity is inevitable.

Another problem sometimes encountered is a failure to listen to those with different perspectives from our own: those from outside the Christian faith and those from differing Christian traditions (see chapter 17). The complexity of so many of the questions we have to confront when discussing human value within biology and medicine demand that we seek as much assistance as possible from those with value systems overlapping our own at significant points. Rather than being a threat, this should be viewed as a source of strength and support. The ethical thinking of Christians does not take place in some watertight compartment, as though there are distinctly Christian stances on many bioethical issues. Even when there are clear distinguishing features between Christians and others, the differences may be modest.

3

Is Medicine Leading Us Astray?

Certain themes emerge repeatedly in discussions of contemporary medicine, especially when concerns are being expressed about what is thought to be its overweening power. The major ones are the control it appears to be exerting over increasingly large swathes of human life, its temptation to play God, and its ability to design and enhance what we are as human beings. All these images are negative ones and I shall look in turn at each in this chapter and the next.

3.1 The power of medicine

The technological sophistication of modern medicine elicits two contrasting responses. At the one extreme there is the picture of medicine as saviour; at the other, that of medicine as destroyer. Of course, one can think of many in-between responses that go to neither of these extremes. Nevertheless, the extremes are always instructive.

In the first mindset medicine will solve all our problems; it enables us to live lives free (or comparatively free) of disease, in that so many of the diseases that brought the lives of our ancestors to an early end have been eradicated, or at least controlled. However, we know that medicine does not solve all our health problems; it may even create a few. But there can be little doubt that the quality of our lives in medical terms is vastly improved compared with those who lived in our societies 100 to 150 years ago. In a limited sense, therefore, medicine is a saviour, even if that term is something of an exaggeration. Unfortunately, some people expect far too much of the medical sciences, and there are those who look to these sciences to, quite literally, bring in human immortality. We shall return to this expectation in chapter 4.

Over against these reactions there are others who respond to the advances and possibilities opened up by medicine in a contrasting fashion. They regard them as threatening and misleading. For them medicine is set to destroy so much of what we hold dear, by undermining how we have learnt to cope with suffering and limitations. Technologically-driven mechanistic processes are replacing the human responses to disease, early death, infertility, and deprivation. For critics of the medical enterprise, medicine is extending its influence well beyond what has traditionally been considered to be the realm of disease, and in so doing is transforming our conceptions of health. Genetics and neuroscience in particular are threatening to change the essence of what we have understood as the human person.

It does not take much thought to realise that both extremes have theological overtones. If medicine is able to solve all our problems and remake us in radically different ways, there may be no room left for the supernatural. Medicine will have taken the place of God and his purposes. Medicine will have become sovereign, not God. In much the same way, dramatically new directions for human living will come from advances in medicine and not from increases in spiritual understanding. The future, therefore, lies in the hands of medicine and biomedical scientists, and not in the hands of theologians or church leaders.

As with all discussions of this nature, far too much is made of the power and possibilities of medicine, and yet one should not attempt to escape from the underlying fears and expectations. The power of medicine stems from the manner in which it allows human beings control over their lives and the lives of others. This is why the issue of control is a crucial one. After all, any effective medical procedure, just like any effective scientific development, will only be effective if it is capable of exerting control over previously uncontrolled forces. There is no medicine worthy of the name without control. Medicine as saviour is medicine the controller. The opposite end of the spectrum also centres on control, this time the perception that medicine is exerting too much control or misdirected control. Such misdirected control is viewed as manipulation, since implicit within it is the quest for freedom from natural limits.

The question of control cannot be avoided, which is hardly surprising since control is a manifestation of what we are as human beings made in the image and likeness of God. I want to consider a number of illustrations of control from medical practice, remembering that the crucial question is: Is the control exerted by today's medicine and medical technology to be welcomed or resisted?

3.2 Should we welcome increasing control over ourselves?

Example 1
A general practitioner prescribes antibiotics for a patient with a respiratory tract infection. The patient is restored to health due to the administration of a short course of drugs to combat the infection and the body returns to its original healthy condition.

Example 2
A general surgeon treats a patient with appendicitis. The patient presents with an inflamed appendix, and the doctor removes the appendix. All proceeds smoothly, and the patient is discharged minus her appendix. Although the change is a simple one, the patient has been modified by utilising the doctor's expertise. Without such interventionary control the patient would have died; instead she resumes life to its full capacity.

Example 3
An orthopaedic surgeon is confronted by a patient with arthritis affecting a hip joint. It is chronic and serious, the patient is in pain, and her mobility is being seriously affected. A decision is taken to replace the hip joint with a prosthesis; the patient has an artificial joint inserted. This functions well, the patient is satisfied, and the surgery is considered successful. This has been accomplished, not only by removing something diseased but by replacing it with something artificial, the aim of which is to mimic the functioning of a healthy joint. This has only been made possible by an array of technological achievements, all of which point to human control of a highly technological nature.

Example 4
An oncologist, confronted by a patient with cancer of the colon, decides to remove the colon and rectum and provide the patient with a colostomy. In this instance, not only has the doctor removed something, but she has also created a means of functioning that does not exist under normal circumstances. From

now on the patient will function in an artificial manner, made possible by considerable understanding of the physiology of the gut.

These four illustrations point to the legitimate use of the powerful abilities of medical technology to restore health. They demonstrate how fortunate we are in terms of what can be done by medical professionals. In spite of the high degree of control underlying these particular operations and in spite of the considerable modification and manipulation inherent within examples 3 and 4, we are grateful for the doctors' expertise. These responses are valid ones, and, in principle, are exemplary in both Christian and ethical terms. These operations are to be commended rather than condemned, because they are good examples of ways in which human responsibility and control are to be exercised. In Christian terms, our emphasis is on health professionals acting as God's agents, as they make use of God-like abilities. I doubt whether we ever depict these operations as examples of doctors acting in rebellion against God.

If we accept these conclusions we are agreeing that some degree of control within medicine is good. We are to be pleased that such abilities are available to us, and we are to be deeply concerned that they are not available to many millions living in societies lacking sophisticated (or even any) medical facilities and trained personnel.

Example 5 (case 2, chapter 1)
A surgeon operates on a frail elderly patient, John, to repair an aortic aneurysm. A few days later it is necessary to operate for the second time as adhesions have formed. Following this John is placed in intensive care, since he is very fragile (or in spite of being very fragile). The patient's family want no further treatment because they feel that what is being done to John is simply 'heroic' and will never benefit him. In spite of this, the surgeon undertakes a third operation for further adhesions. John dies shortly after the surgery.

This is an excellent example to bring out some of the issues inherent within control. It provides us with uncertainty. Even the mission of healing has limits, and biomedical technology as saviour has to be treated with immense caution. We also see here a tension between what surgery might have accomplished (if the patient had lived for a few weeks or months longer), and the actual failure of the surgery in this particular instance. In other words, the outcome was an uncertain one. Even had it been successful in the short-term, the long-term prospects for the patient would still have been dubious. And this introduces what I shall call a 'time dimension'. A few years ago, no one would have contemplated this series of operations, and some years into the future the short-term success rate will probably be much higher than today. In other words, technology is changing, and the technological changes are inevitably accompanied by changing ethical, social, and perhaps even theological perspectives. Frequently, it is not a question of saviour or destroyer, but saviour and destroyer with the balance between the two sides of the equation in continuous flux.

> *Example 6* (case 4, chapter 1)
> Miriam is in a persistent vegetative state (PVS). It is now seven months since the car accident that resulted in severe damage to the higher centres of her brain. Since the accident she has been sustained by excellent nursing, by artificial feeding, and by treating infections as they arise. In normal clinical terms the chances of recovery to any sort of meaningful human existence are nil. She could continue in this state for many years. There is ethical ambivalence on the merits of continuing to keep her alive in the knowledge that she will never again manifest any of the marks of human personhood. The medical and nursing staff want all forms of artificial assistance discontinued; her parents wish it to be continued indefinitely.

The quandary here is that there is no way of avoiding some form of control. Refraining from emergency treatment in the first instance would itself have been an example of control—deciding against using the technology at one's disposal. Alternatively, to commence treatment and then later decide that existence in a PVS is meaningless in human terms, and therefore discontinue treatment, is yet another form of control. There is no escape from serious decision-making.

Can we talk about 'natural limits' in this case? It would be easy to argue that the limits of nature would have been death shortly after the accident: nothing should have been attempted; no technology should have been used. However, this does not sit easily alongside other perceptions we have of medicine. To refrain from using the technology at one's disposal is not an ethically neutral stance; it is a definitive ethical statement, that almost certain death is preferable to life, even if the life may be compromised. The essence of the ethical decision is to determine how compromised the future life is likely to be, and then in the light of that judgment to decide what technology, if any, should be used. The technology itself is not dismissed out of hand, but its usefulness or otherwise is assessed in the light of the patient's condition and its proven efficacy. The ambivalence of the technology stems from its limitations, and not from its terrifying power.

Underlying all these illustrations is an immense degree of human control, without which there would be no modern medicine as we know it. It can be used for good, or it can go abysmally wrong. However, this is implicit to what we are as human beings, who make mistakes and sometimes display poor judgment. It also stems from the ease with which we sometimes put arrogance ahead of the good of others, including the good of patients and of the weak and disadvantaged. And, inevitably, there are genuine ethical conundrums where we do not know which course of action is the most consistent with established ethical principles.

> *Example 7* (case 8, chapter 1)
> 'Surplus' embryos have been produced as a result of Couple McLeod's IVF procedures. Of the ten embryos produced, three have been used in a first IVF cycle, but two of these were found to be unsuitable to be implanted; one was placed in the woman's uterus, and a baby is born. The other seven embryos are frozen and two years later, another four are used; on this occasion, one again survives, and a second baby is born. The remaining three frozen embryos are not required by this couple, and are destroyed (by thawing) after a further five years.

Here, medicine's control has moved beyond that concerned solely with bypassing the infertility, since it has resulted in the production of additional human embryos that are not required by the couple concerned. Is this an example of medicine straying beyond its traditional role of dealing only with ill-health, or can infertility be classed as ill-health? And what about the unwanted embryos? Was their production an example of medical technology as a destroyer of human integrity, or were they an inevitable end-result of a legitimate technological process?

For some writers this is an example par excellence of medicine transgressing the boundaries of legitimate control. For them, this is dangerous territory we should not be exploring, opening up as it does innumerable avenues in gene therapy, genetic manipulation, and even eugenics. It is said that we lack the wisdom to deal morally with such areas, even if we develop the scientific expertise to change and control future life forms. We misuse such developments far more readily than we wisely use them; we destroy others rather provide for their legitimate needs. Additionally, this is medicine as social manipulation.

The arguments in favour of, or against, this use of medical technique will not be readily resolved. However, they should not be allowed to cloud the issue of control. Even if we object to the use of medical techniques in example 7, we should not use this to argue against the legitimate place of control within medicine as a whole. The genie may be out of the bottle, but it is a genie that brings huge benefits as well as huge challenges. From this there is no escape. The role of ethical analysis is to separate the wheat from the chaff, and not throw both wheat and chaff away.

3.3 Is medicine playing God?

This is the second area of profound concern to very many people. Medicine appears to give to human beings the ability to play God, in that they are acquiring powers that belong only to God. They are attempting to become not just like God, but, perhaps even more troublesome, to actually become God. This is an extension of the previous discussion, where we saw the way in which control brings with it power. The concern there was with the element of control. Here it is with the other side of that coin, the element of power.

But what do people mean when they use this term? In all probability most people have not thought deeply about it. What comes through is the fear that things are being done, or are being contemplated, that are beyond the bounds of what we normally find acceptable. These developments may change the future in unacceptable ways, perhaps in ways that will change us all irrevocably. Where are we heading? And why should our futures be put at risk by a small group of scientists? Questions of this ilk are neatly summed up in the phrase 'playing God'. We are going where we should not be going—nothing more needs to be said by way of justification.

This concept seems to be confined to activities that involve direct scientific control over human beings, especially at the beginning and end of human existence. For example, investigations into astronomy don't appear to elicit this condemnation, perhaps because they give the impression of being confined to describing what happens a long way away from us, or events that occurred an unbelievably long time in the past. These things happened, and all these particular scientists are trying to do is fathom their mysteries with ever-increasing precision and sophistication. The same may be said to be true of chemists or geologists or botanists. All these are unravelling the secrets of nature, even if some groups may be unhappy with the interpretations or hypotheses with which these scientists sometimes emerge.

Even architects and engineers who design and build startlingly imaginative and unusual buildings or bridges, don't appear to be playing God. They may be criticised on aesthetic grounds; their designs may not be appreciated, but they aren't usually condemned because they have taken on themselves the mantle of God, by erecting vast skyscrapers or buildings that seem to defy the laws of gravity. These designers are demonstrating enormous creativity, and yet their creativity is not seen to be treading on the toes of a creative God. Whenever I take off in a plane, I am intrigued by how this is possible. I don't understand it, but I'm not inclined to condemn those who make such feats possible on the grounds that they have been playing God.

But once biomedical scientists enter the picture, all this changes. Curing diseases, finding remedies for the common cold or AIDS, and life-saving surgery are acceptable, even though some of these activities have far-reaching implications for individuals and society. These do not generally acquire the opprobrium of going too far and playing God. But tinkering with the genome, interfering with reproduction, and modifying embryos are all typical illustrations of playing God. They touch a very sensitive nerve, and they elicit the deepest of concerns. In some manner they are seen as intruding into what we are, into the very essence of our being, so that we will end up different from what we are now. The very course of human life may be changed, and by definition the change will be for the worse. And so it is important to ask whether we should be meddling at all in God's world, or at least in this particular part of his world?

In order to ground this discussion in reality we need to sort out precisely the type of concerns people have. Take three contrasting illustrations, all from the reproductive area and moving from the generally acceptable to what in the eyes of some is dubious.

Illustration 1

Tom and Sarah have four children. Ten years ago they started their family, not expecting to have any problems. And as they are both fertile they found this to be the case. All the pregnancies were straightforward, with medical technology only utilised in the ways that we would consider entirely normal—via ultrasound, foetal monitors, and pain relief. Yet in planning their family, and in bringing four unique individuals into the world, are Tom and Sarah playing God? Their actions have resulted in the birth of four human beings who could not have existed without their involvement. Tom and Sarah also sought to evenly space their children, rather than conceive at every available opportunity. Does such planning imply they have been playing God?

Illustration 2

Simon and Michelle have one child, a boy who was born with cystic fibrosis. They have always dreamed of having three children but, knowing that they are carriers for the disease, they are terrified that they may have another child with it. They are also unwilling to undergo selective abortion if it was discovered that Michelle was carrying a child with cystic fibrosis. Their doctor informs them that pre-implantation genetic diagnosis (PGD) can be used to screen embryos for cystic fibrosis, with all those affected discarded. They undergo *in vitro* fertilisation (IVF) and after PGD is done six embryos are found to be free of cystic fibrosis. Two of the healthy embryos are replaced and they discover that Michelle is pregnant with a single foetus. In selecting for embryos that were healthy have Simon and Michelle moved too far into the realm of playing God?

Illustration 3

Charles and Megan are a loving couple who cannot have children. Due to a medical emergency Megan had a full hysterectomy and had both fallopian tubes and ovaries removed in her early twenties. Because of this Megan cannot carry children, nor can she provide the eggs. However a close friend has offered to act as a surrogate for Charles and Megan and through an anonymous egg donation embryos are created. The surrogate carries the embryo to term and Charles and Megan are parents at last. But have they played God? Not only has another individual carried the baby but the egg was also donated, thus they have moved even further from the standard form of reproduction. Have they moved into what should be forbidden territory?

In each of these illustrations, a child has been born, but different routes have been followed in achieving this. A few years ago some of these children would not have been born, or other children would have been born with different characteristics and, in the second illustration, a particular illness. The question before us is whether some or all of these couples have usurped God's role as creator. Have they acted responsibly or irresponsibly?

It is easy to get bogged down in the technological, thinking that the temptation to play God is a new phenomenon. It is true that the phrase and all it implies may be a new one, and yet the power of human intervention in the physical and human world is far from new. Relatively primitive technological feats have done exactly the same over recent history. Think of the introduction of clean water supplies to communities, vaccination, adequate nutrition standards, control of mosquitoes, simple hygiene measures, and improved obstetric care. The results have been dramatic, with vast improvements to neonatal mortality rates, survival of children beyond the age of one year, and numerous children alive who would otherwise never have been born or who would have succumbed very early in their lives. Indeed the tragedy of today's world is that this is the situation in far too many countries at this very time, when it need not be. We know what to do, but we do not do it for a variety of reasons.

General comments of this nature are not meant to justify any of the procedures in the three illustrations above. They have to be examined and assessed on their merits and using what we consider to be appropriate ethical principles. These matters are taken up in Section 2. For now the point being made is that we should not bring debate on these procedures to an end simply by denouncing them on the grounds that the people involved are playing God. Let us dig a little deeper into this notion, and ask whether it should always be regarded in negative terms. Can we actually look at it in a positive light?

3.4 Playing God revisited

From a Christian standpoint we are made in God's image, and hence are to function like God. No matter how much our God-likeness has been shattered by rebellion against God, we are still images of our maker, albeit tarnished images. Consequently, we demonstrate a great deal of his creativity and his inquisitiveness. Humans as scientists are humans as God's images, probing and thrusting into the creation, attempting to understand it and re-direct it as stewards of God's creation. Within the medical sphere, the desire is to exercise at least limited control over evil in the form of diseases that would otherwise ravish and destroy all that is beautiful and worthwhile in God's world. Underlying all such attributes is a proviso, namely, that the control is exercised in a responsible manner.

When this is not the case, we see the other side of the picture, namely, that scientists may be arrogant and unworthy, with motives of self-aggrandisement and personal glory. They may show little regard for the welfare of individual humans, even when the realm within which they are working is that of medicine.

From a Christian perspective, we are not to use massive scientific powers for superficial and frivolous ends. There are always dangers, and to risk these for minor gains is dangerous and irresponsible. So much of the criticism of genetics revolves around its possible insubstantial uses, such as gene manipulation for eye colour or facial features. Such criticism is justified, but this is criticism of the misuse of genetics rather than of genetic advance itself. Similar criticism can be made of the misuse of many other technological developments, and even of human abilities themselves. Humans playing God only becomes dangerous when they fail to utilise their God-like capabilities in ways that will deepen and enrich the lives of human beings.

These negative images have to be taken seriously, and yet they fail to negate the overall thrust of much scientific advance. Genetic advance *per se* is not synonymous with pride and arrogance. It is not an aping of God's power, since all forms of genetic therapy owe their rationale to this power. As long as the aim of therapy is the alleviation of human illness, it has the potential to elevate God's images. Nevertheless, there are always dangers, and the notion of 'playing God' should remind us that we are only to modify fundamental biological processes with enormous caution and deep humility. There is much we do not know, and there is much over which our control is tenuous and fragile at best. Playing God is an exercise in responsibility, demanding intelligence, compassion and spiritual discernment. It is not an exercise to be entered into frivolously.

But who is playing God? The general assumption is that it is doctors and scientists. These are the groups who are tempted to transgress boundaries. This is interesting because we don't generally seem to think that artists or composers 'play God' in this negative sense. Did Picasso play God, or Henry Moore, or Jackson Pollock? Probably not. What then about Bach, or Bruckner, or Arvo Pärt? We would probably be more inclined to say that at least some of these glorify God in their compositions; in no way are they usurping his authority. Why, then, do we tend to set apart the activities of scientists?

But this question of who is playing God goes even further than this. Think of those illustrations. It was the couples who were the decision makers. If anyone is playing God, it's them; it's ordinary people, and not arrogant scientists. It is they and we who have to make difficult decisions to help us through difficult situations. What has changed is that so often the decisions are now much more demanding than they used to be, more demanding because the scope of the available technology has become so much wider and more effective. And this is where the playing God picture proves unhelpful. It fails to provide guidance in demanding situations. The result is that it is a motif that makes great headlines, but in practice is ignored.

Ordinary people are forced to play God (if we continue to use that unhelpful term). And this is because of necessity and not arrogance. They have to act responsibly, by choosing what they hope will be the better path, even though—in some instances—they are pitifully aware of the morally tainted nature of any choices they make. Whatever they do, momentous decisions are being taken, and people are playing God because they must play God.

However, the quicker we get away from the negative connotations of this term the better. There is an important positive side to it that stems from a Christian perspective. This is that humans have a God-given mandate to serve others, to care for the vulnerable, and to heal. It acknowledges that humans are to participate in the process of transforming the world, by sustaining, restoring and improving what has been temporarily entrusted to us. The material world (including human beings) could be better than it is, and humans have the responsibility to attempt to achieve this, albeit in a limited fashion. While pride and arrogance are dangers, so are sloth and lethargy. Why highlight the first, but ignore the second? In this positive sense humans are to play God, by being God's representatives. However, it is unlikely that this positive interpretation of the term will ever gain currency, although it should always be borne in mind when developments are being thoughtlessly castigated and rejected for playing God.

3.5 Back to nature?

But there may be a different way, a way that would get us out of all these awful ethical dilemmas. Why not return to the natural way of doing things? Why not reject all these recent technological developments that seem to be getting us into such strife? Why not accept what nature brings? Or what God brings, depending on one's perspective. No matter how the question is phrased the basic assumption is that it is responsible to leave well alone. There is virtue in ignorance; there is something good about a lack of control; there is something of merit in mystery and in the unknown.

The problem with this approach is to determine just when we start acting in this manner. If we decide that the technology we have today is just right, and a moratorium should be placed on any new developments, we are already well down the technological path. We would be accepting a great deal, even if we were turning our backs on the unknown developments that lie in the future. We would have cars, planes, the internet, artificial contraception, computers, neurosurgery, heart and kidney transplants, clean water supplies (in some countries), little in the way of polio or tuberculosis, antibiotics, and so on. Admittedly, we are plagued by Alzheimer's disease, many forms of cancer, cardiovascular problems, and increasing obesity. Why not go back one hundred years, when many of these technological developments were totally or largely unknown, and even some of the diseases were relatively unproblematic? Not only would this be impossible, but we would be plagued by many other diseases that led to much shorter life expectancy, to high childhood mortality rates, and to unsanitary living conditions. Any serious arguments along these lines are doing little more than seeking refuge from decision-making in an enclave of ignorance and disease.

These are quite fundamental issues because they force us to come to terms with our picture of God and God's domain. How much do we leave to God, and how much is it legitimate for us to do? Do we simply sit back and let God sort everything out, or has he given us the responsibility, authority and power to sort out much for ourselves? Humans are to exercise dominion over nature, and we are to free ourselves from its constraints if at all feasible. In carrying out these mandates we are to act as good stewards of God's creation, realising that there is much in his creation that is not as it should be. There are no easy answers, since we frequently have to live with ambiguity and uncertainty. We are torn in different directions, often not knowing which is the best course of action. We may well not know which way is pleasing to God, or which way will best serve other human beings, but there are pointers.

The first is provided by the urge to restore the material world: to improve it, care for it, and cure those with distressing conditions. Inevitably, our attention is on human beings in need of medical help and assistance. If there are current or imminent scientific measures that might realistically be able to alleviate serious illnesses, under normal circumstances they should be pursued. This should be within the bounds of a balanced lifestyle and broad overall interests, and also the character of all those involved in decision-making. How do they live, and how will the decisions that have to be made enrich and extend their lives as human beings?

A second is that we are to be guided by the relationships that make up the human community. Decisions made in any one area may influence human relationships in other areas, as well as our attitudes towards human life in general. Will they enhance or detract from the value bestowed upon prenatal or postnatal human life, the disabled, the marginalised, the chronically ill? There are no clear-cut answers to these queries, and answers may vary in different situations. Once again, delicate decision-making is imperative.

A third pointer that applies specifically to Christian thinking is that of one's dependence upon God. While a global principle like this will not immediately answer very specific questions, it is the fundamental relationship that is the bedrock for all bioethical considerations. Where there are no 'correct' answers, there are answers that demonstrate faithfulness to one's relationship to God and one's position within a community of God's people.

4

Designing and Enhancing Human Beings

It is virtually impossible to read about developments within biomedical science today without encountering references to designer babies and the prospects held out of medically enhancing human beings. The impression one gets is that in the not-too-distant future, there will be people around who will either have been designed in certain ways, or will live until some unimaginable age. Or they may even be both—designed with specified characteristics and also illness-free and with at least another five hundred years to live. These are vastly powerful images that have been the stuff of science fiction for aeons. Now, however, they are becoming the stuff of serious scientific and philosophical discussion, even if this is limited to very select quarters at present. Should we take these discussions any further? Should we too take them seriously, or should we dismiss them as the imaginings of a few benighted people who have nothing better to do? I would like to be able to take this latter course and ignore them. However, I don't think we can do this, since the images are pervading our culture.

4.1 The design trap

Whenever the possibility of designing people is being discussed, the term that is invariably used is 'designer babies'. Why? After all, babies grow up and become children, teenagers, and then adults, and yet we hear little about designer children or designer adults, let alone designer teenagers. I'm sure many parents would love to have designer teenagers, who had been designed to obey them and follow their every whim. Somehow though the designer image appears not to have got past the baby stage. We all know how inviting and innocent babies can be, and so the picture of babies actually designed by us to be exactly as we want them to be is regarded as peculiarly repulsive to some. Perhaps we think of them as small adults made in our image, moulded and created by us.

It may be that concerns about the design motif have not moved beyond the baby stage. They have not grown up and thus are immature and unformed. Like 'playing God' the notion of designing babies is imbued with fear and loathing, and it is almost universally used negatively. It is one of those things we should never contemplate, let alone put into practice. It is beyond the bounds of civilised behaviour, and it is most definitely outside the limits of Christian behaviour. Designing babies is one of the things we should not do, because it is going too far. For Christians this means it is doing something that should be left in the hands of God, where it rightfully belongs. No one with even of the slightest common sense, let alone spiritual wisdom, would countenance the idea.

Whenever something is put as strongly as this, there are two responses: total acceptance or scepticism because of the extreme nature of the response. I fall into the latter category, since in my view dismissing bioethical issues in this way helps no one. We need to get behind the slogans and superficial reactions.

The central problem with all talk about designer babies is that it is unrealistic. It gives the impression that designing babies will be easy, and that we will readily be capable of emerging with the sort of babies we desire. It is just as though we were to look in a shop window and see a range of babies that can be selected off the shelf. There they are displayed and ready to be purchased. Charlotte wants a baby with blue eyes; Emma wants her baby to be fair; Grace wants one with enough intelligence to become a doctor. The fanciful nature of this alleged choice should immediately make us question the whole notion of design and selection. It is one thing to choose clothes in this manner; after all the concept of designer labels is well-known and recognised for what it tells us. But do we really think that producing designer babies is nothing more than manufacturing designer clothes?

Talk about designer babies is unhelpful because it promises far more than it is ever capable of delivering. The science is primitive, and even if this were not the case, designing human beings would involve undertaking some form of PGD, manipulating embryos, and IVF. The costs would probably be prohibitive for most people, and the artificial nature of the processes is not something most people would contemplate under any normal circumstances. Also, the procedures may not work.

In practice, though, most people who use the term 'designer babies' use it to refer to any selection of one embryo over another. Routine PGD is often labelled as such. In other words, designing babies and selecting embryos are treated as equivalent. This is a misnomer since there is no way in which selecting an embryo without the gene that gives rise to a particular disease, for example cystic fibrosis, can meaningfully be called designing that future individual. These procedures can only use genes that come from the parents; they are not manufacturing new genes.

In other words, any manipulation of an embryo and hence a future individual is regarded as going too far. The degree of scientific control is forbidding, and human beings are thought to be becoming far too efficient in their manipulatory abilities, since they are leaving far too little to chance or to God. This is design, and humans should not be in the design business.

But humans are not in the design business in this regard. Compare the production of a particular model of car, which is characterised by precision, equivalence and uniformity. There is no room for individuality on the production line, since each car has to conform to the specifications of that model. To use a biological analogy its manufacture is entirely genetic in character; there is no environmental component, since no development can take place once it has come off the production line. However, an environmental component is implicit in the production and subsequent development of all human beings, and it is this that separates human reproduction (even with impersonal elements) from factory manufacturing processes.

This is why thinking about PGD in terms of biological manufacture is a misnomer. We will never produce babies in the same way as we produce cars, washing machines, or computers. These analogies are seriously misleading. If design involves precision and predictability, there is no way in which babies and future human individuals will ever be designed by people like us.

What then about the *science*? Once again, there are problems. So often the focus appears to be on choosing genes for fair hair, blue eyes, intelligence, physique, and good looks. The ephemeral nature of these longings points to their superficiality, let alone an ignorance of the scientific precision, clinical complexities and expensive resources that would be required to achieve them.

What is required is a rigorous assessment of the merits of what can and cannot be accomplished by biomedical science. Our starting point should focus on the good of the patient, with a commitment to improve the quality of the patient's life and, if feasible, to replace illness by health. This is a positive hope, but it is also a realistic one. The intervention may not work; hopes may be dashed. But the attempt is to be encouraged as long as our expectations are guided by realistic clinical and scientific goals. The dominant value is that of humility, demonstrated by caring for those in need, and of utilising powerful technologies in the service of those potentially capable of benefiting from them.

4.2 Striving for immortality

It is not unusual to encounter stories in serious newspapers and magazines with headings such as 'Anyone for tennis, at the age of 150?' and 'Do you want to live to be 800?' Aubrey de Grey, a biogerontologist at Cambridge University, argues that a future world, perhaps 1,000 years hence, could be populated with people who are alive today and are already around sixty years of age. According to this scenario, the concept of ageing will have become obsolete, with a world populated by people enjoying a state of eternal youth, and no longer threatened by the major diseases of the twenty-first century.

Or think of a typical family reunion at the end of this century. At this reunion there are five generations playing together, with the oldest member at 120 playing a gentle game of soccer with his twenty-year-old great-great-grandson. On the eve of the twenty-second century, diabetes, Parkinson's disease and AIDS will have been consigned to the past, tissues and organs will be readily regenerated, and human immortality will beckon. Technologies utilising stem cells, constructing artificial chromosomes and creating perfect transplants will together have transformed our vision of human nature. The borderline between science fiction and scientific reality will have been obliterated. The former will have become the latter. Indeed, there may be no room for science fiction any more. Anything that can be imagined will be achievable by science. Our wildest dreams will lie within our grasp, including our own immortality.

Wildly speculative as such vistas may be, they are being taken very seriously in some quarters and are causing philosophers and theologians to sit up and take notice, and of course react. And this is precisely what is happening as possibilities such as these are dismissed as examples of grandiose visions of human self-modification, genetic perfectibility, and eugenic aspirations. This is the realm of biological enhancement, the proponents of which are represented by the posthumanists or transhumanists. And it has led to dire warnings that medicine and medical practitioners in the present are going too far.

A sombre note implicit in so many of the responses is the fear that humans are attempting to improve upon God's blueprint for human life. Any movement in this direction is regarded as an irreligious aspiration, and may also be seen as having ill-fated ethical consequences.

4.3 From therapy to enhancement

The extreme type of world envisaged by these speculations stems from processes aimed at enhancing human beings, that is, improving upon what we currently are—how we function, how we age, and the manner in which we succumb to numerous diseases. It is improvement in this sense that causes deep concerns, as opposed to treating diseases with the aim of restoring a person to health and well-being. This is the usual distinction between enhancement and therapy. But what criteria are being employed for deciding the boundaries of normality and human nature and, therefore, the dimensions of therapy?

The distinction is a blurred one, and so often is not tackled head-on. I have suggested three categories of enhancement, as a way of thinking about it and its relation to therapy.

Category 1 refers to the enhancement of a healthy person (H) so that they become super-healthy (SH). What if we were able to protect against early onset Alzheimer's disease (AD), coronary disease, or even mental retardation, by some form of genetic manipulation of embryos? Would such individuals in adult life be H or SH? Is this therapy or is it enhancement? They are not fully SH because they are vulnerable to most diseases; they have only been protected against early onset AD, heart disease or mental retardation. They have not become different forms of human being. They may be healthier than they would otherwise have been, but they are far from illness-free or perfectly healthy. My inclination is to regard these forms of enhancement as variations of therapy, even if they are highly technological variants by current standards. The point here is that individuals whom we would consider today to be SH may come to be classed as normal H individuals in the future.

Changes like this are all around us. Consider the use of vaccines as prophylactics, or the widespread adoption of public health measures such as the provision of clean water supplies. Uninteresting as these examples appear to us today, their 'enhancement' effects on the health of whole populations have been revolutionary. Along with dramatic increases in life expectancy and decreases in neonatal and childhood mortality, the concept of what constitutes good health has been transformed. In other words, enhancement is not simply a future phenomenon; it has already taken place in numerous societies.

Category 2 refers to enhancement that may have nothing to do with health, such as an extension of abilities. In this instance, enhancement encompasses those with super-abilities (SA), as opposed to those with the normal range of abilities (A). The SAs may be more intelligent or may be able to run much faster than they would otherwise have been. Instead of correcting defects, normal functions will have been extended.

Super-abilities may enable individuals to perform better than they would otherwise have performed, the sort of thing that worries education authorities and sports bodies. It is true that enhancement of this type may be unfair on those not in a position to benefit from them. Nevertheless, the enhanced individuals may still perform less well than other highly talented non-enhanced individuals. The bar has been raised, but is this substantially different from the way in which the bar is raised by good nutrition and hygiene, or by superior educational opportunities?

This second enhancement category is more hypothetical and futuristic than category 1. It is pushing the 'natural' barriers more obviously than in category 1, and has moved some distance from any health imperative.

With these thoughts in mind, we should ask where such a well-known procedure as cosmetic surgery fits in. It is not a category 1 enhancement, since it is generally unrelated to health or illness. The desire to look like someone else, to have a lighter (or darker) skin colour or the features of a different racial group, or to appear much younger than one's chronological age, are all category 2 characteristics. Consequently, some category 2 enhancements are with us now; they do not all lie in the future.

Category 3 refers to radical transformation; the individuals are radically transformed (RT) against those who are not transformed (NT). This is exactly what posthumanists (or transhumanists) have in mind when they envisage a massive extension in lifespan, hearing wavelengths previously beyond their capabilities, wiring brains directly to machines to amplify muscle movements, or providing new kinds of sensory experience.

Radical enhancement has no boundaries, not surprising once finitude and mortality have been overcome. Once into this realm, medicine can be used to deconstruct and reconstruct the human body, providing the capability of controlling everything we are or want to be. Regenerative medicine is repeatedly looked to as a means of greatly extending longevity, since ageing is a disease, and can therefore be treated and even vanquished. The goal of medicine becomes transformed into a means of waging war against death. Mortality will be replaced by immortality, endless bodies in an age- and disease-free world.

What, then, are we to make of therapy and enhancement? This is where the problem lies. Having rejected these extreme scenarios, some move immediately to a rejection of any interventions in the genome or brain. This is because any use of technology to improve the quality of life, say, or improve mental functioning, can be viewed as part of a much broader endeavour, that of extending the lifespan indefinitely or giving individuals unlimited mental powers. No room has been left for category 1 measures, which are viewed solely in terms of the far more radical and idealistic goals of category 3. The underlying assumption is that the ethos of medical practice and research has already been transformed: instead of caring for patients, its only interest lies in curing people of every conceivable malady, including ageing and death.

So often it is assumed that the distinction between therapy and enhancement is clearly defined; similarly with the distinctions between normality and abnormality, and health and disease. The assumption also appears to be made that whatever these distinctions may be, they are unchanging. They are the same today as they were in 1950 or 1850, or they are the same now across all societies.

However, this is not the case. Routinely accepted biological limits are wide and the concept of normality is broad and tenuous. Psychopharmaceuticals can be used to combat everything from shyness and forgetfulness, to sleepiness and depression. Are any of these diseases? Is depression normal? Clinical depression may be a disease entity, but what about the low-grade, sub-clinical depression that afflicts so many people? If it is not a clinical phenomenon, and therefore not an illness, is treatment with drugs a form of enhancement? Similarly, should we treat hyperactivity in children who are difficult to handle? Are their behaviours normal or abnormal? Ritalin administration may be therapy or it may be social manipulation. The line between the normal and the pathological can be a very fine one, and we may be far from sure which side of the line we are on.

And then there is the slight deterioration in memory that accompanies ageing, demonstrated by minor forgetfulness in everyday activities: so-called *age-associated memory impairment.* Mild memory losses may be a prelude to *mild cognitive impairment* and ultimately the dementia of *Alzheimer's disease*, or they may not.

Drugs influencing memory could prove useful in younger age groups, where improvement in test scores at school and university would be the driving force. This use of memory-enhancing drugs appears to be a category 2 enhancement measure. It also highlights the way in which society's values and desires can shape the direction and interpretation of scientific endeavour.

It is impossible to escape the blurred nature of the normal/ abnormal, and therapy/enhancement boundaries, a blurring that becomes even more problematic when a time element is introduced. Present day expectations of what constitutes good health and normal life expectancy have changed out of all recognition since the early years of the twentieth century. Moreover, our expectations bear no resemblance to those of many people today living in the developing world. Whose expectations are normal?

The reality is that we ourselves are enhanced. Technological interventions into the human condition did not commence in the latter years of the twentieth century. If our forebears of three thousand years ago (or even three hundred years ago) could see us, they would think we were futuristic beings, truly enhanced version of themselves.

4.4 Thinking again about enhancement

It would be a great pity if Christians ended up inadvertently defending the *status quo* and the present state of biomedical understanding and control for fear of highly speculative posthumanist scenarios. There are ways of working towards a better future that are far more modest than that based on a posthumanist agenda, and that take serious account of theologically helpful pointers. Those working within a framework of faith should be prepared to joyfully embrace category 1 and at least some category 2 enhancements, while vigorously arguing against category 3 varieties with their veneer of posthumanism.

We need to ensure that we develop a paradigm that leaves room for the serious discussion of ethical issues around stem cell research and therapy, PGD, and gene therapy, where the focus is on possible clinical applications (either now or in the future). Whether one labels some of these as enhancements or therapy is of little relevance to medical treatment, where patients capable of benefiting from the procedures are the objects of attention.

We are not to rush in the direction of enhancement technologies, but neither are we to reject all of them out of hand. It may be right to be suspicious of the grandiose claims, and even of some of the more moderate ones—the optimism of some commentators is astounding. Nevertheless, we have broad principles that should be put to good use in this discussion. There is nothing inherently evil about being finite, such that we have a mandate to overcome it. Our finiteness should be both our starting and end points. It is basic to what we are as humans. Hence we are not to look for technologies to 'heal' our finiteness or eliminate suffering as an intrinsic feature of our finiteness. Therapy aims to diminish suffering within the context of accepting that the human response to suffering is a crucial feature of our humanness. Herein lies our freedom alongside our finiteness.

General as these considerations are, they serve as useful pointers for any theological perspective. In themselves they do not preclude any particular modifications, which are to be assessed using the therapy-enhancement categories I have outlined. The blurring of boundaries between the two reminds us that we are to take therapy seriously, at the same time as we dismiss the speculative and unhelpful extremes of some forms of enhancement theorising.

Important theological strands are provided by wisdom and prudence, alongside humility and weakness. It is right to be cautious, but this by itself does not lead to outright opposition to all forms of exploratory therapy and the modest categories of enhancement. In our concern to respond to the overweening ambitions of some scientists and thinkers, we should not succumb to the temptation to bless the *status quo*, as if it were perfect. The *status quo* is far from that; indeed, it is frequently filled with human misery, some of which is genetically caused.

But am I ignoring the power of present-day science, and am I failing to consider sufficiently seriously the future directions of science? Perhaps I am. However, the line between where science is today and where it will be in thirty years' time (let alone three hundred years' time) will probably be a tortuous one. Future scoping exercises are fraught with uncertainties, and have a poor track record. As little as thirty-forty years ago, discussions of reproductive cloning concentrated on the manner in which it would result in the redirection of human evolution; no thought was given to its role in agriculture and the pharmaceutical industry.

The scientific enterprise, by its very nature, is creative, aiming to find new ways of approaching medical and allied problems. Its approach to problems is a strictly limited one, driven as it is by its reductionist methodology. In no senses is this antagonistic to the giftedness of life, even when the realm is the reproductive one. The challenge is to hold human creativity and the gift of life in tension, something which many feel is not happening, particularly in those areas where the science is driven by pharmaceutical and commercial interests. I accept this, but I do not accept that this is an argument against the creative impulse within science. Viewing scientific investigations as part of a posthuman agenda will not solve any challenges that lie at the border between therapy and enhancement, whether one seeks to prohibit or advocate them.

Discussion of enhancement would be more helpful if we accepted that we are already enhanced, at least at the category 1 level. Ethical discussion could then be grounded in the present, and not in some unclear and largely untenable future. We could then see that fundamental moral values, such as the benefit of the individual, justice and fairness, are central, no matter whether therapy or enhancement is contemplated.

While theological considerations do not provide specific answers concerning what is or is not acceptable, they serve to provide a framework by which it is possible to accept our finiteness and mortality. While acceptance of realities like these could lead to fatalism, it is balanced by an awareness of the magnificance and grandeur of human beings that is also integral to the Christian faith. It is the duality of these characteristics that leads to scientific achievements as we know them, together with humility regarding their vast but limited dimensions. In these terms, enhancement technologies can be assessed and critiqued, utilising those that appear to advance human welfare and arguing against those whose aspirations appear to be counter-productive.

But perhaps we need to say finally that those advocating these extreme forms of enhancement need to get real. Walk around a hospital any day and see all the conditions that bring lives to an end at relatively young ages even today. Think about breast cancer, prostate cancer, heart attacks, strokes. And then think about the degrading conditions that ruin the lives of the elderly, particularly Alzheimer's disease, and even debilitating and painful joint conditions, various forms of arthritis, and osteoporosis. Take your pick. We are so far from the idealistic world of posthumanism that one sometimes has to wonder whether the protagonists should be taken seriously. The world in which we live is riddled with conditions that limit life in affluent societies, quite apart from the far more devastating conditions that ruin human existence in other societies. A little realism might help both those who advocate extreme scenarios and those who object to them, and in the process object to any significant improvements in health care.

Section 2

Beginning of Life Issues

5

The Importance of Human Embryos

Up until the 1970s little interest was shown in human embryos, either by the public at large or by church communities. They were not the object of ethical interest, let alone ethical debate. This was hardly surprising since they were generally far removed from the public gaze. The central interest at that time was on abortion, and the destruction of foetuses from eight weeks or so of gestation (the latter stages of the first trimester of pregnancy). At that time it would have been exceedingly difficult to predict that the polarisation of opinion over abortion would be transferred into an equally divisive polarisation over what can be done with, and to, embryos.

The change was brought about by the abilities of scientists to maintain embryos in a laboratory environment in special media that enable them to grow and develop *in vitro*, that is, in an artificial environment. It was this that led in the 1970s and 1980s to the emergence of IVF as a viable procedure for bypassing infertility and for providing childless couples with children they could not otherwise have had (see chapter 7). Like all such developments the scientific prowess did not elicit any major negative response at the time. Debate about IVF was muted in its early days, since its potential and repercussions went unrealised. However, this initial subdued response has been replaced by vigorous opposition, as the possibilities opened up by research on human embryos and embryonic stem cells, have come to fruition. The result is that the vigour and antipathy shown towards abortion is now shown towards any manipulation of early embryos.

It is no exaggeration to state that the frontline in the ethical battle over what inroads should or should not be made into prenatal human life has shifted in large measure from the foetus (in abortion) to the embryo (in embryo research). It is also pertinent to point out in the context of this book that opposition to the use of embryos for research, or even therapeutic purposes in the future, comes largely from the churches and Christian groups. In other words, many see this battle as a theological and faith battle as much as a purely ethical one. I do not view the debate in these particular terms, but I can appreciate why this is such a common presumption.

These few remarks demonstrate very clearly that debate over the status and value of the human embryo is a very practically-oriented one. Forty years ago it may have been a largely theoretical debate; today that is most certainly not the case. The debate is often viewed as narrowing down to the age-old question of when human life begins. Unfortunately, the simplicity of this question belies the complexity and problems enshrined within an answer, since any answer will have to take account of myriad clinical situations where the value placed upon embryos may be pitted against the value ascribed to other human beings.

The chief problem is that there is no way in which it is possible to achieve consensus within pluralist societies. It is not even possible to achieve consensus within relatively homogeneous church communities, although this is often not acknowledged publicly. The divergence of views on the embryo is striking. To some it is self-evident that human life commences at conception or fertilisation, with the result that human embryonic and foetal life is to be given the same degree of protection as human life after birth. To others this is far from self-evident. As we have seen this disagreement has traditionally come to the fore in discussions on abortion, when the foetal life in question is anything from around six weeks' gestation to at least twenty weeks' gestation. However, the reproductive technologies focus our attention on early embryonic life, as early as three to six days after fertilisation and never beyond fourteen days of development. Do the same principles apply? Should someone who is anti-abortion also be anti-IVF or against any form of research on surplus embryos?

The difficulty with this debate is that it is not strictly a scientific one, but neither is it strictly a theological one. It is a mixture of the two, with a host of clinical, philosophical, social and policy dimensions thrown in for good measure. This is not easy for anyone to handle, and it is hardly surprising that it emerges as such a murky area. In this book I do not intend addressing directly any biblical teaching on life before birth (see Further Reading for the books and articles where I have covered this). Instead, I shall focus on the science and ethics.

5.1 Embryonic development

To begin to understand the issues involved we first need a brief background on embryonic development. Fertilisation is the fusion of a sperm and an ovum. This is achieved by the sperm penetrating the outer layers of the ovum, a process that takes between twenty-six and thirty hours to complete. The resultant fertilised egg is a single cell, the zygote, and is totipotent, that is, it has the potential to give rise eventually to a complete new individual (the foetus plus placenta).

The moment of zygote formation is regarded as the beginning of embryonic development. The egg becomes active and the genetic individuality of the embryo is established by the combination of genes from each of the parents. This single cell undergoes cleavage, during which it divides with little intervening growth to produce two, then four, then eight smaller, identical cells. These are the blastomeres, which at the eight-cell stage are only loosely associated with one another, and each has the potential to develop into complete adults if separated from the other blastomeres. By the thirty-two-cell stage, they have become increasingly adherent and closely packed, and have almost definitely lost this equal developmental potential.

As the number of cells continues to increase, those on the outside of the group become firmly attached to one another, with the internal ones remaining unconnected. At this stage, at around five to seven days, we have the blastocyst, an entity that has come to assume major importance in scientific terms and ethical debate. The outer cells of the blastocyst are in the process of differentiating and forming a surface layer, the trophectoderm, which becomes the trophoblast when implantation occurs into the wall of the mother's uterus (completed by fourteen days). These trophoblastic cells eventually give rise to the placenta. By contrast, the inner cells of the blastocyst constitute the inner cell mass (ICM) and are still undifferentiated; it is from a small number of these cells that the future individual arises.

By fourteen days after fertilisation, a structure known as the embryonic disc develops, and it is this that becomes the embryo proper. At fifteen to sixteen days a few thousand cells in the disc migrate to the midline where they form the primitive streak, which is a transitory developmental structure. This instigates the appearance of the neural plate, from which arises the first rudiment of the nervous system early in the third week of gestation. By about twenty-eight days, the beginnings of the central nervous system are present, although individual parts of the brain are not recognisable until five to six weeks' gestation.

The primitive streak has assumed a position of major importance in ethical debate. Its appearance at around fifteen to sixteen days has been widely regarded as marking a point of transition, with some arguing that no coherent entity exists prior to this, so that it is misleading to refer to anything earlier as a human individual. Conversely, commitment to developing into an individual embryo is present before the primitive streak stage, from which point onwards a spatially defined entity capable of developing into a foetus and infant begins to exist. While these points are made within a scientific framework, they send out powerful ethical and regulatory messages, so that in those societies where research on human embryos is permitted the dominance of the fourteen-day upper limit to research is currently unchallenged.

This scientific description only begins to hint at the different ways in which developing embryos are regarded ethically and theologically. Nevertheless, it should not be downgraded, since the precision of scientific studies and clinical procedures throw these different stages into relief all the time. As a result, ethical analysis which currently concentrates on embryonic potential at fourteen days may have to start taking seriously the ethical significance of the three or six day stage.

5.2 Ways of looking at embryos (and foetuses)

5.2.1 Embryos are moral persons

Many people believe that even the earliest embryos, from fertilisation onwards, have the same moral status as other people—in other words, embryos are moral persons, capable of being harmed and benefited just like us. Those who hold this view consider that destroying embryos counts as murder, and is ethically commensurate with killing a person.

According to this perspective, the process of embryonic development is simply the development of a person. There is no stage in human existence when we are not persons. From this it follows that embryos and foetuses are to be treated as persons with absolute value. Underlying these conclusions is the idea of potentiality: whatever we now are, was present in potential form in the embryos from which we developed. But do we do this in any other area of life? Is a caterpillar the same as a butterfly, and is a three-day-old human embryo the same as a thirty-year-old adult? In each case numerous processes both internal and external are required before the one becomes the other.

The intentions of those who hold the 'foetus is a person' position are exemplary, with their desire to enhance the value and moral standing of embryonic and foetal life. From a Christian perspective it is a very important position, since it is frequently seen as the one most in accordance with biblical and church teaching. But the issue is not this simple; biblical principles cannot be neatly encapsulated in positions such as this one. Nevertheless, its absolutist facade has enormous attractions for many Christians.

Some Christians employ a 'benefit of the doubt' approach. According to this, if there is any question about the value to be ascribed to an embryo or foetus, give it the benefit of the doubt by ascribing greater rather than lesser value. Although it is impossible to prove that personhood begins at fertilisation, the argument is that we should err on the conservative side (of protection) and conclude that this is indeed its starting point. There is then no chance that we will be committing murder. The aim of this approach is to protect the weak and disadvantaged. Nevertheless, care should be exercised to ensure that it does not simply bring an end to serious thought.

On this view, the promise of human embryonic stem cell research in terms of developing new therapies is irrelevant. This is because any research on human embryos is equivalent to murdering human beings, and this is untenable. Moreover, the routine destruction of embryos to provide a source of embryonic stem cells would constitute a further step towards the instrumentalisation of human life. It would be little more than exploiting human embryos (human persons) as a resource for our own ends, and hence would be objectionable.

5.2.2 Embryos are not moral persons

Others view the embryo at its blastocyst stage as a mere collection of cells that should not be considered as a moral person, and thus has none of the rights of other humans. On such a view, embryos are not capable of being either harmed or benefited. Their use for any purpose whatsoever is ethically defensible, so long as other issues such as consent are adequately addressed. If this view of the moral status of embryos is correct, it might be unethical *not* to use surplus IVF embryos, at least for research that aims to alleviate human suffering.

This position stems from the generally-held viewpoint that we do not consider it wrong to destroy either the ovum or sperm before they have united. On this basis, some conclude that we are not morally obliged to preserve the life of the embryo or foetus. Both can be regarded as a thing, and not a person, until that point in development when brain function or sentience can be established (which itself is highly debatable and has been put at anything from six to thirty-six weeks' gestation). Once sentience has been acquired, an embryo or foetus has sufficient moral status to make it wrong to inflict unnecessary pain upon it. A variation of this argument is to place emphasis upon when a nervous system can first be recognised. Some more extreme writers argue that infants do not become persons until around two years of age.

A central problem with this approach is that it ignores our moral obligation as people to nurture the very young within our midst. It fails to take account of the commitments we have to the welfare and survival of infants and also, to varying extents, of foetuses. Consequently, this position is almost unknown among Christians. The human family has obligations to the prenatal and neonatal, and in more general terms to those unable to look after themselves, since all these are totally dependent on the actions of responsible moral agents committed to their care. Apart from such actions, neither foetuses nor the newborn would survive. What this approach emphasises is the importance of relationships within the human community, including relationships with those who, using neurological and behavioural criteria, are barely members of that community. In other words, neurological and behavioural criteria alone are not sufficient to tell us how we should act towards foetuses and infants, since they fail to take account of the commitments so crucial to our life together within the human community.

5.2.3 Gradualist position

Many adopt a stance somewhere between these two extremes, considering that embryos have rights and are owed protections, perhaps due to their potential to become moral persons or due to shared genetic heritage, but that these rights and protections exist to a lesser degree than those of full moral persons. On this view, an embryo's rights and protections must be weighed against the potential benefits of using the embryo for research. Each research project using human embryonic stem cells will therefore be ethically defensible to a different degree, depending on the research's potential benefits.

In these terms a human embryo or foetus is a potential person, in that it has some claim to life. Emphasis on this sort of potential takes seriously the continuum of biological development. There is no point in development, no matter how early on, when the embryo or foetus does not display some elements of personhood—no matter how rudimentary. The potential is there, and because of this both the embryo and foetus have a claim to life and respect. This claim, however, becomes stronger as foetal development proceeds, so that by some time later on in development (probably during the third trimester for practical purposes), the claim is so strong that the consequences of killing a foetus are the same as those of killing an actual person—whether child or adult. This mirrors most people's responses in ordinary life, where we recognise a difference between the accidental loss of an embryo and the birth of a stillborn child. Both entail the death of a human being, and yet under most circumstances the loss of a life-which-almost-made-it is felt much more acutely than that of a life-which-had-hardly-begun-to-develop.

As with all intermediate positions, the gradualist position satisfies neither extreme. It is seen as being too liberal by advocates of the 'embryo is a person' viewpoint, and too conservative by the 'embryo is not a person' school. Not only this, but the 'potential person' stance is itself open to varying interpretations. Nevertheless, its gradualist emphasis strikes a chord with many on biological, philosophical, intuitive, and pragmatic grounds. It helps many through the maze of problems in the difficult prenatal and neonatal areas, and constitutes a helpful ethical basis for tackling specific ethical issues here. I find myself at ease within the broad limits of this position.

Within a gradualist perspective there are some who distinguish between the first fourteen days of development and everything subsequent to that point. There are numerous reasons for placing the emphasis here, but they narrow down to the thought that, using a variety of criteria, nothing resembling an individual can be discerned prior to fourteen days. And so they conclude that what is present is more akin to human tissue than to anything recognisable as a 'me'.

But is this a Christian position? The biblical accounts touching on prenatal human life do not take us nearly as far as some Christians would like. Embryos and foetuses are extremely important; they fit within the human community and are to be treated with a great deal of seriousness. Nevertheless, it is well-nigh impossible to use the Bible to provide watertight rules regarding the precise value of embryos under difficult, competing situations.

5.3 What are we to make of the natural wastage of embryos?

Pregnancy wastage is defined as the loss of an embryo or foetus during the period of gestation. In other words, it is the failure of a fertilised egg to result in the birth of a living newborn. Spontaneous abortion, foetal death, trophoblastic disease, ectopic pregnancy, and prematurity are all forms of pregnancy wastage. Of these, spontaneous abortion is the predominant form, with ninety per cent of pregnancy wastage occurring during the first trimester of gestation. Research into the frequency of pregnancy wastage estimates this to be around sixty to seventy per cent. The significance of the rates of spontaneous foetal death is that, for a twenty-five per cent mortality, 1.3 pregnancies are required per live birth. For a fifty per cent mortality, two pregnancies are required for one live birth, while for a seventy-five per cent mortality four pregnancies are required. In order to illustrate what these figures mean in real terms we can use, as an example, the American figures for live births. In 2004 there were 4,112,000 live births in the USA. If a sixty per cent prenatal mortality rate is assumed, this means there would have been

10,280,000 pregnancies in order to achieve 4,112,000 live births (2.5 pregnancies for each live birth). By the same token, there would have been 6,168,000 spontaneous abortions. If a seventy per cent prenatal mortality rate is used, the number of pregnancies rises to 13,707,000 for the same 4,112,000 live births (3.3 pregnancies for each live birth). In this case, the number of spontaneous abortions is of the order of 9,595,000.

In using figures such as these, I am not attempting to give to rough estimates a facade of accuracy they most certainly do not possess. I am also aware that, in some respects, these figures are simplistic. They do not take induced abortions into account, although if this was done the figures for spontaneous abortions may actually increase. On the other hand, there are factors besides spontaneous abortion responsible for some pregnancy wastage, and these would reduce the figures a little.

The question which needs to be asked in the present context is why there is this astronomically high rate of pregnancy wastage. The crux of the answer is to be found in chromosomal abnormalities. The frequency of these in spontaneous abortions has been reported to vary from eight to eighty-three per cent, the most frequently quoted overall figures being forty to fifty per cent. This variation stems largely from the ages of the abortuses examined.

It has also been found that both the rate of spontaneous abortions and the frequency of chromosomal anomalies among abortuses increase with maternal age. For instance, it has been estimated that among recognised pregnancies spontaneous abortions rise from sixteen per one hundred pregnancies among twenty to twenty-four-year-old women to thirty-seven per one hundred pregnancies among thirty-five to thirty-nine-year-olds. In a similar manner, the frequencies of chromosomal anomalies per one hundred spontaneous abortions rose from fifty-nine to seventy-four in the same age groups.

The mechanisms for eliminating chromosomal anomalies during pregnancy are extremely efficient. For instance, it appears that over ninety-nine per cent of chromosomal abnormalities are eliminated through spontaneous abortion or foetal death. This figure is arrived at by comparing the number of chromosomal abnormalities at birth (six per 1,000 live births) with the number at implantation (estimated at 890 to 1,113 per 2,226 implantations required for 1,000 live births). On a percentage basis, 99.3% to 99.5% have been eliminated.

Over ninety per cent of chromosomal anomalies fall into three categories. Trisomy (the presence of one extra chromosome) accounts for forty to forty-five per cent of chromosomally abnormal specimens in humans, the most common occurrence being trisomy 16. The absence of a sex chromosome (45,X anomaly) is found in twenty to twenty-five per cent of spontaneous abortions. This has a prenatal mortality of ninety-eight per cent. Polyploidy refers to the presence of complete extra sets of chromosomes. Of these, triploidy occurs in fifteen to twenty per cent of chromosomally abnormal abortuses, and tetraploidy in another five per cent. Only about one per cent of triploid conceptuses reach term.

No matter how pregnancy wastage is viewed, it poses a major challenge to those with a high view of the embryo, and especially those who hold the view that a person in the fullest sense of that term comes into existence at fertilisation. Some dismiss this problem by comparing the prenatal loss of human life to the high infant mortality rates in the Middle Ages or in developing countries today. However, there is a difference. To attempt to save every foetus about to be spontaneously aborted would mean allowing into life an astronomically large number (perhaps 2.5 million per year in the US) of abnormal children. While this is not even feasible at present (even if anyone wished to do it), the question facing us is whether, theoretically and theologically, this would be justifiable. In this instance, to save life is to produce handicapped life. The 'protective mechanism' of spontaneous abortion would be overridden, thereby uncovering vast sources of developmental abnormalities. It is this element in the pregnancy wastage debate that makes it so different from efforts to decrease perinatal mortality rates, where to save life is (in most instances) to save healthy, normal life. This is the crux of the ethical and theological dilemma of pregnancy wastage. By its very nature it raises imponderable issues for the status of the embryo.

5.4 Embryos today

Interest in embryos at the present time centres on their potential for research and therapy, with the thrust of the ethical debate revolving around their use as a source of embryonic stem cells. This is because the extraction of stem cells from embryos inevitably involves their destruction. This situation may change in the future, but that is not the case currently. The manner in which anyone responds to the destruction issue will depend on the status they ascribe to embryos (as discussed above).

5.4.1 The source of embryos

There are a number of sources of embryos from which embryonic stem cells can be obtained. The first of these are *non-viable embryos created via IVF*. These have no potential to develop into a living individual and may be regarded by some as clusters of human cells. They represent human tissue, and should be treated with respect but have no potential to implant.

Second, and far more important in practice, are *surplus embryos created via IVF*. These were created for potential implantation into a woman but are no longer required for reproductive purposes, and hence are destroyed. They are distinct from non-viable embryos in the fact that, were they transferred into a woman, they would have the potential to form a living individual. Allowing the creation of surplus embryos inherently means that some of the embryos created will be destroyed. Legislation in many countries prohibits the indefinite frozen storage of surplus embryos, and thus many embryos are destroyed by thawing.

Allowing the use of surplus embryos may well be the least contentious path, as they were created for reproductive purposes, as part of an IVF program, and not purely for research ends. It is also possible to procedurally separate the decision to destroy surplus embryos from the decision to use them for research. Thus a couple can choose to destroy their surplus embryos, having no longer any reproductive use for them, and then be given the opportunity to donate them to research. Procedural separation is important in seeking to prevent exploitation and coercion.

The third source of embryos are those *created via IVF specifically for research purposes*. The ethical difference between the creation of embryos specifically for research purposes and the use of surplus embryos lies in the fact that with those created for research the destruction of the embryos is premeditated, and there can be no separation of the decision to destroy the embryo and the decision to use it for research.

The arguments for allowing one and not the other are not concerned with the harm to the embryo itself. They focus primarily on the intended use of the embryo rather than the outcome, which is the same in both cases. Surplus IVF embryos were created for potential implantation into a woman but are no longer required for reproductive purposes. In contrast, where embryos are created for research there is no intention that they will ever develop into human beings, thus they are a means to an end, not an end in themselves. A significant number of people consider the creation of embryos for research as inconsistent with the principle of respect for human dignity, representing a further step in the instrumentalisation of human life. Creating embryos for research is viewed as treating them as a commodity, rather than bestowing dignity and respect on viable embryos as potential members of the human race.

However, arguments over dignity and respect must be tempered by the realities of what is considered the appropriate use of the embryo within our societies. In very many societies, procedures such as IVF, prenatal diagnosis, pre-implantation genetic diagnosis (PGD), and the creation, storage and destruction of surplus embryos are allowed, so that only limited respect is given to the early embryo. What has to be asked is whether there is inconsistency in allowing the production of surplus embryos in IVF but rejecting research possibilities. The result of both is the creation and destruction of embryos. It has to be decided whether the creation of embryos via IVF for research purposes diminishes the respect bestowed upon embryos and whether there is a significant difference between creating surplus embryos in IVF and creating embryos for research.

A fourth source of embryos is via their *creation using somatic cell nuclear transfer (SCNT),* or therapeutic cloning, for research purposes. Arguments for and against the creation of embryos via SCNT are similar to those for the creation of embryos via IVF. The difference between three and four lies merely in the way in which the embryos are created.

An argument against allowing therapeutic cloning is based on the view that it is the beginning of a 'slippery slope' toward reproductive cloning. The argument is that while SCNT research may be considered acceptable, it will inevitably lead to reproductive cloning and a devaluation of human life in general. In order to justify this position, it has to be demonstrated that there is a necessary connection between therapeutic and reproductive cloning. Some argue that it is entirely possible to legislate in favour of the creation of embryos for research via SCNT but against reproductive cloning. Another area of concern is that SCNT could result in the improper use of women's bodies by creating a demand for human eggs, as the technology would create a market for them. Of further concern is the fact that offering money for eggs could lead to the exploitation of poorer women, who would presumably be most likely to sell their eggs.

A fifth source is that provided by *hybrid and chimeric embryos created for research purposes.* While the notion of hybrid and chimeric embryos evokes images of man-beast animals, this is light years away from where researchers are at. Seeking to look beyond such images is important to determine the ethical context for such a proposal. As in positions three and four above, hybrid and chimeric embryos would only be used for research purposes. If it is decided that the creation of embryos for research is permitted, the differences between embryos created via IVF, SCNT or hybrid and chimeric embryos appear to be minor

Yet a further source of embryos is where they have been *created for research purposes but lack the potential to develop further.* Altered nuclear transfer (ANT) was first proposed as a way around the moral concerns that arise when considering embryo research. Proponents of ANT suggest that creating embryos that have no potential to develop avoids the controversy because they are not embryos. However, questions have been raised as to the truth of this claim. It has been suggested that in reality ANT would simply be creating disabled embryos programmed for an early death. This position appears to satisfy nobody. On the one hand, those who deem the early embryo to have full moral personhood are likely to object, arguing that the creation of non-functioning embryos is offensive. And on the other hand, those who promote embryo research are unlikely to be satisfied with a proposal that is likely to significantly limit research possibilities.

Let us now look at the ethical issues around the way embryos are obtained. There are two issues here which are immediately apparent. First, is the issue of consent. And, second, is the issue of compliance with regulations in the country of origin.

All research using human tissue raises consent issues. In general, the requirement to obtain informed consent recognises the need for researchers to show respect for persons, the persons in this instance being of those who have brought the embryos into existence. This even applies where embryos may be used for the extraction of human embryonic stem cell lines (see chapter 10). In this instance, additional requirements may be made for obtaining consent from the embryo donor. Human embryonic stem cell lines may be cultured for long periods of time and used in a number of different research projects, some of which will not be able to be envisaged when consent is sought. The consent obtained from the embryo donors should indicate an understanding and acceptance of this fact. The embryo donors should also be made aware that once a cell line is created using their embryo, they will have no control over the research uses to which the cell line is put and will thereafter be unable to withdraw their consent for the use of their embryo. Finally, donors should understand that products with a commercial value may be created using cell lines derived from their embryo and should accept that they will not receive any compensation for profits made from these products.

There are two questions relevant to deciding whether a research project using human embryonic stem cells is justified. The first question is: Can the research objective be met by using other approaches that do not involve human embryonic stem cells? Examples of possible alternative approaches include using animal embryonic stem cells or adult stem cells. If the research objective can be met by other means, then approval should not be given to using human embryonic stem cells for that purpose.

If the research objective cannot be met by using other approaches, then we must ask the second relevant question: Are the benefits of this research likely to justify the use of human embryonic stem cells? It would clearly be inappropriate to allow research that was expected to provide trivial or insignificant benefits to be carried out using human embryonic stem cells.

In spite of this safeguard against unnecessary use of embryonic stem cells for research, it is important to recognise that a huge amount of basic research will be necessary in order to obtain sufficient knowledge of human developmental pathways to allow therapies to be designed. This basic research will need to involve as many different types of stem cells as possible, including human embryonic stem cells. It is important that the need to ensure that human embryonic stem cells are used appropriately is balanced with the need to ensure that this basic research can go ahead.

5.5 Embryos in context

This chapter has taken us a great distance from traditional discussions of the moral status of the embryo. To some I will have transgressed boundaries that should not be crossed. The discussion of embryos today, with its focus on research using embryos, should not be interpreted as suggesting that societies have to move in these directions, nor that any of us as individuals have to approve of them. I have attempted to paint a picture of what is either happening or is proposed across the world. Different countries allow various procedures, and few, if any, allow all the ones I have outlined. Nevertheless, this variety of sources of embryos for research purposes highlights the boundary of the current debate.

One of the problems with far too many discussions of the value to be placed on human embryos is that they are considered in isolation of everything else. It is as if their moral status stands in grand isolation from any other human considerations. This is misleading, since embryos are members of the human community, even when they are not regarded as full human persons. As members of this community they are subject to the vicissitudes of what it means to be human. The consequences in practice include the following.

Embryos only have the potential to become new individuals if they exist in an environment conducive to this development. For instance, embryos in a laboratory setting lack such potential, since this depends upon their being placed in a woman's uterus. It can be argued, therefore, that the status bestowed upon embryos is actually bestowed upon embryos within a congenial environment. And so the different ways of looking at embryos discussed above actually apply to embryos plus an appropriate environment. This consideration may well have implications for ethical and theological debate.

The value placed upon embryos is a comparative value, in that it should be placed alongside the value of other human lives. This is part of what is implied by treating embryos as members of the human community. It is against this background that some justify research on surplus embryos if there is evidence that that research may in the long run benefit those with serious illnesses. A balance is being struck between embryos and others in need within the human community.

We are under no obligation to look at embryos in these terms, but I would suggest we cannot ignore completely the communitarian pressures. It can be argued that this is inherent within a Christian emphasis upon stewardship, where we do our best to assist those in need using our abilities and resources. Of course, there is tension here between our treatment of embryos and our treatment of others. Regardless of the conclusions we arrive at, this tension has to be faced.

6

Reproduction: Prevention of Fertilisation

Western cultures are dominated by two opposing drives in relation to fertilisation. One is the prevention of fertilisation, and along with this the desire to avoid introducing a child into the world. Opposing this is the reverse drive to overcome infertility by whatever means are necessary. This encapsulates the all-encompassing desire to have children of one's own. Of these drives, the first is generally the domain of the young, those wanting to develop their careers and enjoy the benefits of life without the prospect of children, or those waiting to find their life partner. The second encompasses those who have infertility problems, with in recent years a growing number of older women who have delayed child-bearing until their careers are on track. Since age plays a significant role in decreasing fertility, many of those who wait to have children until their late thirties have problems conceiving.

Underlying both drives is a common theme, namely, that children are a gift of God. Hence, procedures aimed at decreasing fertility as well as those devoted to facilitating it, come under the umbrella of this underlying concept. The question is what does it signify, and what is its relevance to either of these directions?

6.1 Children as gifts of God

The phrase 'children are a gift from God' is used repeatedly within many circles—from the religious to the secular media. As with all such terms it is frequently difficult to know in what sense it is being used and where the idea comes from in the first place. Another problem is that at face value it conveys a static feel. A gift is something to be accepted; no one is forced to give it to us, and we are to be grateful no matter what we think of it and whether we do or do not want it. Furthermore, when I have been given a gift, it becomes mine; I now own it. It is difficult to escape such ideas since they are implicit within our understanding of gifts in everyday life. But are they helpful when dealing with children? My answer is that they are useful in part, but only in part.

While the term has strong religious overtones, it does not feature nearly as prominently in the Bible as one may think. In the Old Testament Hannah demonstrates the agony, despair and social ostracism of the infertile (1 Samuel 1:5–20). When her prayer was answered and she bore a child she regarded the child as a special gift from God. Also in the Old Testament one encounters other instances of children as a gift of the Lord, usually in the context of faithfulness. More generally one can argue that we receive children in trust from God, in that they have been entrusted to us by God. This involves acceptance of our children as we find them. The relevance of this for our discussion is that children are gifts and not products. They are ends in themselves and are not simply instruments for achieving the ends of their parents.

It is this *giftedness* that is crucial ethically and theologically. They come as they are and are to be accepted as they are and not as we may wish them to be. They will also develop as themselves: developing their own sense of self, moving away from their parents, and becoming responsible (or irresponsible) human beings in their own right.

As with any gift it is significant to ask: to whom is the gift given? Are children given to parents? Are they given to the church? Or are they given to wider society? Perhaps the answer to these questions is that they are gifts to all. Wider society, as well as the immediate family, are participants in the nurturing and developing process. They are also God's gift to themselves in that they have been given the gift of life. No one owns them—not their parents, nor the church, nor society. They stand before God in their own right. In the light of these thoughts, how are children to be viewed within the reproductive realm? Are we being led to adopt a hands-off approach to bringing children into the world, or does that not follow from these considerations?

First and foremost, the idea that children are a gift from God highlights the importance of children. Jesus' words in Matthew 19:14 speak of this, 'Let the little children come to me, and do not stop them; for it is to such as these that the kingdom of heaven belongs'. The children among us, those who are on their way to becoming one of us in a full sense, are significant. They are never to exist on the margins. Second, children are not gifts to be owned; they are entrusted to us—to be cared for, protected, and provided for. Third, acceptance of children is vital, even if they are not entirely what we may initially have wanted—another daughter, a child at an inconvenient time in our lives, a disabled child who will not be able to run like all the other children, a short child who will never make a basketball player.

In none of this can I find anything that would preclude human intervention in bringing a child into the world. The giftedness motif limits what we will or will not do, but it does not paralyse us and prevent any action to improve the lot of children. On the positive side, it will encourage us to improve the health of children as much as we can (just as we attempt to improve the health of adults), to have balanced families that are capable of looking after their children as well as they can, to nurture children, and to give prominence to their needs. In constraining us, the motif will lead us to conclude that we cannot treat children as commodities, to be bought and sold; we cannot reject children on flimsy grounds; we cannot attempt to mould children so that they become replicas of their parents or are made to fulfil their parents' every wish.

In other words, the giftedness motif takes us far beyond any simple allegiance to the natural and rejection of the artificial. Regardless of whether or not artificial means are employed to prevent or encourage child bearing, it is the way in which children are viewed and treated that is central to a Christian ethic. As gifts they are to be handled with care, and this has nothing to do with how they were conceived or when they were conceived. Once here and in our midst, they are important; they are one with us in the human endeavour.

In the following pages I shall regard all children as gifts of God, regardless of the way in which they were brought into the world.

6.2 Significance of fertilisation

Do the different methods of contraception used have significance from a Christian standpoint, especially as far as any embryos are concerned?

Let's look at some examples (see case 6, chapter 1):

> Four young couples (Allan, Brown, Cardrew and Davies) were recently married, and not one of them wishes to conceive. Couple Allan decides to use the rhythm method, thereby hoping to prevent the birth of a child. Couple Brown has intercourse; an oral contraceptive is being used, fertilisation does not occur, and no child results. Couple Cardrew has intercourse. Since the wife is using an intrauterine contraceptive device, fertilisation does occur, but the embryo is prevented from implanting; no child results. Couple Davies has intercourse. No contraceptive is being employed since they think they are infertile and have no reason to expect to conceive. However, on this occasion fertilisation occurs. A child is not wanted on account of the wife's serious and chronic ill-health, and so a first trimester abortion is carried out; no child results.

These four couples pose immense challenges to our ethical decision-making, and demonstrate clearly the stress placed on fertilisation. The intention of all four couples is the same, since not one of them wishes to conceive and bring a new human being into existence. The result in all four cases is the same, and yet in two of them fertilisation occurs. This immediately poses a challenge. Is there any moral difference between the actions of these couples?

An intuitive response is that there appears to be a difference between the actions of couples Allan and Brown on the one hand, and couples Cardrew and Davies on the other, since in these latter cases, an embryo or foetus has been prevented from developing further or has actually been destroyed. Are either of these actions tenable for Christians? For many people, the actions of couples Cardrew and Davies may sometimes be acceptable, although their actions are more problematic than those of couples Allan and Brown. In turn, the actions of couple Davies pose greater problems for many than do those of couple Cardrew. If, however, fertilisation is used as an absolute landmark, the actions of couples Cardrew and Davies will be regarded as equally unethical.

Should Christians regard fertilisation in these terms? In each case, there is a couple demonstrating their love for each other but not wishing to conceive at this time. This may be supremely ethical and deeply spiritual. In the case of couple Davies, the love of the two for each other leads them to want to protect the life of the wife. Her life is seen as being of greater value than the possible life-to-be of the foetus. Their desire to maintain intact a loving and committed relationship is a profound act of human commitment, even though its accomplishment involves sacrificing the future life of a foetus.

6.3 Contraception: from natural to artificial

Natural methods of contraception are just that. They are methods aimed at avoiding conception. This immediately poses a religious question for some people: Should one attempt to avoid conception under any circumstances? Might not this be thwarting the purposes of God? In other words, any form of contraception is attempting to control reproduction; control is not confined to artificial methods of contraception. The issue within contraception, therefore, is not between control and no control, but between natural and artificial forms of control.

Natural contraception can only be found in one area: abstinence. Natural family planning uses periodic abstinence, when fertilisation is most likely to occur, to prevent conception. But does even this have an artificial element to it, since it is deliberately avoiding intercourse at the biologically optimal time, albeit via abstinence?

Leaving abstinence and natural family planning to one side, we are catapulted into the realm of the artificial, filled with numerous forms of contraception. Artificial contraceptives can be separated into two categories: those that prevent fertilisation, and therefore conception; and those that act after fertilisation, and therefore fail to prevent conception.

6.3.1 Pre-fertilisation contraceptives

- *The combined oral contraceptive pill (COP):*

This contains synthetic forms of the hormones oestrogen and progestin. This prevents ovulation, leading to the prevention of fertilisation as there are no eggs to fertilise. The hormones in the pill also influence changes in the histology of the endometrium (which occur normally during the menstrual cycle), making it unsuitable for implantation. A third effect, brought about by progestin, is to increase the viscosity of the cervical mucus making it less receptive to sperm traveling to the uterus. Other forms of hormone release, such as the vaginal ring, contain the same hormones, and act in the same way as do COPs.

- *Some forms of the mini pill:*

These only contain the hormone progestin, and so act similarly to the COP. Some forms of the mini pill prevent ovulation, and hence fertilisation. Injectable forms of progestin are also available, and if injected every twelve weeks, prevent ovulation. Implants are another option that act in the same way. These are match-sized plastic rods, which are implanted under the skin in the upper arm and last for three to five years.

- *Barrier methods:*

Male and female condoms, diaphragms and cervical caps. These prevent the sperm from getting to and fertilising the egg.

- *Spermicides:*

These kill sperm on contact and come in many different forms. By killing the sperm, fertilisation is prevented.

- *Sterilisation:*

Either tubal sterilisation for the female or a vasectomy for the male. This ensures that either ovulation is unable to occur or no sperm is released.

6.3.2 Post-fertilisation contraceptives

- *Most forms of the mini pill:*

As previously stated, these contain the hormone progestin. Ovulation may be prevented up to sixty per cent of the time. Like the COP the mini pill acts on both the lining of the endometrium and the cervical mucus. Thus, when ovulation is not prevented and the thickening of the cervical mucus does not prevent the sperm from reaching the egg, the hostile environment in the uterus prevents implantation.

- *The morning after pill / emergency contraceptives* (ECPs):

These contain higher doses of hormones than those contained in birth control pills. ECPs can contain only progestin, or both oestrogen and progestin. They prevent ovulation if it has not already occurred, but if fertilisation has taken place they also prevent implantation. ECPs will not terminate an early pregnancy that has already implanted into the uterus.

- *Intrauterine devices (IUDs):*

These consist of flexible plastic devices with that are inserted into the uterus, where it can stay for up to five years. They either contain a copper wire or work by releasing a progestogen. Although literature on the IUD suggests that fertilisation may be prevented and perhaps the copper in the IUD kills sperm, there is no evidence to support the hypothesis that sperm are killed or that fertilisation is prevented. IUDs prevent the fertilised egg from implanting in the lining of the uterus. They are also used for emergency contraception, when the device must be placed in the uterus within seven days following unprotected sex.

The table on the next page provides an overview of the efficacy of different forms of contraception. While these figures may be regarded as of practical interest and little more, they have ethical implications since efficacy is a component within ethical deliberation. If something is being used in order to achieve a particular end (contraception in this instance), an ethical procedure would be expected to be as efficient as possible. Inefficient procedures are, by definition, dubiously ethical.

Pregnancy rates within first year of use [1]

	Typical Use (%)	Perfect Use (%)
No Method	85	85
Hormonal Methods		
Combined oral contraceptive pill	5	0.1
Progestin-only pill	5	0.5
Depo-Provera injection	0.3	0.3
Implant	0.09	0.09
Barrier Methods		
Male condom	14	3
Female condom	21	5
Cervical cap (women with no previous births)	20	9
Cervical cap (women with previous births)	40	26
Diaphragm	20	6
IUDs		
copper coil	0.8	0.6
progestin releasing	2	1.5
Spermicides	26	6
Female sterilisation	0.5	0.5
Male sterilisation	0.15	0.1
Withdrawal	19	4
Natural family planning	25	1-9

1. US Food and Drug Administration 'Consumer-friendly birth control information'. Available at: <www.fda.gov/fdac/features/1997/conceptbl.html>. Accessed 20 February 2007.

6.4 Range of Christian perspectives

Until the 1930s Church teaching universally condemned contraception. In more recent times a theological divide exists between Roman Catholic teaching, which still considers the use of all contraception to be morally wrong, and that of most Protestant denominations. In other words, there has been a dramatic change in viewpoint over the past fifty or so years in some Christian quarters, and probably far more so in practice (if not in theory). Shifts of this nature are, as we shall see, common over bioethical issues. It is intriguing to consider why this shift has occurred, and why one church has maintained its opposition.

The position of the Roman Catholic Church in relation to contraceptives has remained unchanged. As Pope Pius XI wrote in 1930, in reaction to the decision by the Anglican Church to allow the limited use of contraceptives:

> Since, therefore, openly departing from the uninterrupted Christian tradition some recently have judged it possible solemnly to declare another doctrine regarding this question, the Catholic Church, to whom God has entrusted the defence of the integrity and purity of morals, standing erect in the midst of the moral ruin which surrounds her, in order that she may preserve the chastity of the nuptial union from being defiled by this foul stain, raises her voice in token of her divine ambassadorship and through Our mouth proclaims anew: any use whatsoever of matrimony exercised in such a way that the act is deliberately frustrated in its natural power to generate life is an offence against the law of God and of nature, and those

> who indulge in such are branded with the guilt of a grave sin.[2]

The Roman Catholic Church considers the Old Testament teaching of the Sin of Onan to prohibit all forms of contraception. As St Augustine notes, 'Intercourse even with one's legitimate wife is unlawful and wicked where the conception of the offspring is prevented. Onan, the son of Judah, did this and the Lord killed him for it.' The Roman Catholic position holds that we should not separate *love-making* from *baby-making*. There is, therefore, no place for any artificial methods of contraception, nor IVF or any other form of assisted reproductive technology. This is one extreme interpretation of a stance based on what is natural, with a particular interpretation of the child as a gift of God concept. We must not interfere with God's designs. If taken to its logical conclusion it also allows no room for natural contraception. The implications of this stance for every aspect of reproductive technology are far-reaching.

While the Roman Catholic Church considers sinful any sexual act devoid of the possibility of generating life, Protestant churches have changed their stance. The Anglican Church was the first to relax its view on contraceptives, declaring in the 1930 Lambeth Conference that:

> Where there is clearly felt moral obligation to limit or avoid parenthood, the method must be decided on Christian principles. The primary and obvious method is complete abstinence from intercourse (as far as may be necessary) in a life of discipline and self-control lived in the power of the Holy Spirit. Nevertheless in those cases where there is such a clearly felt moral obligation to limit or avoid parenthood, and where there is a morally sound

---

2. Pope Pius XI, *Casti Connubii: Encyclical of Pope Pius XI on Christian Marriage to the Venerable Brethren, Patriarchs, Primates, Archbishops, Bishops, and other Local Ordinaries Enjoying Peace and Communion with the Apostolic See.* Available at: <www.vatican.va/holy_father/pius_xi/encyclicals/documents/hf_p-xi_enc_31121930_casti-connubii_en.html> Accessed 20 February 2007.

> reason for avoiding complete abstinence, the Conference agrees that other methods may be used, provided that this is done in the light of the same Christian principles. The Conference records its strong condemnation of the use of any methods of conception control from motives of selfishness, luxury, or mere convenience.[3]

This limited approval of contraceptives was later broadened. By the 1958 Lambeth Conference, contraception had become generally accepted among Anglicans. As a result, what was seen as important was that Christians took upon themselves responsibility for deciding before God on the number and frequency of children within a marriage.

Other denominations soon followed the example of the Anglican Church, until today when condemnation of contraceptive use among Protestants is unusual. Among most Protestant believers debate over the use of birth control is not over whether or not to use it, but, rather, which methods of contraception are acceptable. As we have previously discussed there are two views generally held among Christian circles: that life begins at fertilisation, and that life begins later probably at implantation. Obviously, those who hold to the first position will only consent to the use of contraceptives that act prior to fertilisation. Those who hold to the latter position may approve of the use of all contraceptives that act prior to implantation.

There is, however, a small but growing group of Protestants who attest that the use of all contraceptives, including the use of natural family planning is wrong. They claim that to use contraceptives is to curtail the will of God and prevent Him from deciding when and how many children each family should have. Other evangelicals today come close to the Roman Catholic position. As one writer puts it:

---

3. Resolution 15, 1930 Lambeth Conference of Anglican Bishops. *The Life and Witness of the Christian Community: Marriage and Sex.* Available at: <www.lambethconference.org/resolutions/1930/1930-15.cfm> Accessed 20 February 2007.

> In the use of contraception, the sexual act is impoverished by the removal of its procreative significance if undertaken within the marital bond, it is abused if the sexual act is undertaken outside of the marital bond and is degraded if the unitive aspect is absent. I conclude that the use of artificial contraceptives frustrates God's desire and will to hand out the gift of life; but in the use of ARTs, the sexual act is rendered superfluous for procreation, and thus human procreation is degraded to the product of scientific innovation rather than the fruit of human intimacy. In this instance, God is asked to accept the child when he has not given that gift of life.[4]

A position such as this one appears to owe more to an interpretation of *natural law* than anything in the Scriptures. As such, any procedure designed to negate a natural outcome is unacceptable.

In any form of family planning, the couple in question is trying to prevent the conception of children. If it is wrong to employ methods to prevent and regulate the timing of children, then no matter if these methods are artificial or natural it is still wrong. However, if there is nothing wrong with preventing or regulating the timing of conception, then there is no difference between artificial or natural means. The question comes down to whether it is right to separate the possibility of procreation from the sexual act. This is not a biblical precept, and so it appears that we cannot conclude that such separation is wrong, unless one is following particular church teaching.

6.5 Weighing up contraceptive usage

The arguments for and against the use of contraceptives cover a wide spectrum of thought, with a host of pressures thrown in for good measure. One thing is certain: they are not isolated claims; they have

4. EC Hui, *At the Beginning of Life: Dilemmas in Theological Bioethics* (Downers Grove, Illinois: Inter-Varsity Press, 2002), 187.

repercussions for many other bioethical agendas, and they stem from a range of considerations.

Arguments against contraceptive use revolve around what are essentially natural law arguments: opposition to any separation of love-making and baby-making, and overt opposition to the introduction of artificial devices into what is a natural process. For many years this area could be considered in isolation of any other reproductive considerations, but this is no longer the case. An anti-contraceptive position now leads to opposition to any other interventions at the beginning of human life—from artificial insemination by the husband to IVF in its many guises. Inevitably there is also resistance to donor insemination (DI) and to any form of surrogacy. Surprisingly, there is some support for embryo donation on the grounds that this amounts to saving human life, even though the artificial element and the crossing of marital boundaries are paramount (see chapter 7).

The main assumption behind the previous paragraph is that there must be consistency in the application of basic ethical principles. If this is not the case, one can imagine holding a strict position on preventing conception, but not on means of overcoming infertility. It is in this context that we need to be reminded that the natural-artificial distinction is not used in other areas within the biomedical sciences and clinical medicine. Its use in the reproductive domain at the beginning of life sets that domain apart from all others, and this needs to be justified both ethically and theologically.

Additional arguments against the use of contraceptives (especially oral contraceptives) include their contribution to social malaise, through the weakening of long-term committed relationships, a general lowering of moral standards, and disruption of family life. It has to be admitted that over the past forty years there has been a devaluing of the family, a lowering in moral standards and an increase in infidelity and premarital sex, but does it follow that these are a direct consequence of the use of contraceptives? One could perhaps suggest that availability of contraception and abortion has aided those seeking to hide infidelity, and that it has given some the impression that they are able to indulge in unhealthy activity with no consequences for themselves or others. But it seems that the availability of contraceptives themselves is not responsible for this, rather that society as a whole has moved in this direction. These are not arguments against the responsible use of contraceptives within a loving committed marital relationship.

As with many of the biomedical technologies we are concerned with in this book, the misuse of contraceptives elicits a longing for the old days before their availability. If only the oral contraceptive had not been developed, societies today would be so much more moral than they are; marital infidelity would be far lower, and there would be a much lower incidence of sexually-transmitted diseases. The assumption here is that science is to blame for moral and social malaise. While the oral contraceptive has undoubtedly had social consequences, one only has to look at many developing countries, where oral contraceptives are little used, to realise that any direct cause and effect relationship is only part of the story. The impetus for moral behaviour is not dependent upon the availability or non-availability of scientific devices. We are to act morally whether or not contraceptives are available. This, surely, is a central feature of the Christian message.

7

Reproduction: Artificial Reproductive Technologies

From one to three million in under thirty years is quite an achievement. Such is the cataclysmic change that is the revolution of *in vitro* fertilisation (IVF). Who would have thought in 1978 that by the age of twenty-eight Louise Brown would be just one of three million IVF babies? But this is what the reproductive revolution has wrought, and with it has come a legion of related technologies. The world of the artificial reproductive technologies (ARTs) is now well and truly with us, bringing with it a swathe of technological and social repercussions. However, before we look at these, we should set the scene by spelling out what is involved in natural fertilisation.

Biological Parents:	F1 and M1
Fertilisation:	Natural insemination into F1
Gestation:	F1
Social Parents:	F1 + M1

Our couple, F1 and M1 (F stands for the female and M for the male), are a fertile couple. The gametes (egg and sperm) come from them, making them the biological parents. Fertilisation occurs by natural insemination of sperm into the female, who then carries the foetus to term. Additionally, they rear the child themselves, so that their influence extends throughout the years of childhood. The two people concerned are, therefore, the social parents as well as the biological parents.

As we consider the various ARTs, it will be important to look closely at the similarities as well as dissimilarities with natural fertilisation. This will demonstrate where the ethical pressure points lie.

7.1. Various forms of artificial fertilisation

The many forms of artificial fertilisation available today have developed in response to a variety of clinical and social demands, and have differing degrees of technical sophistication. Nevertheless, they have in common an artificial element aimed at overcoming or bypassing inherent obstacles to the birth of a child.

Case 1. Artificial insemination by donor: DI

Biological Parents:	F1 and M2
Fertilisation:	Artificial insemination into F1
Gestation:	F1
Social Parents:	F1 + M1

In this case, the sperm comes from an anonymous donor (M2) and is artificially inseminated into the female partner, and gestation occurs normally. The male partner (M1) contributes nothing and so is not the biological father, although he is the social father. The mother (F1) is both the biological and social mother. Since a third party has been introduced into the reproductive process, the resulting child will have three parents. In practice, however, society has attempted to reduce this to two parents, the social parents, since the anonymity of the biological father (M2) has, until recently, been assiduously protected. Even when it is possible for the child to trace the biological father, there is no hint that he is a parent in any meaningful sense.

Case 2. Surrogate motherhood (without IVF)

Biological Parents:	F2 + M1
Fertilisation:	Artificial insemination into F2
Gestation:	F2
Social Parents:	F1 + M1

The female partner of our couple is infertile and is also incapable of carrying the child through gestation. For both these functions she has been replaced by another woman (F2) who is inseminated with the sperm of the male partner (M1). This second woman carries the child to term, and then hands over the child to the social parents. The novel features of this arrangement are that conception of the child in a third party is intentional, on the understanding that the third party's involvement will be confined to the period of gestation. A radical separation has been deliberately introduced, therefore, between child-bearing and child-rearing. In this instance, the resulting child has some of the genetic characteristics of the surrogate (F2).

Case 3. IVF: simple case

Biological Parents:	F1 + M1
Fertilisation:	IVF
Gestation:	F1
Social Parents:	F1 + M1

This is IVF in its standard or simple form. The biological parents are the social parents, and gestation occurs in the female partner. In all these respects it is identical to natural reproduction. The one crucial divergence from natural reproduction is the manner of the fertilisation, which occurs in the laboratory under controlled scientific conditions.

Before a woman's eggs can be obtained for IVF her ovaries are generally stimulated with hormones. Then, while the patient is sedated, eggs are aspirated from the ovaries under ultrasound guidance. The eggs are then fertilised in the laboratory with the male partner's sperm. In most IVF programs surplus embryos will be frozen, raising the inevitable ethical quandaries as to what to do with embryos no longer required by the couple. Consequently, they will have to face a demanding range of clinical procedures on the female partner, as well as serious ethical considerations regarding the ultimate fate of any embryos not required by them.

Case 4. IVF: with intracytoplasmic sperm injection (ICSI)

Biological Parents:	F1 + M1
Fertilisation:	IVF
Gestation:	F1
Social Parents:	F1 + M1

IVF is constantly being refined through the development of further techniques, some of which have emerged as major players in the modern IVF armamentarium. One of these is ICSI, which involves the direct injection of a single sperm into an egg. This is now a much utilised procedure, accounting for around fifty per cent of all IVF procedures. Other procedures sometimes employed include the use of (immature) sperm from the epididymis or testis rather than (mature) sperm obtained by ejaculation. All these procedures are aimed at increasing the success rate of IVF.

Case 5. IVF: sperm donation

Biological Parents:	F1 + M2
Fertilisation:	IVF
Gestation:	F1
Social Parents:	F1 + M1

The male partner (M1) is infertile and so a sperm donor (M2) is used. Although the female partner produces eggs, DI has failed. Despite this, fertilisation does occur following IVF. The resulting embryo is implanted in the female partner, and pregnancy occurs in a straightforward manner. The resulting child has three parents.

Case 6. IVF: egg donation

Biological Parents:	F2 + M1
Fertilisation:	IVF
Gestation:	F1
Social Parents:	F1 + M1

The female partner (F1) is infertile but is capable of carrying a foetus to term. Another woman (F2) donates an egg, and this is fertilised in the laboratory by the man's sperm (M1). The resulting embryo is placed into F1, in whom gestation takes place. The child has three parents, since the biological mother differs from the social mother. This is the converse of DI, although anonymity cannot be maintained to the same extent as with sperm donation. This is because the menstrual cycles of the two women have to be synchronised, a requirement that will continue in force until it is clinically commonplace to freeze and thaw eggs.

Case 7. IVF: embryo donation

Biological Parents:	F2 + M2
Fertilisation:	IVF
Gestation:	F1
Social Parents:	F1 + M1

Both members of our couple (F1 and M1) are infertile, although the woman is capable of sustaining a pregnancy. An embryo that, under present circumstances, would be a surplus embryo from another couple (F2 and M2) on an IVF program is placed in the woman and gestation proceeds. Since the biological and social parents are different, this is sometimes referred to as prenatal adoption, although this is probably a misleading term.

Case 8. IVF: surrogate motherhood

Biological Parents:	F1 + M1
Fertilisation:	IVF
Gestation:	F2
Social Parents:	F1 + M1

This is similar to number 2 above, although the introduction of IVF makes surrogacy a far more radical procedure. This stems from the possibility opened up of the transfer of an embryo (rather than sperm) to the surrogate mother (F2), who will then serve solely as an incubator for the couple's embryo.

Apart from this consideration, the major justification for using IVF would be sub-fertility on the husband's side. IVF may lead to fertilisation even if artificial insemination has proved unsuccessful. As in 2, above, the essential prerequisite for surrogacy is the wife's inability to sustain a pregnancy. Additional permutations of the IVF surrogacy arrangement can include sperm or egg donation. Obviously two women would not be required if the egg donor was also the surrogate mother, as in 2. IVF makes possible the separation of the donor and the surrogacy roles, which can help the surrogate to mentally and emotional distance herself from the child she carries. If both the male and female partners (M1 and F1) are infertile, embryo donation can be considered. The resulting child in this instance has five parents. In considering surrogacy the assumption is being made that it is altruistic and hence is non-commercial. Commercial surrogacy raises a host of additional considerations.

Case 9. IVF: with pre-implantation genetic diagnosis (PGD)

Biological Parents:	F1 + M1
Fertilisation:	IVF/PGD
Gestation:	F1
Social Parents:	F1 + M1

This technology takes IVF a step further. PGD is used before an embryo is placed in the uterus of the woman. It works by taking a cell from the early embryo and screening this cell. The sex of the given embryo can be determined along with its chromosomal make-up, and disabilities such as cystic fibrosis can be detected (see chapter 8, where further details are given). The point of including it here is to show that the parentage is straightforward. Any ethical issues revolve around the selection of embryos.

7.1.1 IVF

It is evident from the above that IVF has been the harbinger of revolutionary developments within the reproductive technologies. Single-handedly it has given rise to the ARTs, and to a whole new way of looking at human reproduction. The original impetus behind IVF was to enable young infertile couples to have children when all other approaches appear to have failed. It is still used in this way.

The most common causes to infertility are: male factor infertility or female factor infertility—including tubal disease, ovulatory disorder, diminished ovarian reserve, endometriosis, uterine factors. It is not uncommon for there to be multiple female factors or for both male and female factors to contribute to infertility. A significant number of cases are unexplained.

However, since IVF is a technological procedure, it can be used in many other ways as well, and this has resulted in post-menopausal women, single women, and lesbian couples using it. It has also been used to enable couples, who already have children by previous relationships, to have children with their new partners, and even for couples to have a large family as opposed to a family (following, say, a hysterectomy after the birth of a second or third child). Since increasing numbers of women are delaying motherhood until later in life (early-mid forties) when there is a precipitous decline in fertility, it is being increasingly used to enable this growing sub-population to have children.

The clinical and ethical ambivalence of IVF is startling. Its success is bought by focussing attention onto embryos rather than onto one or both partners where the source of the infertility lies. IVF depends upon making available human embryos in a laboratory environment, where they can be studied and analysed in previously unimaginable ways.

The challenging ethical issues associated with IVF have elicited quite different responses from those within the Christian community. These centre on the moral status of the embryo, especially with regard to the selection of embryos that occurs in routine IVF treatment and the production of surplus embryos within IVF programs. The latter has come far more to the attention of theologians and policy makers since the potential of embryonic stem cells was realised in the late 1990s (see chapters 5 and 10). Also inherent within IVF is the separation of sexual intercourse from fertilisation, a theme previously discussed in connection with artificial methods of contraception (see chapter 6), and with this the tension between divine and human control (see chapter 3). Hence, IVF makes explicit concerns that have been encountered for many years within reproduction, but in this instance they are over attempts to enhance fertility rather than counter it. The context therefore has shifted quite dramatically.

Where do we start? It cannot be denied that IVF is a way around infertility rather than a cure for infertility. The technological expertise solves the problem in a technological manner. Children produced by this technique have to be produced technologically. This is the basic reality from which there is no escape.

The element of human control in IVF has elicited different responses to the procedure. The amalgam of human intervention and a laboratory environment has led some to condemn IVF as dehumanising, on the grounds that *baby-making* and *love-making* have been separated. Others, however, have seen the planning as being supremely human, especially since an obstacle to marital and human fulfilment has been overcome. This in a nutshell is the essence of the debate over what constitutes legitimate human control.

Some have gone as far as to argue that the laboratory production of human beings is no longer human procreation, because the technological inroads have replaced the profoundly human characteristics of normal procreation. It has even been argued that once we start making human beings in this way, we stop loving them. This is because any movement away from the physical and sexual may deprive procreation of its human connotations, since it no longer involves the diversity of factors constituting human sexual love. This has led some to argue that this could have implications for the family as a biological unit. It is noteworthy that these criticisms of IVF are pragmatic and social ones; they are amenable to being tested. Since there are currently over three million IVF children in existence, the detrimental social and moral effects of IVF should be readily demonstrable—if they indeed exist. I would suggest that they do not exist. To argue that the desperately wanted children produced by IVF are little more than technologically-produced creatures bears no semblance of reality to the clinical situation.

An argument sometimes raised against IVF is that it is an artificial means of conception, as opposed to the natural means, which is regarded as the only acceptable one. The concept of 'natural' is, however, highly relative. If it is argued that it is not natural to have a baby by IVF, it is equally unnatural to use any technological form of contraception (as some would argue), to employ any medication during pregnancy to protect the developing foetus, to resort to neonatal intensive care units, or to vaccinate infants (intrusions that are not generally condemned). Many facets of modern medicine are unnatural, and yet this by itself does not make modern medicine *per se* unethical.

The failures of IVF have also been used as ammunition against it, since some couples may be presented with false expectations. Some couples have unduly high expectations in spite of the far more cautious advice given by the clinic. Of course, IVF is quite often a failure (see below), and its successes have to be balanced against its failures (the same applies to natural fertilisation). The human face of IVF is to be seen in this balance, and not simply in the children born to happy and grateful parents.

In the end, arguments for and against IVF tend to stem from one's willingness or otherwise to use technological means to alleviate infertility and produce children. There is no doubt that some strands of Christian thinking are vigorously opposed to any scientific or clinical intrusion into bringing new human life into existence. Children are gifts of God, and any human intrusion into reproduction is seen as threatening this, somehow interfering with God's purposes and resulting in subhuman children. In my view this is far too narrow an interpretation of the concept of gifting which does not eschew an artificial component (see chapter 6).

Any technological contribution can be well used or misused. It will contribute in helpful ways if it is regarded as one ingredient within a rich human-divine framework. Alternatively, if it becomes nothing less than a technological solution to wide-ranging human problems, it will prove deceptive. My conclusion is that IVF holds out the prospect of enhancing the procreative process as a whole, just as many forms of routine medicine hold out the prospect of enhancing human well-being when it has been lost. The potential of IVF lies in its ability to rectify a missing element in the union of man and woman (husband and wife), so that it may be a legitimate means of healing in certain situations. Nevertheless, this does not justify its use as a way of bypassing the normal means of human procreation in the absence of a therapeutic rationale. Neither does it mean that we can do anything in the reproductive area. Christians are always to balance technological intrusions with other considerations, seeing such intrusions as inferior to natural means of reproduction and to be resorted to only when 'natural' reproduction fails.

But what about the fate of the embryos used in IVF procedures? This doubt is a three-pronged one: the sacrifice of embryos during the development and continued improvement of the technique; the dilemma about whether to implant an embryo observed to be abnormal; and the multitude of embryos surplus to the requirements of those undergoing IVF.

The first problem has much in common with many clinical research programs. In these, initial treatment using a new procedure in human patients is frequently relatively unsuccessful. The rate of success increases with experience as modifications are introduced in the light of the results of earlier trials. This has certainly occurred in the case of IVF.

The second problem is what to do when embryos are found to be abnormal. In routine IVF practice decisions are made every day about which embryos to implant and which to discard, not on some ideological eugenic basis but simply to improve the chances of having a successful pregnancy. Hence embryos thought to be non-viable in that they are not dividing properly are discarded. It is difficult to see what arguments can be raised against this practice, since it mirrors what must be occurring all the time in nature. This has a great deal in common with what happens naturally where up to seventy per cent of embryos are lost in the form of spontaneous miscarriages (see chapter 5).

This leaves the third issue, that of surplus embryos, which forms the crux of the ethical and theological issues for many people.

7.1.2 Surplus embryos

The hormonal regimen prescribed for women undergoing IVF causes them to superovulate and produce a number of eggs (up to fifteen) in a single cycle. Doing this reduces the likelihood that a woman will have to undergo the uncomfortable and potentially dangerous process of hormonal stimulation again. Currently, embryos and sperm can be frozen and defrosted easily without significant damage but eggs cannot, although this is changing. The reasons why it is desirable to produce so many embryos are: the transfer and implantation of the initially chosen embryos may not be successful and so more are needed; not all the embryos will be suitable for transfer and so having a pool of embryos from which to choose is beneficial; and saving the woman from having to undergo ovarian stimulation again should she want more children in the future.

However, usually a successful pregnancy occurs before all the embryos have been implanted, leaving embryos surplus to the couple's needs. These frozen embryos can be stored for a maximum period of time in most countries; ten years is frequently the period selected. Other than storage for a limited length of time embryos can be: destroyed, by allowing them to thaw; donated to other couples; or used in research. Once again, what can or cannot be done varies between countries.

At 31 December 2003, there were 104,917 frozen embryos in storage in Australia and New Zealand. In March 2003 there were 116,252 frozen embryos in storage in the United Kingdom. A survey in the US found that in April 2002, 396,526 frozen embryos were in storage. Storage of embryos incurs an annual fee is many regimes.

7.1.3 Complications with IVF

From the figures already given it is clear that IVF is very widely employed in many countries. One of the major problems with it over the years has been the increased incidence of multiple births. This is due to the fact that in the past up to three or four embryos were replaced in women. Until a few years ago this was necessary because of the inefficiency of IVF procedures. However, as the efficiency of these has increased, there have been numerous births of twins, triplets and quads, creating further problems. Today it is becoming increasingly accepted that only one embryo should be replaced.

The chance of congenital abnormalities in children born as a result of IVF is similar to children conceived naturally, and this is a little less than three per cent. However, there is evidence of a slightly higher rate of chromosomal abnormalities in children born as a result of ICSI. Studies suggest that IVF and ICSI are associated with a high risk of rare disorders associated with the 'imprinting' of genes, occurring in approximately 1 in 2,000 children compared to 1 in 10,000 children conceived naturally.

7.1.4 Costs of fertility treatment

The cost of IVF treatment and funding available varies between countries, from some where there is support for an unlimited number of cycles to others where there is no support at all. Most support one or two cycles. In the United Kingdom a cycle of IVF treatment costs around £3000, with additional charges for consultations, drugs and tests and other procedures, such as embryo freezing. About twenty-five per cent of IVF treatments are funded by the NHS (National Health Service). In the US the average cost of an IVF cycle is $12,400 (US). In Australia the average cost of an IVF cycle is $7,117 (AUS), and IVF funding is not limited by age or cycle number, though IVF clinics must be accredited to receive funding. The average cost for a couple of New Zealand is around $7,300 (NZ) for IVF, $9,000 (NZ) for ICSI and $14,000 (NZ) for PGD. If an infertile couple qualifies the New Zealand government will pay for up to two cycles of IVF/ICSI treatment.

In most countries IVF is not universally available, since costs limit its availability. Its expense means that many health services are unable to afford it. Allied with this is the belief in some countries that infertility is not an illness and so should not be supported using public funds. Both these considerations raise ethical concerns.

7.1.5 Success rates

In 2004, 41,904 treatment cycles were carried out in Australia and New Zealand. In the same time period, in the US, more than 127,977 cycles were carried out. Between 1 April 2003 and 31 March 2004, there were 38,264 treatment cycles in the United Kingdom. Overall the success rate of IVF is around twenty-five live births per 100 cycles started. However, the success rate varies according to the mother's age. For women under thirty-five the percentage of live births per cycle started is around thirty to thirty-five per cent, dropping to twenty per cent for women aged thirty-eight to forty, ten per cent for ages forty-one to forty-two, and down to a dismally low four per cent for women over the age of forty-two.

7.2. Gamete donation (GD)

Both egg and sperm donations are used in clinical practice. Of the two, sperm donation is by far the more common, since donor insemination (DI) has been used for the past hundred years. Egg donation only became possible with the advent of IVF and was first used in 1984. In addition to these embryo donation is also available.

There is no doubt that GD enables a couple, where there is an infertility problem on one side, to have a child they can bring up as their own and who is a biological child of one of them. Moreover, the female partner has gone through all stages of the pregnancy, and so there has been bonding between mother and developing child. Therefore, although the child is only fifty per cent the couple's child in genetic terms, it is entirely the couple's child in environmental terms. This is also an important consideration where the man or woman does not wish to pass on a genetic defect to the child. In this situation GD is an alternative to having no children of their own.

What makes DI attractive is that it is a relatively non-invasive procedure. Egg donation, on the other hand, is far more invasive, requiring IVF on the part of the donor and hormonal medication for the female partner (to replace that which is normally derived from a natural ovarian source).

All ethical arguments in favour of GD are dependent on one basic premise: that the source of the reproductive cell is of less importance than the love, care and nurture of children. In these terms, children constitute an essential element of marriage, so that the means by which they were conceived is of secondary importance. Arguments against GD revolve around objections to the introduction of a third party into the marriage relationship. These objections are of two main types: one based on a particular view of marriage, and the other on psychological considerations.

For some, the introduction of a third party into the marriage relationship, even when limited to the sperm or egg of an anonymous donor, means that a foreign element has intruded into what should be an exclusive relationship. The concern has frequently been expressed that this amounts to adultery, although if adultery is defined as voluntary sexual intercourse of a married person with someone other than his or her spouse, GD does not constitute adultery. Since it is carried out with the consent of the two partners, it can be regarded as a mark of the stability of a marriage rather than the converse.

The second category of objection to GD centres on the reactions of the partner to a child that is not biologically theirs. The male partner with a DI child may reject the child on the grounds that the child may be a constant reminder to him of his own inadequacy and weakness. A very large literature now exists on this matter, and, as one would expect, the results vary. However, the objections are largely unfounded, and there are many instances where there is remarkable degree of acceptance and gratitude on the part of parents and child for the gift of this new life that otherwise would not have come into being. The issue of non-genetic relationship to the resulting child highlights, not so much an argument against GD, as an argument for adequate counselling of the couple in preparation for GD and the birth of a GD child.

A very important consideration in looking at GD, as at all other reproductive technological procedures, is the position of the child. A feature of GD, particularly sperm donation, in the past was the secrecy that surrounded the technique, and the deceit that has sometimes been entered into by parents and family.

7.2.1 Christian responses to gamete donation

For some Christians, GD by mutual consent of married couples is not regarded as a moral evil. It may even be viewed as a great good in some instances, since it can be used to promote and preserve whole human personhood. Other Christians, emphasising the third party element, recognise it as adultery in essence, even if not adultery in fact.

In GD the partners are participating in the social creation of a child—as opposed to the biological creation of a child. In this sense, they can legitimately refer to the child as 'our' child, since it is their decision that has resulted in the creation of a new human being. The child is indeed, a creation of their relationship. It is the element in GD that separates it so decisively from adoption, with its stress on the involvement of the couple in GD, even though one of them is no more than an onlooker biologically. When these two contradictory trends can be accepted the relationship may well be strengthened. Conversely, the result may be disastrous when there is not acceptance of the separation of the procreative and sexual sides of human existence.

Perhaps the most contentious issue within the GD family (both immediate and extended family) has been the secrecy and deception of GD. This has been practically endemic within DI. Although many individual families undoubtedly do handle GD children, and the secrecy surrounding them, very well, the issue of deception remains. Recent studies have found that nearly half the parents have not told, or are unlikely to tell their children they are 'donor-assisted' babies. This situation is currently changing, with increasing emphasis upon the necessity of openness on the part of all involved, including the donor and his/her identity. This points to a child's right to know something of its origins, in the same way as adopted children have this right. This may be regarded as an outworking of the Christian emphasis on the equal dignity of all human beings regardless of their origins.

My conclusion is that GD should not be condemned on ethical grounds in every instance; equally, I believe GD is not a viable option simply on the grounds that the resulting child will be loved and cared for. GD must be viewed within the context of both family and society, and this is a challenge within every community.

7.3 Embryo donation

Embryo donation generally involves the use of surplus embryos from IVF programs. These embryos were originally wanted embryos, produced with the intention of leading to the birth of children. Those who consider all embryos to be full human persons are showing considerable interest in this possibility. From this perspective they should not be destroyed, since this is akin to murder. Neither should they be used for research purposes. That leaves only one avenue: donation to another couple. This desire to give 'human life' to an already existing human embryo has been expressed by some evangelicals, and even by some within Roman Catholic circles.

The similarities between embryo donation and adoption in the conventional sense stem from the 'wanted-ness' of a human organism. The adoption of an embryo enables the adoptive mother to experience the developing organism within her throughout gestation, an experience denied the adoptive mother in postnatal adoption. The mother is also able to give of herself to the developing foetus, since its environment is that of her own body. In many respects, therefore, she provides for that foetus in the most profound of ways. She is not the genetic mother, but she is the carrying and nurturing (social) mother. The adoptive father, too, is able to make a more direct contribution to the growing foetus than ever would be possible when adopting a child.

The practicalities of embryo donation are far more onerous than sometimes appreciated in countries where such procedures come under state control, since every effort has to be made to protect the child-to-be. This leads to checks at least as stringent as those imposed upon adoptive parents-to-be. It is unfortunate that considerations of this nature are so often overlooked in discussions that regard embryo donation as an idealistic answer to the surplus embryo syndrome.

However, fascinating further issues are introduced by this procedure, namely, the intrusion of third and fourth parties into the marriage relationship. Embryo donation takes the separation of biological and social parenthood much further than any other procedure. The reproductive process is artificial, while neither of the adoptive parents has any genetic stake in the embryo/foetus. This raises the question of whether this particular intruder is a foreign element hostile to the exclusivity of the marriage relationship, and even whether the female partner is not, in essence, acting as a surrogate mother for the genetic parents. The tension arising from these considerations and that of 'saving the life' of surplus embryos is largely unresolved at present.

8

Reproduction: Beyond IVF

IVF has become the showpiece of the human control of reproduction. Nevertheless, there are many other ways in which reproduction is modified. Before the advent of IVF artificial insemination by husband and by donor had long been practised. Hormonal regimes in the form of fertility drugs had been employed in attempts to improve the chances of conceiving for those suspected of having infertility problems, for maintaining pregnancies in danger of failing (spontaneous abortion/miscarriage), while in order to improve pregnancy outcomes obstetric procedures were utilising an increasing array of technological interventions. As a result of increasing technological sophistication it has proved possible to save the lives of ever-younger premature babies, in spite of the uncertain outcome (with high levels of morbidity) for the youngest of them. In other words, reproduction has been associated with varying degrees of technological intervention for a very long time. This does not mean that all these have been readily accepted by everyone, with objections to at least some of them coming from groups as far apart as the Roman Catholic Church and secular feminists.

Apart from procedures aimed at enhancing fertility and pregnancy, the overarching modification has been that of bringing a pregnancy to an end, namely, induced abortion. And it is around abortion that the bulk of ethical and theological debate has raged for the past fifty years. Also of concern has been the increasing sophistication of contraceptive measures, depending increasingly upon hormonal interventions and in some instances amounting to very early abortion (see chapter 6). Behind the scenes technological modifications have been developing apace, but in general have elicited comparatively minor amounts of ethical debate when compared with abortion and contraception. The assumption appears to have been that positive measures taken to improve the prospect of bringing new life into existence are less problematic than negative measures aimed at bringing life to an end. Put in these stark terms it is easy to appreciate why this has been the case, and yet even life-saving measures may not be without their own ethical quandaries. Ethical ambiguity reigns supreme.

Some of these ambiguous procedures will be covered in this chapter, with the major focus being on pre-implantation genetic diagnosis (PGD).

8.1 Prenatal diagnosis

While it is PGD that receives all the attention today, prenatal diagnosis (PND) has been in use for many years. Diagnostic testing has long been used during pregnancy to assess the wellbeing of the growing foetus. Until 1989 PND was the only available option for detecting abnormalities. Various diagnostic techniques are available, including ultrasound, blood tests, amniocentesis and chorionic villis sampling (CVS). The first two procedures are non-invasive, but the latter two are more invasive and pose risks to the foetus. Ultrasound can be used to detect an anatomical abnormality, or, in the case of Down syndrome, to measure nuchal translucency. A blood test can isolate and test foetal blood cells or cell-free foetal DNA found in the maternal circulation. Amniocentesis involves the insertion of a hollow needle through the mother's abdominal wall into the amniotic cavity to withdraw a small amount of amniotic fluid containing foetal cells for analysis. To perform CVS a catheter is inserted through the vagina to sample cells from the placental chorionic villi. Amniocentesis and CVS are carried out in the second trimester or late in the first trimester respectively, and carry with them a risk of miscarriage (approximately 1 in 200), although this has reduced in recent years. The blood test and ultrasound are low risk, but for many conditions they are not as accurate as amniocentesis or CVS, and so the latter procedures are often used if a foetus has been identified as high risk.

These techniques can be used to identify a number of abnormalities including neural tube defects, chromosomal abnormalities (for example, Down syndrome) and genetic disorders (for example, cystic fibrosis, sickle cell disorders, thalassemia). Prenatal diagnosis will often be performed if one parent carries an inheritable genetic condition, if the mother has previously had babies with birth defects, or if she has certain health issues. In the case of chromosomal abnormalities such as Down syndrome it is commonly recommended that mothers over the age of thirty-five are routinely screened, as the risk of chromosomal abnormalities increases with maternal age, with the rate of Down syndrome reaching at least 1 in 270 for mothers over thirty-five. Recently the American College of Obstetricians and Gynecologists recommended that all pregnant women be offered screening for Down syndrome regardless of age as the more accurate tests have become less risky. There is often considerable pressure for pregnant women to undergo such tests, and the issue of informed consent is pertinent here.

If a foetal abnormality is found the parents are faced with the choice of terminating the pregnancy. Such terminations are legal in most countries under abortion law. New Zealand law permits the termination of a pregnancy after twenty weeks only when the mother's life is in grave danger or she will be permanently injured, physically or mentally, if the pregnancy continues. The abortion laws in Australia and the US are different in each state or territory, with some far more restrictive than others. Abortion law in the United Kingdom sets no time limit on terminating a pregnancy if there is a substantial risk that the child born will be seriously handicapped, and one per cent of all abortions are carried out because of this. Of these abortions, about a third are for chromosomal abnormalities, and about half are for congenital malformations. Down syndrome is the most common chromosomal abnormality, accounting for twenty-two per cent of all the abortions for serious handicap. The definition of 'serious handicap' is vague and often left to the doctor's discretion, allowing for the abortion of foetuses with relatively minor handicaps such as cleft lip, club foot, and extra digits, which can all usually be readily corrected with surgery after birth. In these situations it is imperative that the prospective parents are fully informed of treatment possibilities and the probable quality of life of an affected child. Other foetal interventions, such as *in utero* surgery, may be considered after prenatal diagnosis of a serious foetal condition, but the most common intervention is termination.

These possibilities raise important, if initially unlikely, queries. Is it possible to abort a foetus for its own sake? Is it right to inflict upon a foetus the consequences of a particular disability, whether it be Down syndrome or a far more severe condition such as Tay-Sachs disease? Will abortion benefit the foetus, the parents, society, or none of them? Some genetic disorders are so severe that it is sometimes argued that abortion is for the good of the foetus. In other words, non-existence will benefit the foetus by preventing intolerable suffering, severe retardation or gross malformation. Elimination of future suffering in this manner introduces a new (and for some disturbing) dimension into medical practice, since its goal is to overcome abnormality and suffering by means of non-existence. A disease is 'cured', not by making the patient better, but by bringing that patient's existence to an end.

Some realism is called for, since we do not possess the ability to eliminate all the genetic abnormalities we should like to eliminate. We have to recognise the limits of our responsibility. We are nowhere near being totally competent at eliminating or rectifying genetic abnormalities, and so less than godlike abilities should be accompanied by less than godlike responsibility.

Very easily the good of the foetus becomes the good of the parents, who are most involved in the care of a retarded or malformed child. But it may be difficult, or even impossible, to decide in advance whether experience with suffering and the often overwhelming care of a severely defective child will strengthen or disable a particular family. It may well be that some families will be unable to cope, although it is extremely difficult to predict the outcome in any specific instance. For other families in similar circumstances it may prove a difficult, but humanising, experience.

Objections to prenatal diagnosis and subsequent termination are of course allied with traditional anti-abortion arguments, but also centre around the perception of disability and people with disabilities. It is argued that eliminating foetuses with disabilities reinforces a negative view of people with disabilities who were not identified and aborted. Reducing the number of children born with disabilities may also make life harder for existing people with disabilities by reducing public awareness of disabilities and access to resources.

However, prenatal diagnosis can also benefit parents who decide to continue the pregnancy, allowing them and their clinicians to manage the health needs of the foetus and newborn, and also helping parents to prepare themselves for the birth. Research suggests that mothers who learn they are carrying a Down syndrome foetus will cope better psychologically once the child is born than mothers who learn of the disorder at the time of birth.

8.2 Pre-implantation genetic diagnosis (PGD)

While PGD is hardly a mainstream technique and will be unknown to many, it is worth considerable attention because it represents a shift in perspective by directing far more attention than any other procedure onto embryos. In this it is an extension of the world opened up by IVF, and with it the prospect of actually manipulating embryos and thereby altering crucial aspects of future individuals. As we shall see the degree of manipulation is small, but the very thought of being able to do this leads many commentators to dub resulting children as 'designer babies'. As indicated previously (see chapter 4), I consider this erroneous, and yet it points to a level of concern that should be taken seriously.

PGD can only be used in conjunction with IVF, even when there is no evidence of infertility. In other words, it is never going to be a procedure that will be used routinely in order to achieve limited ends. During PGD those embryos found to have a serious genetic condition are discarded. This is the extent of the selection currently undertaken. The live birth rate per embryo transfer after PGD is around twenty per cent, not dissimilar to the live birth rate for IVF in the United Kingdom.

The first live births of healthy babies after PGD analysis occurred in the early 1990s. Since then PGD has been used increasingly in the detection of three types of abnormalities: single gene disorders, familial sex-linked disorders and familial chromosomal disorders. In addition, it is being used increasingly for nonfamilial chromosomal disorders associated with advanced reproductive age, where there may be specific numerical chromosomal disorders, including Down syndrome. Some examples of disorders for which PGD may be used are:

Familial single gene disorders:

- Cystic fibrosis
- Huntington's disease
- Myotonic dystrophy
- Sickle cell anaemia
- Spinal muscular atrophy
- Thalassaemia

Sex-linked disorders:

- Duchenne's muscular dystrophy
- Haemophilia
- Fragile-X syndrome

Familial chromosomal disorders:

- Patau syndrome (trisomy 13 syndrome)
- Prader-Willi syndrome

This procedure was initially offered only to couples with genetic predispositions to certain conditions. Currently, however, many PGD clinics also offer aneuploidy screening to couples having trouble conceiving or carrying a baby. This is because this type of screening appears to improve the live birth rate of couples with fertility problems.

PGD involves the extraction of one or two cells (blastomeres) from the very early embryo, when it is between four to eight cells; this can also be done at the blastocyst stage, when the embryo is five days old. The extracted cells are then tested, via one of two methods, for the presence of chromosomal or gene disorders.

It was first developed using polymerase chain reaction (PCR). Today PCR is generally used to detect single gene defects, and the misdiagnosis rate is very low. Fluorescent *in situ* hybridisation (FISH) is a process in which the extracted blastomeres are incubated with chromosomal-specific DNA probes, which have a fluorescent marker attached. By using fluorescence microscopy coloured spots can be detected on the sample, which enables the easy identification of chromosomal abnormalities. For example, a normal probe of chromosome 21 results in a sample with two spots; in contrast, three spots are visible in Down syndrome. FISH is used to determine the sex of embryos, where sex-linked conditions are suspected, and also to detect structural chromosomal abnormalities and numerical errors (aneuploidies). The misdiagnosis rate for FISH is also very low.

At present it is not possible to screen for all forty-six chromosomes using PGD. Between nine and eleven chromosomes can be tested, although this number is increasing all the time. Therefore, even if an embryo is replaced on the assumption that there are no numerical abnormalities on the chromosomes tested there is still a possibility that one or more of the remaining chromosomes are affected.

One of the features of PGD is that it enables the sex of embryos to be readily determined. This is both an advantage and a disadvantage. The advantage is that, when dealing with sex-linked genetic conditions, it enables embryos of the appropriate sex to be selected so that the resulting child will not suffer from the condition in question. The disadvantage is that sex selection can be used for social control of the next generation by providing parents with a child of the preferred sex. Since this form of sex selection has nothing to do with any medical condition, it demonstrates the paper-thin boundary between medical and social drivers.

A further use to which PGD may be put is to avoid the implantation of an embryo with a late onset genetic disorder, such as Huntington's disease, or one with a predisposition to develop conditions like diabetes, high blood pressure, breast cancer, or even—hypothetically—Alzheimer's disease.

In the United Kingdom the Human Fertilisation and Embryology Authority (HFEA) has recently allowed the use of PGD for lower penetrance, later onset inherited conditions, such as breast, bowel and ovarian cancer. This has been extremely contentious since the new individual would not suffer from any disease for many years and perhaps not at all. This means that embryos are being selected against because of the *possibility* that they will develop into individuals who may suffer from a particular condition. This is moving a long way from any conventional form of therapy.

Even more challenging is the birth of so-called 'saviour siblings', where one baby is brought into the world in an attempt to save the life of an already existing sibling (with a condition like Fanconi's anaemia). Human leukocyte antigen (HLA) tissue typing is used in addition to PGD to select embryos that are both free of the familial disorder in question, and are a tissue match for the older sibling. This double requirement of embryos means that more embryos are discarded than in straight-forward PGD, including embryos known to be biologically normal (those free of the disorder but not a tissue match). At birth, the umbilical cord blood of this newborn child will probably be used to treat the older ill sibling. This appears to be using one child for the benefit of another and has clear overtones of exploitation.

In this instance, the ethical issues revolve around the manner in which the resulting child is treated. If the child was to be looked upon as little more than an 'organ farm' for the ill sibling, no justification could possibly be found for moving in this direction. On the other hand, if the child is treated with as much care and love as the ill sibling, and if they are given every opportunity to develop and be themselves, it is far more difficult to see what basic ethical values have been abrogated. Of course, for those who oppose the selection of embryos as a matter of principle, there will be no place for going down the 'saviour siblings' path. The double selection will be more objectionable than the single selection of PGD by itself.

What are we to make of PGD? In the first place, it is not a panacea for all the ills of either humanity or individuals, even our genetic ills. This should be obvious, and yet the ethical literature is awash with vast generalisations concerning either the redemptive or abusive powers of any form of genetic selection. PGD should be seen for what it is: another means of partially tackling certain genetic conditions, limited in scope, even if associated with considerable potential. It will always be ethically ambiguous.

Second, PGD will never provide us with perfectly healthy children. Idealistic expectations like this are deceptive. And yet within them is a noble desire: to do the best for our children. Such a worthy goal is difficult to refute, until it is realised that it is medically unrealisable. The acceptance and love of our children, wanting the best for them and seeking to see them flourish in all aspects of their lives, have nothing to do with genetic perfection.

A third issue is the doubly artificial nature of PGD. When contemplating PGD, one is faced with IVF-plus-PGD. This has two consequences. Reproduction has become a seriously laboratory-based exercise, which will not in all likelihood be undertaken for anything other than pressing reasons. Associated with this is its cost, since both IVF and PGD are expensive technical undertakings. Most people will not be able to afford this, especially if the grounds for moving in this direction are insubstantial. Even for good reasons, there would need to be extensive government support, and this raises numerous funding issues for all health service providers.

Will future generations look back positively on PGD, or will it be seen as a slippery slope to sex selection for superficial reasons, to unwarranted manipulation of human embryos, and to eugenic directions? We don't know, and science alone will not provide an answer. Ongoing ethical reflection, informed by accurate and detailed science, is needed to balance the prospects for good against what seem to be the dangers.

8.3 The dilemma of selection

Inevitably, PGD involves selecting embryos: selecting those that are not genetic carriers of the disease trait, and discarding those that have the gene responsible for the disease. Certain embryos are chosen; others are rejected. Put like this it is not difficult to appreciate why PGD so readily acquires theological overtones: chosen and rejected, in the way in which God is sometimes depicted as choosing and rejecting. Against this backdrop, how can we possibly allow mere humans to choose some and reject others? The theological thrust becomes even more pressing when embryos are equated with people; it is not embryos that are chosen and rejected, but people like us, who are either set on the way to life or consigned to early destruction. While only some will argue in this manner, this gives a feel for the territory into which PGD has moved.

For those to whom all embryos are full human persons, one embryo should never be selected over another. And yet as we saw in chapter 5, some embryos are discarded under natural conditions, usually on account of chromosomal or genetic abnormalities. This is part of the natural wastage phenomenon described in that earlier chapter. This is a form of embryo selection, in which the embryos chosen are those that appear to be 'fit' to proceed throughout gestation. Some are fit to survive; others are not. While what happens naturally cannot be used as an argument about what is ethically permissible in the laboratory, neither can it be completely ignored.

Outside the reproductive area, we routinely select one person over another—in education, health, and employment. But is selection at the beginning of human life different from selection after birth? The crux of the difference is that selection at the embryonic stage is that of existence versus non-existence, whereas postnatal selection simply modifies an existing person. In the case of PGD, we have to ask how selection is being used. Many of the diseases currently tested for are devastating in their effects, and the pain and suffering of those with the conditions, as well as their families, are enormous. However, some of the conditions that are tested for are not necessarily in this category. For example, some syndromes can result in relatively minor impairment. For other conditions the onset of the disease does not take place until later in life, for example Huntington's disease, which usually occurs when the individual is between thirty and forty-five years of age. Hence, the selection against Huntington's disease is a decision that a mid-life illness, debilitating when it sets in, is reason enough to select against embryos. Phrased differently, non-existence is preferable to a healthy existence for thirty to forty-five years, followed by a serious disability. This is an unnerving conclusion.

This demonstrates that selection in PGD is far from ethically neutral, but neither is any other form of selection. Individuals and societies make wrong choices. Selection can be on ephemeral grounds, and this is widespread. Consequently, it would not be surprising if this were also to occur with PGD. But as I have indicated the rigours and costs associated with PGD may limit the more extravagant uses of it. Nevertheless, selection remains.

The advantage of PGD is that it allows the analysis of the very early embryo, at only five days of age. Therefore, affected embryos can be discarded before a pregnancy has begun. Hence PGD may have advantages over a much later abortion after prenatal diagnosis. However, this postulated advantage will only ring true for those with a developmental view of the value of the human embryo.

Some view PGD as discriminating against people with disabilities, and promoting the view that the birth of such people should be prevented. Concern has been raised that by selecting against certain disabilities, negative perceptions of disability in society may be strengthened and this may result in pressure being put on couples to use PGD. However, others contend that it is important to distinguish between 'disability' and 'people with disabilities', and that selecting against embryos with disabilities does not necessarily imply that those with disabilities are living lives that are either less valuable or less meaningful. It is also argued that for many years couples have had the option of prenatal diagnosis to test for the same kinds of abnormalities that PGD can now detect (see above).

It is unfortunate that far too much discussion around PGD concentrates on ephemeral and unrealistic goals. And so one reads a great deal about using it to select *against* homosexuality, obesity or hyperactivity, or *for* intelligence, beauty or athletic ability. If only people would realise that the use of PGD for these purposes is not currently scientifically possible nor is it legally permissible. Some of these uses may never eventuate. It is discussion of this ilk that leads on to talk about 'designer babies', overlooking the fact that the selection of embryos prior to implantation via PGD is selection from existing options without any meaningful design component.

Any particular theological response to PGD tends to parallel views held on the status of human embryos. For those who view embryos as human persons, discarding such embryos in PGD is unacceptable, as is the selection of one embryo over another. For Christians with a gradualist view of an embryo's developing personhood, PGD will probably be seen as acceptable under some circumstances, since it involves a balancing of goods, and takes account of the health and wellbeing of future children and adults.

Theological insights would be expected to emphasise the importance of the voluntary nature of a procedure like PGD, and hence would argue against coercion. We would also expect them to seriously question any ephemeral use of PGD, but to applaud therapeutic goals as long as these do not jeopardise the integrity of human personhood. Striving for health has been an underlying rationale in much Christian-based health care, and this would play a prominent role in the use of PGD in spite of the inevitable ethical challenges posed by the procedure. But we would not expect the allegedly eugenic nature of PGD to feature in theological arguments.

It is important for Christians to examine the reasons why society encourages PGD. Much of this comes from the desire to have healthy children and all that that entails. The problem here is that expectations of health continue to escalate, transforming the notion of health itself. The result is that PGD is being used for an ever-increasing range of conditions. This is where PGD becomes questionable, since it is guided by both good and bad motivating factors. We can focus on the burden that the parents will be placed under upon the birth of such a child—including financial burdens. Or we can discuss the life that a child born with a debilitating condition will have to endure. Such emphases have to be balanced by acceptance of all individuals, no matter what disabilities or diseases they may suffer from. Christians will wish to respond with compassion to families struggling with these issues.

8.4 Maternal-foetal conflict

For this final section of the chapter I shall turn to what at first glimpse appears a completely different realm from that of PGD. And so it is, in that it is dealing with issues far removed from the very beginnings of human life. Nevertheless, this is an area of conflict within the reproductive sphere albeit within the uterus of a pregnant woman. No longer are we in the laboratory, but now the 'laboratory' is the intact functioning uterus. While this is generally referred to as maternal-foetal conflict, it may on occasion include the embryo. This is a growing area as technical sophistication increases, allowing more and more to be done to protect the interests of the foetus. However, this immediately raises the question of who determines these interests? One also has to confront the issue of informed consent, since there is no way in which the foetus is able to provide such consent even where all are in agreement that a procedure needs to be carried out.

The first example of a conflict area is where a pregnant woman's intentions or actions do not coincide with the needs, interests, or rights of her foetus as perceived by others—most often her obstetric caregivers. A current illustration of maternal-foetal conflict is the discovery that maternal transmission of HIV to newborns can be cut by seventy per cent when infected women are given the antiviral drug AZT during pregnancy. The question this poses is: can or should pregnant women be forced to undergo HIV testing?

In the US alone, a few hundred women have been criminally prosecuted for taking drugs known to harm the foetus, *in utero* child neglect or abuse. In addition, pregnant women have been forced to undergo Caesarean section delivery, maternal blood transfusion, invasive foetal monitoring for suspected foetal distress during labour, intravenous administration of agents to inhibit pre-term labour, and intrauterine foetal transfusion. In some American states there are foetal protection laws that allow courts to detain pregnant women who engage in conduct, such as drinking alcohol, that may harm their foetus. In all these cases, foetuses are regarded as patients.

There are arguments on both sides of the fence. Either way, the value of one of the parties is being placed above that of the other. Critics of attempts to criminalise, restrict or regulate the behaviour of pregnant women in this manner argue that women are being relegated against their wishes to the status of 'foetal containers'. They are also being viewed as enemies of the foetus. The medical needs of one person (the foetus) are overriding the autonomy of the woman. Pregnant women are being forced to assume medical risks that would not be forced on competent non-pregnant women and competent men. The most common justification for this approach is that restricting pregnant women will do less harm to them than the harm that would befall their foetuses.

The underlying assumption for acting in this manner is that the foetus is already a person, with rights and interests that require protection. The interests of the foetus are equal to those of the pregnant woman; both are to be valued in the same way. But this is not possible. If pregnant women are forced to undergo treatment they would not choose for themselves, or if they are prevented from acting in ways they would normally choose, they are being valued less than the foetus. It is impossible to treat both in precisely the same way when their interests come into head-on conflict. One or the other has to give way.

If the two have equal status, the interests of the foetus cannot automatically be placed ahead of the interests of the woman; they have to be assessed on their merits. We do not generally circumscribe the actions of a mother or a father on account of the interests of their children, if say a father takes his family to work and live in an area with high levels of chemicals or radioactivity. These may damage his children's health, in the same way as a pregnant woman's lifestyle (drinking alcohol, smoking cigarettes) may damage her foetus' health. Such damage should be prevented if possible, but a foetus' dependence upon its mother is a major limiting factor if the mother's autonomy, dignity and responsibility (or irresponsibility) are given due weight. The conflicting interests of those made in the image of God bring us face-to-face with self-centredness, and rebellion against God. It would be preferable for the interests of a foetus to be given very high weight, but coercion of the mother overrides her standing before God.

The tension becomes even greater when the major technological advances that allow open surgery on the foetus are considered. This can be undertaken for conditions such as congenital hydrocephalus, urinary obstruction, cardiac defects, spina bifida, twin-twin transfusion syndrome, and the repair of a diaphragmatic hernia. The early onset of these conditions can cause irreparable tissue or organ damage, requiring *in utero* intervention. Such interventions are being developed, and at the present stage many, such as that for spina bifida, are yet to prove more successful than postnatal surgery.

The surgery poses a significant risk of premature delivery or death to the foetus, and there are also risks to the mother who may suffer serious bleeding or infection, or lose her ability to have further children. *In utero* haematopoietic stem cell (bone marrow) transplantation has been used for the treatment of haematological disorders including X-linked severe combined immune deficiency (SCID) with some success. In contemplating *in utero* therapy, the clinician needs to consider the likely benefit of the procedure to avoid unnecessary intervention on either a foetus that is not likely to survive or for which postnatal therapy would suffice. The field of *in utero* therapy is still in its infancy, and research is continuing on animal models to develop less invasive endoscopic surgery and also *in utero* gene therapy. Endoscopic surgery is also being contemplated to treat cleft lip and palate *in utero* to take advantage of the foetus' enhanced and scar-less wound healing. Exciting as such advances are, this technique may only be possible by personalising the foetus and depersonalising the woman. Not only this, intervention of this sort may allow foetuses to be carried to term that would otherwise have been spontaneously aborted, or the resulting children may be left with a moderate or severe level of disease rather than be cured.

Were *in utero* surgical techniques to become standard procedures, a situation may be reached where pregnant women who refused to undergo them may be criminally prosecuted for a failure to provide care. In these cases the mother may in no way be responsible for the foetus' ill-health, and so the gulf between the interests of the foetus and those of the mother will have widened alarmingly with implications not only for the mother but also for other members of the family.

When procedures like these become commonplace, there will have to be flexibility on both sides. There are no ready-made solutions, either for Christians or for anyone else. Foetuses, like every other human being, are to be valued as highly as possible, but in some circumstances, we shall have to work very hard indeed to decide precisely how this manifests itself in practice. There is no escape from this, since pregnant women are also to be valued as highly as possible. What is required are altruism and self-sacrifice, grace and servanthood; the Christian virtues of hope and living for others will be urgently needed if destructive impasses are to be avoided.

9

Reproductive Cloning

Reproductive cloning is all about the production of people like you and me, and this is often referred to as the replication of people like you and me. And so one encounters numerous pictures in magazines and TV programs of large numbers of identical babies (generally smiling idyllically at you), and of identical famous people from footballers to film stars, from politicians to media stars, and from scientists to musicians. Unfortunately, all this is misleading, since clones will not be identical in the way in which identical twins truly are identical. Were human clones to exist they would have many of the characteristics of the person from whom they had been cloned, but they would not have all their characteristics, quite apart from the fact that they would have been brought up in a different generation from the originating person. Putting together all these factors, we can say that they would not be replicas of their originators. Similar they may be, but identical they would not be.

What fascinates and appals so many people is the notion of producing people to order, and even more of producing them in someone's image. This strikes at something very deep within us. Normally reproduction is a lottery; we don't know what we will get; there will be some of the mother's characteristics and some of the father's, all mixed up. This is what natural reproduction provides us with—a bit of him and a bit of her. But cloning is different; it will give us him or her (although in reality it would be a large part of him or a large part of her). The fear is that little Johnny will not be a new creation, but far too much of a chip off the old block. Added to this is the concern that as little Johnny grows up he will not be able to live out his life as his own person, since he will merely be reliving someone else's life (everything he does will be retracing big Johnny's steps).

Cloning has taken on mythical proportions, since it encapsulates concerns about the manipulation of human beings. This truly is 'playing God' (see chapter 3), where medicine has taken on itself the mantle of creation by bringing into existence creatures who would not otherwise have seen the light of day. Will clones be human? Will they have souls? Will they be nothing more than subservient slaves to do the will of those with power and prestige? Quite literally, this is designing new human-like creatures in our own image. No wonder cloning is despised and almost universally rejected.

However, as I have already hinted, I am not enamoured with many of these responses. I have no desire to advocate reproductive cloning, but equally I would like to see this debate grounded in a more reasoned scientific context. Also, I would like the religious questions that it inevitably raises discussed in a dispassionate way.

9.1 Cloning people like you and me

For most people the current debate on human cloning commenced in February 1997 with the publication of a now famous article in the science journal *Nature*. This reported the birth of Dolly the sheep, the first mammal cloned from a cell of an adult animal. Dolly was produced by taking a cell from the udder of an adult sheep and fusing it with an egg that had had its nucleus removed. The birth of Dolly demonstrated that a cell that previously had limited functions could be reprogrammed to form an entirely new animal, just as if it was a fertilised egg. This overturned a fundamental scientific dogma, that it is biologically impossible to clone mammals.

The idea that humans will one day be asexually reproduced according to order has been around for a long time, although mainly in the annals of science fiction. The serious scientific work has been far removed from the human arena, concentrating instead on sea-urchins, salamanders and frogs, and even in these cases interest has been on the way in which cell differentiation takes places in embryos. And so, even when the focus was on cloning, the aim was to find out more about how early cells become specialised during the course of early development. The move to mammals, using mice, was far more difficult and in the mid-1980s some concluded that cloning in mammals was biologically impossible. However, just after this surprisingly positive developments were beginning to appear using not mice in university laboratories, but sheep in agricultural laboratories.

However, even when these serious strides were being made, if slowly, there were distractions. The major one of these took place during the late-1970s with the publication of a fraudulent claim that a human clone had actually been born. This had all the hallmarks of fantasy, and yet was portrayed as scientific fact. It took a few years for one of the scientists named in the book to win a court case against both the author and publisher. The story was indeed a fraud. It is a pity so many journalists and newspapers seemed to be unaware of this incident when the spurious claims of the Raelian cult surfaced a few years ago. But such is the power of cloning to mesmerise, tantalise and mislead. It is almost as if many people actually want these claims to be true. Human cloning is a bit like a macabre peep show—its wickedness intrigues and fascinates us. The trouble is this makes it very difficult to undertake serious debate on the many important features of the biological phenomenon of cloning, features that have nothing to do with producing real live human clones.

In the early 1990s human cloning again hit the headlines when it was revealed that human embryos had been successfully duplicated. Abnormal embryos were separated soon after fertilisation, when they had divided into two cells. Each of the cells developed into an embryo (just as happens with identical twins). Scientifically, this wasn't particularly interesting, but ethicists started writing about it. They discussed important issues which are still central in the cloning debate: the presumed loss of individual uniqueness, the possibility of causing harm to the interests of the child, the creation of embryos for the purpose of genetic diagnosis, and public policy issues.

While this debate was going on, considerable scientific progress was quietly being made in a few agricultural research laboratories interested in sheep and cattle, picking up on the tentative start that had been made on sheep in the 1980s. At the Roslin laboratories outside Edinburgh, several cloned sheep embryos were produced in an attempt to learn more about basic cellular processes. The Roslin studies showed that the cell cycle, particularly that of the donor cell, is what is critical in the cloning process. This was a major breakthrough, the one required to bring mammalian cloning closer to reality.

For many, it was the announcement of the birth of Dolly in 1997 that transformed the character of the cloning debate, since this was an adult mammal that had been cloned. However, the fundamental breakthrough in cloning technology had actually come earlier, with the birth of two other sheep reported in a 1996 *Nature* paper. Although these were produced from embryonic donor cells, their birth established the validity of the cloning methods. Later clones included transgenic sheep, pointing the way to the rise of 'pharming'—the manufacture of pharmaceutical products from genetically modified animals.

None of this work was carried out in secret, all the results were published in standard science journals, and it had nothing to do with the cloning of humans. Underlying it was an ardent desire to better understand fundamental developmental processes. Normally, such a venture would have elicited little interest outside the scientific community, but the association with human cloning changed it into something horrendous and terrifying.

It is deeply unfortunate that some clinicians and scientists insist on making claims that they have cloned a human, and that some women somewhere are carrying cloned foetuses. To date none of these claims has transpired, and they remain as claims. However, claims of this nature, no matter how dubious and even fraudulent they are, raise the ethical temperature, by giving the impression that it is only time before a cloned human will be born. If not today, it will be tomorrow; if not this year, it will be next year. This makes wonderful media fodder, stamping cloning with an even more dubious status, but none of this helps serious ethical analysis.

The response of just about every official political and scientific body throughout the world has been startling. It is perhaps the only issue on which they all agree: reproductive cloning should be banned. The European Parliament, UNESCO, and bioethics councils of all varieties in one country after another speak in unison; all that differs is the strength of the words used to condemn cloning. It is contrary to human dignity, it denies people their right to their own genetic identity, it violates all that is at the core of being human, it is an exercise of unrighteous power. While these are condemnations of the cloning of individuals, they also apply in some cases to therapeutic or research cloning in which there is no intention to reproduce people (see chapter 10).

One thing should be made eminently clear, and this is that the risks attached to cloning mammals at present are so great that it would be totally unethical to attempt to clone human beings. This statement has nothing to do with any other arguments. Currently, the chasm of unknowns is prodigious, with an overall success rate around two per cent of cloned mammal embryos producing live births. Even when there are live births, there is a very high incidence of abnormalities. These figures are ample justification for condemning human cloning at present and into the foreseeable future. There is no justification for proceeding with any procedure unless there is clear evidence to justify its use clinically.

This, of course, is a pragmatic argument, and the situation may change with time. But that will depend on a vast amount of animal experimentation and a considerable increase in understanding the scientific processes involved. To me, this is the definitive argument against human cloning in current debate. By itself, it is not a sure argument against cloning for time immemorial.

9.2 Why clone?

Why would anyone want to clone? In current debate, the reasons tend to have a reproductive flavour to them, rather than some idealistic thrust (with the exception of the Raelian cult with their science fiction way to redemption and eternal life). Nevertheless, for some cloning is viewed as a route to a form of immortality, because it allows an individual to cheat death. The foolhardy nature of this view should be obvious, for the simple reason that a clone would be a different person from his or her progenitor, for whom death will be as inevitable as it is for everyone else. An individual who is cloned will only live on in his or her clone in the same way as we currently live on in our naturally conceived children. There is no possibility that cloning could be a way to cheat death.

A more mundane reason for cloning would be the desire of infertile or lesbian couples to have children genetically related to one of them. There would be no question of imposing a particular plan on the child. Were the cloning of humans ever to eventuate, this would probably be the reason for its initial introduction. This in no way justifies it, and there are numerous alternatives that would be more likely options.

What about other reasons? Some parents may long to replace a dead baby, or a child killed in an accident. This would elicit strong sympathetic support from many were it to become feasible. Similarly, there may be parents looking for a sibling to be a compatible tissue or organ donor for a child dying from leukemia or kidney failure. Or think of a couple with a recessive lethal gene, who wish to have a genetically-related child and want to avoid the use of donor gametes or selective abortion. Another scenario sometimes painted is that of a wife whose husband is dying and who wishes to have biological offspring of the dying husband. And so one can go on.

In each of these cases, the birth of the children would be to satisfy the desires and wishes of adults, no matter how sympathetic we might be towards some of them. Each one prompts us to ask whether the children are being loved primarily for their usefulness, rather than for what they bring to the world as unique individuals. Each places the spotlight on the needs of individuals (parents, siblings) other than the children to be born. The prospects of using children to serve the purposes of others are extremely high, although not inevitable. It is this element in these hypothetical scenarios that shows cloning for what it would probably be. At one level the situations elicit our sympathy, but the cost of addressing them through cloning may well be far too high. And then of course the replacement child, that is, the cloned child, would never be the same as the one lost. The parents would not be getting back the child they had lost, simply because the cloned child would be as truly unique as any other child.

9.3 Should Christians be concerned?

A major message that I hope will emerge in this chapter is that reproductive cloning is one of the more theoretical topics being discussed in this book. Unhappily one gets the impression that it is the most important issues in bioethics—at least, alongside abortion and euthanasia. This is not the case. However, most Christian writers see things differently. They are implacably opposed to the merest hint of it, so that they are in no doubt that it should be prohibited.

What is it that leads Christians to be so negative about cloning? Are these views informed by the teachings of Jesus, or are they principally a reflection of prevailing attitudes, or are they a mixture of the two? One generally encounters the following concerns, that cloning:

- oversteps the limits of human dominion;
- violates human dignity;
- reduces the cloned offspring to a sub-personal status;
- requires experiments on human embryos;
- makes children as opposed to begetting them;
- subverts the uniqueness of human beings;
- attempts to exert excessive control over biological processes.

For a number of writers a Christian approach starts with the creation story in Genesis, where the differentiation of the sexes and the begetting of a child are linked to one another. From this it follows that children should only be conceived as a result of a sexual relationship between man and woman. This is regarded as essential for the health of both that relationship and the offspring. This leaves no room for any form of artificial reproduction, including of course, cloning. Some go as far as to maintain that producing cloned children would amount to nothing other than narcissism on their part, fulfilling highly questionable goals that ignore the welfare of the resulting children. In acting like this, so the argument goes, some human beings would become the controllers of other human beings.

This introduces what some regard as the crucial distinction between begetting and making. While 'begetting' (natural sexual reproduction) results in someone like us, 'making' (artificial reproduction) results in someone unlike us. Begetting signifies equality between parent and child, whereas making suggests that the parent(s) has produced an inferior being. While these are criticisms of the artificial reproductive technologies (procedures like IVF), cloning is viewed as an extreme form of production.

A related argument is that cloning exceeds the limits of the dominion delegated to the human race by God. This assumes that humans were not given authority to alter their nature or the manner in which they come into existence. Consequently, cloning has been likened to eating the fruit from the forbidden tree in the Garden of Eden: it is delving in a dangerous manner into the knowledge of good and evil.

Underlying most of this opposition to cloning is a deep concern that there should be no interference in natural processes. Reproduction should be left well alone. While this is not always a desire to leave nature to itself, since many of the same writers would not object to a host of other developments in modern medicine, the conception of a child fits into a category of its own. Somehow, lack of control is seen as being more akin with what God has ordained.

9.4 Looking again at cloning

As stated previously, I have no desire to advocate reproductive cloning. I regard it as a red herring and of little true bioethical interest. But I think it is worth looking a little further at some of the arguments used against it, because they raise important principles that we need to think about. And so it is in this spirit that the remainder of this chapter should be read. There are no right or wrong answers in biblical terms, but I have no doubt that we can bring Christian perspectives to bear on all the issues that arise.

Many people regard cloning as inherently tainted because they think clones will be treated as objects and not as people. This is a valid concern, since the temptation to control the future direction of children's lives is very high, with parents achieving their own ambitions through their children. Regardless of whether children are conceived naturally or artificially, they should be accepted and loved for who they are. Existence should always be in the best interests of the children, which requires giving them the room to develop as unique individuals. Cloning may well raise problems in this regard, but there is no inevitability about this.

One of the most frequently expressed concerns is that clones would lack genetic uniqueness, because they would be identical to someone already in existence. But does our uniqueness as individuals stem entirely from our genetic uniqueness? Identical twins demonstrate unequivocally that whatever the relationship may be between human and genetic uniqueness, it is not a direct one. Clones with identical genetic make-up would have different brains.

This is because the organisation of the brain is as much dependent upon soft wiring (influenced by the environment) as upon hard wiring (built-in genetically). Environmental influences are not mere after-thoughts or unimportant add-ons, but are essential for the final form of any brain. Our identity is shaped by the history of our relations with others, and by our biographies. The two individuals concerned would be different people, with a different sense of self, different thought processes, and different ethical responsibility (just like identical twins). Their biological uniqueness would remain, as would their spiritual uniqueness, which lies in their relation to God. Theologically, our personhood, identity, and value are God's gracious gift, and not something that humans can manufacture or copy.

By itself, a lack of genetic uniqueness cannot be a threat to our freedom. It has to be overlain with other factors forcing us to conform to the whims of other people, who would have to force us to see what they want us to see, read what they want us to read, view the films they want us to view, and listen to the music they want us to listen to. It may be possible to manipulate someone's brain to be the sort of brain we want it to be, but that demands far more from behavioural pressures than from genetic ones. A person's uniqueness is placed in jeopardy by forcing them to perform in some preordained manner. This goes well beyond cloning.

As in other areas, a critical element is that of the attitudes and motives underlying our ventures: we are to treat others as equals, and as beings of dignity, regardless of their method of fertilisation. To some this is a contradiction in terms, since the production of clones has already deprived them of their dignity; but this is far from self-evident. Human clones would be derived from people, would undergo gestation in a woman, and would be brought up by normal humans. The whole context of their upbringing and lives would be that of human families. The onus on those around them would be to interact with them as with any other fellow human being. Any downgrading of human clones would be imposed post-conception and post-birth, far more so than at their inception by cloning. Christians, in particular, should vigorously oppose even the merest hint that human clones could be treated in sub-personal ways, but this applies just as forcibly to all other groups—from the handicapped and demented to those holding diametrically opposing political and moral stances to one's own.

But what about the control element within cloning? For some Christian writers, there is conflict between the human control of reproduction and God's way of creating. Any increase in human control leads to God's way being usurped (see chapter 3). The two are at loggerheads. In view of this, the uncertainties of the genetic lottery come to constitute the central plank of God's way of creating; remove this and God's involvement is threatened and even removed.

But why look to mystery rather than understanding? When the genetic lottery goes seriously wrong, resulting in distressing diseases, we have traditionally attempted to rectify the errors. This is what much of modern medicine is all about. Although this has been done indirectly, by manipulating the results of the genetic errors, there appears to be no difference in principle between this and directly influencing genetic combinations (as long as the science is reliable).

Why is there this fear of human abilities? The power exerted by humans in weaponry and information technology is truly awesome, and the consequences for ill are sometimes all-too-evident. And yet for many, the reproductive technologies represent the crossing of the Rubicon from the apparently legitimate realm of control external to the human person, to control of the human person itself which should be outside the bounds of human interference. But is the boundary as significant as this? I tend to think that it isn't, as long as the resulting children (and adults) are provided with opportunities to flourish as those made in God's image. For me, it is this, rather than the mystery of ignorance, that is important.

Control is a two-edged sword, because while some forms may be beneficial, others are to be avoided and condemned. To think that one can use technology to totally alter human nature and the way in which human beings function and interact with one another is deeply misguided, and in all probability unachievable. Such vistas do nothing to advance serious debate on cloning or any other artificial reproductive intervention. Biological control is far less powerful than is often depicted. Even with human intervention, there will be mystery, since mystery is inherent within so many facets of human existence, from our commitment to one another, to worship and great creative achievements.

In considering the limits of the dominion delegated to human beings by God, we have two biblical perspectives. In Eden human beings are given dominion over the garden, having responsibility for tilling and keeping it (Genesis 1:26; 2:15). Nevertheless, it is a limited dominion. This tells us that the world was not created by us or for us, but we are to enjoy it and are to develop it judiciously as stewards. The other side of the picture is provided by Babel (Genesis 11), with its depiction of unrestrained ambition and the desire to be like God. Here there is no room for the role of steward; everything is trampled underfoot, and the lust to control and master is allowed sway. In these two images we have the contrast between directed and undirected control.

Many Christian writers resort to the Babel image when discussing cloning, stressing the dangers of excessive human control in the reproductive realm. From this, they argue that a procedure like cloning should be placed beyond the reach of scientific investigation. Some go further and state that humans are not to touch our prenatal existence. Such an interpretation is only made possible by ignoring the balancing perspective provided by the Eden image.

If we cling to these two biblical pictures, we have to try and take both of them seriously, because our abilities can be harnessed for good, as well as for destructive, ends. Neither will tell us in unequivocal terms whether it is appropriate to go in the direction of human cloning, or to stand back and totally reject it. What they do is present us with a profound challenge. If we take seriously the Eden picture we will not abdicate our responsibilities for the created order and will not adopt a fatalistic attitude and refuse to put our God-given skills to good use. If we take seriously the Babel image we will not use these skills in an arrogant fashion and pretend we are gods with unlimited abilities. Neither course of action is an easy one, and neither allows us to sit back and close our eyes to the world of the reproductive technologies.

Underlying this discussion is an even more fundamental issue, and this is whether humans should interfere with the natural world at all. Is it legitimate for humans to manipulate the world? Or, to phrase this question theologically, is God's creation a completed act, or is it legitimate to improve it if that proves possible?

When discussing the reproductive technologies, many Christian writers take the former position, whereby the natural world as we know it reflects the world created by God. Our biological nature, the way of bringing humans into the world, and the organisation of our bodies and brains are all 'given'. Since creation is a given, humans are not to tamper with it, nor with the make-up of humans themselves. By definition, God's likeness cannot be improved upon, and therefore human nature is not to be modified.

Viewing creation as a completed act leads to an acceptance of the world as we know it, and yet this interpretation appears to be a malleable one. It features prominently in the genetic and prenatal areas, but is largely ignored in other biomedical areas. It leads to an emphasis on rectifying disease and that which has gone wrong, as opposed to attempting to improve upon that which has been given. This is a useful guide in most situations where disease is the focus, but does it inevitably lead to the conclusion that all interventions into the reproductive process (especially cloning) are out of bounds to Christians? This is the conclusion of some, but are they being consistent in their application of the 'creation as a completed act' principle?

What about going beyond this act and viewing creation as a transformative process, according to which God moved the world from a chaotic nothingness to an ordered, light-filled, life-bearing place? If we view God's creative activity as ongoing, we come to recognise a divine-human partnership in our stewardship of creation. In these terms, the emphasis shifts onto God's good purposes and away from a particular form of creation. In turn, what becomes important are the creativity and inventiveness humans display as images of God. Acting as stewards of God's creation, we put our creativity to work to assist in major endeavours: to overcome disease, alleviate poverty and hunger, expand the wealth of human achievement, and develop technology across many broad fronts. This is what so much in modern medicine is about, and while its aim is to cure or alleviate diseases, it frequently employs highly creative measures to achieve these ends. True, it is not attempting to design some new form of humanity, but its overall effect on the quality and length of human life is dramatic. The contrast between human life today and 500 years ago in, say, Western Europe, probably demonstrates qualitative and not simply quantitative differences. Cloning may well add another dimension to this contrast, by taking transformation yet further. What we have to ask is whether there is a clear gap along the line between continuity and transformation, or is it a continuum?

I have come to the conclusion that, while continuity is the predominant element in creation, we cannot discount a transformative aspect to it. If this is the case and if we have a part to play in bettering our world, our assessment of human cloning will depend on the manner in which it is employed. Can it ever be used for good ends, or is it so inherently evil that only evil ends will result? If the former is true, the motives and end-result of cloning will emerge as crucial. If the latter, there is no way in which the cloning process can be redeemed. In my estimation, there is no clear answer to this conundrum at present.

Can sinful human beings be entrusted with control of this order, especially when this is genetic control? Once again, there is no assured answer. The world has been transformed for the better by the control of many diseases, although even this has negative facets. On the other hand, to bring children into the world as mere technological showpieces would be a travesty. Unfortunately, children have always been brought into the world for fatuous and irresponsible reasons, so that the divide between the natural and artificial is far from clear-cut.

As we contemplate the givenness of our world and our ability to transform parts of it, we come to realise both our enormous abilities and our definite limitations. We work within very constrained parameters, no matter which technologies we are contemplating. And this includes the cloning of human individuals. We should seek to transform what needs to be transformed, while gratefully accepting much else as given. In these terms, there is no place for unthinking acceptance of cloning, but neither is there for unthinking rejection of it.

Since cloning is an extreme technique, we should not devote too much attention to it. The trouble is that it proves too alluring and we use it as a benchmark by which to judge all the other reproductive technologies. The problems and dangers of these forms of technology are writ large in cloning, and the temptation is to recoil in horror. The challenge for Christians is to determine whether a reaction of this type stems from essential Christian convictions or from a fear of the unknown and untried.

10

Stem Cells and Therapeutic Cloning

By far the major emphasis in this chapter will be placed on stem cells, although since they are so often discussed in connection with cloning, the role of cloning in connection with stem cells needs to be clarified. When the issue of cloning is raised in this context it is therapeutic or research cloning that is the object of attention. Unlike reproductive cloning, as discussed in the previous chapter, the intention of using this other form of cloning will be the preparation of specified cell lines and possibly one day tissues. It will have no connection with the production of new individuals. In this instance cloned embryos will be maintained in the laboratory for only a few days. During this time, research will be conducted on them, or they will serve as a source of stem cells (undifferentiated cells). The aim of such work will be to find out more about: why the development of embryos so often goes wrong (leading to infertility), abnormal developmental mechanisms that may lead to cancer, and the potential of stem cells to serve as a cure of numerous diseases (including heart disease and Alzheimer's disease).

The dual use of the adjectives therapeutic and research is confusing. Therapeutic implies that this form of cloning will give rise to therapies, whereas research concentrates on their uses in research programs. These descriptors tend to be used interchangeably on the assumption that this form of cloning will ultimately lead to therapies for the alleviation of a range of disease conditions. However, it should be acknowledged that this lies in the future, so that the immediate prospects are limited to research. Most of what we are talking about is research cloning rather than therapeutic cloning.

But where do stem cells enter the picture? In order to answer this question we need to look at embryonic stem cells, that is, those derived from embryos. As we shall see below, these can be derived from a variety of embryonic sources, one of which are clones derived for research and/or therapeutic purposes. These clones would be produced in the same way as in reproductive cloning, that is, by inserting the nucleus from an adult cell into an egg with its nucleus removed. This is the process known as somatic cell nuclear transfer (SCNT). Stem cells would then be removed from embryos cloned in this way, and the cell lines or tissues derived from them could be introduced into the body of the individual who provided the adult cell (and its nucleus). The theoretical advantage of this process is that the cloned tissues would be compatible with the tissues of the host individual—there would be no rejection.

The last chapter demonstrated unequivocally that most authorities vehemently reject reproductive cloning. Research or therapeutic cloning occupies an ambivalent position in people's thinking. Some are unnerved by the possibility that were this form of cloning to be accepted (as it already is in some countries), it would prove impossible to prevent reproductive cloning from occurring; the only difference between the two is implantation of the cloned embryo into a woman's uterus. Others view the two has having different moral and scientific drivers so that the one would not lead inexorably to the other. Underlying these arguments is a more fundamental contrast; between those who oppose any research on human embryos, and those who advocate such research under circumscribed conditions.

10.1 Embryonic stem cells

10.1.1 What are embryonic stem cells?

Human embryonic stem (ES) cells burst into the limelight in 1998, when they were first successfully derived. The attention they have subsequently received, on account of their potential to alleviate a range of debilitating illnesses and give rise to a new genre of medical therapies, has been bewildering. These positive vistas have been counter-balanced by a welter of concerns, ranging from the ever-present ethical dilemmas precipitated by the moral status of the human embryo, to a confusing array of conflicting claims regarding the scientific superiority of adult stem cell sources. What comes to the fore here is the balance between beneficence and maleficence: beneficence towards those with serious illnesses (who could possibly benefit from stem cell therapies) and maleficence towards embryos (which would be destroyed in the act of extracting stem cells from them). Unfortunately, the place of beneficence is raised only occasionally in theological discussions of ES cells.

It is now well recognised that stem cells are unspecialised cells, with the ability to renew themselves indefinitely, and under appropriate conditions can give rise to a variety of mature cell types in the human body. They have multiple sources, ranging from embryos to umbilical cord blood, foetal tissues, and a variety of adult tissues. More recently it has been claimed that they are found in amniotic fluid. For the sake of simplicity, stem cells from all sources other than embryos are termed adult stem cells (as opposed to ES cells).

ES cells are derived from the inner cell mass (ICM) of early embryos at the blastocyst stage, which occurs at about five to seven days after fertilisation (see chapter 5). At this point in time the blastocyst has differentiated into just two cell types, ICM cells and the surrounding trophectoderm cells (which will later form the placenta). The ICM cells are frequently considered to be totipotent, in that they have the capacity to give rise to a complete individual. However, this is only the case if the blastocyst, with its trophectoderm cells, is maintained in an intact state, and if it is eventually placed in a woman's uterus. Isolated ICM cells in the laboratory will not form a new individual. This means that ES cells are pluripotent, with an ability to create all the cell lines of the individual (embryo, foetus) but not the individual itself. Placement in a woman's uterus provides the only suitable environment we know of at present for the development of an embryo and later foetus into a viable new life.

A fundamental ethical consideration is that in order to obtain ES cells the blastocyst (early embryo) has to be destroyed, since the ICM is disrupted. At present, there is no way of obtaining ES cells and maintaining the embryo as a living entity. The embryo will be destroyed; it will be unable to develop any further. In the future it may prove possible to eliminate the blastocyst stage altogether. But that is not where we are at currently. The question for now concerns the reasons why the blastocysts were created. This may have been specifically for research or therapeutic purposes, or they may be surplus to the requirements of couples in IVF programs. In the former case, they were brought into existence in order to serve as research or therapeutic tools; their creation and destruction as a source of ES cells are intimately linked. In the latter case, they were created in an attempt to bring a new human being into existence, but they are no longer required for this end and so will be discarded; their creation and destruction as a source of ES cells are not linked.

In neither case is there an opportunity for these blastocysts to give rise to new individuals; their future life-giving role is non-existent. There is no intention that they should do so, while their laboratory environment ensures they will not do so. Although extracting stem cells from blastocysts will destroy them, these particular blastocysts were slated for destruction anyway. Decision-making will revolve around the respective merits of blastocysts that have been deprived of their life-giving ability, and benefits that could accrue to humanity from research and therapy using ES cells. There are ambiguities on both sides of this equation. The production of blastocysts that become available for use in ES cell research, plus the research itself, have to be justified ethically, theologically, and clinically; neither is a value-free activity.

10.1.2 Embryonic versus adult stem cells

In contrast, the process of obtaining stem cells from adult tissues is minimally invasive. Hence, there is a major category difference between embryonic and adult stem (AS) cells, especially in ethical debate, where the adult variety is seen as being far less problematic ethically than the embryonic variety. What this highlights is their source, for example, blastocysts (embryos) versus skin cells or mucosa from adults. This is cut-and-dried, and yet the actual identification of stem cells depends to some extent upon the environment. Indeed, there appears to be a dynamic interplay between all types of stem cells and their immediate microenvironment. The components of this microenvironment have an impact on stem cells, because they affect the precise directions in which they subsequently develop. In other words, both AS and ES cells demonstrate considerable plasticity.

One conclusion that could be drawn from this is that the plasticity of AS cells renders the use of ES cells unnecessary. However, there are a number of scientific reasons to suggest it would be unwise to draw this conclusion. Even though there are a few confirmed reports of truly pluripotential human AS cells, what is required is far more understanding of the fundamental biological issues raised by this research. Scientifically, therefore, research with both adult and embryonic sources should continue, bearing in mind that AS cells are probably more limited in the range of cell types and tissues into which they can differentiate than are their embryonic counterparts.

While it is easy to lump AS cells into one category as though they were all the same, this is deceptive. They are derived from a number of sources:

- germ cells or organs of aborted foetuses;
- blood cells of umbilical cords at the time of birth;
- some adult tissues (such as bone marrow);
- mature adult tissue cells reprogrammed to behave like stem cells.

Each of these sources presents a different picture, since each has different potential with different abilities. While these do not concern us here, they are very important scientifically and clinically.

In light of this evaluation, considerable care should be employed in advocating, on allegedly scientific grounds, the advantages of AS over ES cells as the source of replacement tissues. In other words, it is short-sighted to attempt to circumvent discussion of the moral status of the blastocyst by concentrating on the scientific potential of AS cells alone. Whatever merits this may have ethically and theologically, it will not have much impact on scientists.

10.2 What makes stem cells so interesting?

The answer to this is two-fold. The one that is constantly touted in the popular press is that they hold out the prospect of curing numerous diseases. In the long term there could be considerable potential for the use of tissues derived from stem cells in the treatment of a wide range of disorders by replacing cells that have become damaged or diseased. Examples might include the use of insulin-secreting cells for diabetes, nerve cells in stroke or Parkinson's disease, or liver cells to repair a damaged organ. Additionally, as we have already seen, stem cells which are genetically compatible with the person being treated could be derived from cells created by SCNT. Further advances in understanding how organs regenerate would increase the range of possible treatments that could be considered.

In addition to this potential to develop tissues for use in the repair of failing organs, or for the replacement of diseased or damaged tissues, the technique of SCNT might be applied to the treatment of some rare but serious inherited disorders. Repairing a woman's eggs by this technique gives rise to the possibility of helping a woman with mitochondrial damage give birth to a healthy child, which inherits her genes together with those of her partner.

The other reason, of which one hears remarkably little, is that they are of immense scientific interest. Their fascination for scientists arises from their research potential, since they provide a tool for investigating very fundamental questions about the way in which developing cells differentiate and how it might prove feasible to change the direction of differentiation. Control of such fundamental processes opens the way into a fascinating new universe in developmental biology. Research of this nature may have spin offs in therapy, but the driving force is the research itself.

Expressing the situation in these dispassionate terms misses much of the argument swirling around stem cells, and mainly of course the embryonic variety. The moral and scientific sides of the debate have been unhelpfully stirred together with almost unbridled passion. And the fault lies on both sides. On the scientific and clinical side are voices determined to be heard by exaggerating the potential of ES cells—cures galore lie just around the corner, patients with Parkinson's disease will once more be able to live a full life, patients with spinal cord damage will walk normally again, and even those with Alzheimer's disease will be able to throw off the shackles of memory loss and confusion. Whether any of these will one day be achieved is an unknown. One thing is certain: most of these outcomes do not lie around the corner. To suggest otherwise is tragically misleading. On the other side the argument can be just as misleading. ES cells are dismissed as useful therapeutic agents since they have contributed to no cures, in contrast to AS cells that have. No attention is paid to the fact that research on ES cells is still in its infancy, first being described in only 1998, whereas some categories of AS cells have been in therapeutic use for fifty or more years. It is most unfortunate when this type of spurious argument is used to bolster an ethical argument by those who would be opposed to the use of ES cells no matter what the therapeutic outcome was.

The episode of Hwang Woo-Suk in South Korea provides a tragic example of what can go wrong when status and unrealistic expectations are rolled into one. The desire for quick results and glory led to unethical behaviour and gross, outright fraud. Carried out in a hothouse of unbridled longing for a vast scientific breakthrough in research cloning and ES cells, both within his own country and also by the editors of leading international scientific journals, his work was too good to be true. The result was a disgrace for the scientific community, on top of which it added fuel to the fires of distrust on both sides of the ES cells furore. Tragic as it was, it does not indicate that all scientists are dishonest, nor that the scientific enterprise is inherently flawed. Neither should one conclude that nothing good will ever come out of research cloning or ES cells. On the other hand, it points eloquently to the need for extra caution when dealing with revolutionary data and ideas. We are all fallible and we are all tempted to exaggerate and put our case in the best possible light. Listening to one's antagonists is a salutary step to take.

10.3 Do Christians have special insights into these topics?

No common consensus exists among Christians as to what is right and what is wrong regarding cloning and stem cell research; different groups have reached hugely diverging conclusions. However, it is worth examining the reports of two different Church bodies, both of which have sought to thoroughly and systematically address the issues raised by stem cells and research cloning. The first is the 2006 Church of Scotland report on 'Embryo Research, Human Stem Cells and Cloned Embryos'. The second is a 2002 report by a committee for the Anglican Synod of Canberra and Goulburn in Australia on 'The Cloning of Human Cells: A Response to the Scientific Issues from an Ethical and Theological Perspective'.

The Church of Scotland report spends much time on the question of when life begins. The following question is asked 'when should the embryo or foetus be regarded as a brother or sister for whom

Christ died?' The report raises three objections to viewing fertilisation as the point at which personhood begins, these are:

1. Genetic uniqueness does not have inherent value in itself.
2. The huge loss of early embryos.
3. That 'such a view implies priority over other factors in the development of the embryo and foetus that might have at least as much moral and theological significance'.

The report notes how Jesus made difficult choices, and these may provide guidance. In looking at the gospels, the report highlights the way in which keeping the Sabbath is listed alongside the prohibition of murder and adultery in the Ten Commandments, and yet healing is not mentioned. It goes on to comment that all four gospels make significant mention of occasions when Jesus heals on the Sabbath. These examples of emphases made by Jesus occur within the context of human beings being made in the image of God.

While acknowledging the lack of consensus within the church, and within the working group, the report gives support to some embryo research. 'For the majority of the working group . . . a more gradual view of the moral status of the embryo allows some embryo research.'

It is fascinating that the outcome of this report is in stark contrast to the previous report of 1996. That report found that 'despite natural wastage . . . from a biblical point of view human life begins at conception, at which point the human embryo is genetically complete'.[1] And it stated that, 'every other human being from the moment of conception is a person in Christ, called into personal relationship with Christ, and must be so regarded and treated with sanctity'.[2] One has to speculate on why this change has come about over a ten-year period by the same church body. While different reasons could be given, a contributing factor is probably the passage

---

1. Church of Scotland, Church and Society Council, *Report of the Working Group on Embryo Research, Human Stem Cells and Cloned Embryos* (2006). Available at: <www.srtp.org.uk/cloning.shtml> Accessed 19 February 2007, 28.
2. *Ibid,* 28.

of time with its opportunity to reflect further on the science and theological implications stemming from this.

The 2006 Church of Scotland Report recommends that the General Assembly should 'oppose the deliberate creation of human embryos for research by IVF methods or nuclear transfer cloning methods, except into serious diseases and only under exceptional circumstances'.[3] And it should also 'oppose the creation and use of human embryos as a source of cells in the treatment of diseases'.[4] I wonder whether this position will undergo modification over the next ten years.

The 2002 report for the Anglican Synod in Australia does not spend a great deal of time discussing the personhood of the early embryo. It suggests that 'some Christians have come to believe that there are two "books" of revelation. The first book is the Bible . . . the second book is the book of nature which science reads.'[5] The report goes on to state 'living with these two books is a tension, but it can be a creative tension if tackled with a faithful and open mind'.[6]

The report focuses on creation, the image of God, sin, and redemption in seeking to find a way forward in the discussion of the cloning of human cells. The committee concludes the report saying:

> We accept the arbitrary fourteen-day period from fertilisation as the limit of the time in which it should be permissible for the human embryo to be the subject of experimental cloning procedures. Though this time line is later than fertilisation itself, we consider the moment of penetration of the sperm into the ovum as equally arbitrary from the point of view of the existence of a new human being. We see no theological or philosophical basis for seeing

---

3. *Ibid*, 52.
4. *Ibid*, 52.
5. F Bergersen, J Clarke, P Ewing, G Garrett and J White, *The Cloning of Human Cells: a Response to the Scientific Issues from an Ethical and Theological Perspective for the Anglican Synod of Canberra and Goulburn by a Committee* (2002). Available at: <www.canberragoulburn.anglican.org/HTML/publications /CLONING.PDF> Accessed on 19 February 2007, 18.
6. *Ibid*, 18.

> that process as instantaneous. Importantly, the view that we have accepted has been presented for more than two years in the Anglican Church.[7]

Two of the recommendations of this report are that:

1. The cloning of humans even to the foetal stage be unlawful.
2. Research on both embryonic stem cells and the alternative approaches be permitted to proceed.

Both the Australian Anglican and the Church of Scotland Reports emphasise the need for the churches to become informed and to be involved in the debate on these issues.

I have included these as examples of two church reports. One can readily find others that come to diametrically opposite conclusions. These though have taken the science seriously and have made valiant attempts to view scientific findings and concepts alongside theological principles. There is no consensus in Christian circles and one may end up by concluding that Christians have no special insights. Nevertheless, I believe that theological principles provide an important balancing perspective.

In the last analysis we are not dealing here with merely theoretical issues. Governments have to draw up policies on what is allowed and not allowed in their countries, and this is where embryo research and ES cells enter the public policy arena. How might theological insights help?

10.4 Stem cell regulations: theological input

As one scans the regulations on ES cells worldwide, four dominant positions emerge. These vary from position A, the prohibition of all embryo research, to position D, which allows the creation of human embryos specifically for research via both fertilisation and SCNT. In addition, there are two intermediate positions. Of these, position B confines the use of ES cells to those currently in existence, in that they were extracted prior to some specified date, thereby

---

7. *Ibid*, 26.

prohibiting the extraction of ES cells and the utilisation of ES cells derived in the future. Position C allows for the use and ongoing isolation of ES cells from surplus IVF embryos.

Do these positions have any theological correlates? Position A is compatible with the stance that human life commences at fertilisation, allowing nothing to be done to the embryo that is not in its best interests. Such a stance would also be expected to disapprove of IVF, on the grounds that its development and further refinement have necessitated research on embryos. Further, IVF programs that incorporate the production of surplus embryos would also be unacceptable since these programs inevitably result in the production of numerous embryos that have to be discarded. By the same token, this position fails to contribute to any research or subsequent therapy dependent upon the use of ES cells, and it must be asked if adherents of position A should condone access to such potential therapies. Consequently, its emphasis is entirely on the harm done to embryos, ignoring the good that might accrue to others in the human community through the therapeutic potential of ES cells.

It is in this latter context that position B comes into its own, in that it allows some research on human embryos, but at the same time setting out to protect human embryos. This is achieved by allowing research only on stem cell lines already in existence. In other words, the embryos from which these lines were extracted have already been destroyed. Nothing can be done about that, and so it may seem reasonable to utilise those stem cells in scientific research. On the other hand, this position forbids the destruction of any further embryos. In one stroke it gives the impression of placating both sides of an exceedingly contentious argument. Research can continue in a limited way, and some good might emerge from this research. Hence, it is not deaf to the plight of people with severe degenerating conditions who could, possibly, benefit from scientific advances. What is more, those advocating protection of human embryos can feel that their case has been supported, by preventing the destruction of any more embryos for research (and possibly therapeutic) purposes. Position B represents an uneasy compromise, made possible only by accepting the use of 'ethically tainted/unethically-derived' material.

How should this compromise position be viewed theologically? Christians who view human life as commencing at fertilisation have reacted in two contrasting ways. One school of thought has berated the position on the ground that it gives away too much. In their eyes it appears to accept embryo destruction, even though the destruction occurred in the past. For this school of thought position A is the only theologically acceptable position. In contrast, a second school of thought has welcomed the compromise as a way of taking science seriously while also protecting the interests of embryos.

However, there may be a problem with consistency of policy. Position B proves problematic in societies that permit IVF programs that produce surplus embryos, most of which will be discarded. Hence, restrictive ES cell guidelines do nothing to protect the large numbers of embryos that are being destroyed by IVF procedures. They simply prevent research on embryos destined to be destroyed. It would appear, then, that position B introduces an unnecessary compromise that has neither a substantial ethical nor theological base.

These considerations suggest that, for those whose theological stance emphasises the importance of personhood from fertilisation onwards, position A is the more consistent of the two positions. However, this position suffers from neglect of any interests beyond those of the very early embryo. This fails to do justice to the obligations of servanthood, living in community, loving our neighbours as ourselves, and seeking to bring healing and wholeness to those in need. It has to be questioned whether the whole of our focus should be on the very earliest stages of embryonic development to the exclusion of all other stages.

What about position C? This provides a protective view of the human embryo, within the framework of a more consistent ethical stance. This is because ES cell research is limited to surplus embryos from IVF programs, with a procedural separation between the initial decision to discard embryos and the subsequent decision to donate them for research. This allows both the utilisation and extraction of new ES cells, and eliminates arbitrary time limits on extraction.

Can this position be justified theologically, since it accepts the destruction of embryos? As outlined previously, the destruction is of *in vitro* blastocysts that have no future as human individuals.

Although produced in IVF programs, in order to give rise to new individuals, these early embryos are no longer required to achieve this. There are some similarities between this situation and that found in normal fertilisation where many embryos are incapable of developing further through abnormalities. In my view position C fulfils a broader range of Christian imperatives, seeking to improve the health status of numerous individuals suffering from common debilitating conditions, as well treating early embryos with the care and respect due to human tissue.

But what about the creation of embryos for research purposes, either by fertilisation or SCNT, and the move to position D? On the surface, this represents a dramatic shift in moral perspective since embryos are being created solely for research purposes. I accept this and have reservations about this position. Nevertheless, the differences between positions C and D may be less than sometimes thought.

Position D is important in reminding us that a Christian perspective should ensure that we confront the intentions and motives of researchers, clinicians, and patients. What is the rationale for carrying out certain procedures on blastocysts rather than on other cells or tissues? Is there any reason for using human, as opposed to mouse, blastocysts? If we choose human blastocysts, what are the reasons for wishing to use specifically created blastocysts for research as opposed to using surplus ones from IVF programs? In what ways do we think this research will elevate our concept of humans as beings made in the image of God?

Whatever view we emerge with on the respective merits of positions C and D, we should look closely at our character as people before God. Specific answers will depend on a close analysis of ethical and scientific considerations, but only within the context of how we act as people seeking to live as worthy stewards, asking repeatedly what might be in the best interests of those for whom we have some responsibility.

11

Genetics and the Blueprint of Life

In the previous chapters we have encountered a number of topics that I refer to as mythologies: playing God, designer babies, cloning. In this chapter we come up against another of these, the gene mystique. The world of genes has unbelievable power—or so it seems. Everything can be explained by reference to our genes, those basic units of heredity, the DNA in our cells. Indeed we are our genes. At one level there is nothing wrong with this, since so many of our physical characteristics do indeed have a strong genetic basis: our height, the colour of our eyes or hair, our physique, the shape of our nose, and so on. Aspects of our personalities also have a clear genetic basis. We may even act in certain ways on account of our genes: or at least in part on account of them. But this is where the power of genes becomes questionable. Is it true that my violence is nothing more than a manifestation of certain of my genes? Or if I am compassionate, is this due to nothing more than a set of genes that makes me compassionate? In other words, is everything that makes me what I am no more than an expression of my genetic make-up? Genetic determinists will answer this question in the affirmative. This is precisely what we are; we are gene machines.

From here it is a small step to the assertion that our fate is in our genes; they are the master molecules responsible for all facets of our behaviour, from the moment of conception to the point of death. No wonder understanding the human genome has been described as biology's holy grail. Explain our genetic make-up and you describe the persons we are. If we are nothing more than our genes, so much else that we have traditionally considered important vanishes into obscurity. Once genes assume all-explanatory powers, other explanations for the human condition become redundant. The person has been reduced to a collection of genes—our religious sensibilities are genetic in character, our moral responsibility is an outworking of genetic combinations, artistic abilities are chance features of our genome. Social conditions and environmental factors become mere accretions to core genetic drivers.

When taken to extremes like this, one can understand why many are concerned at the vast swathes of gene hype that confront us every day. Beside them all else pales into insignificance. This is the new world of genetic control, with its aura of the engineering of our very essence through genetic manipulation, where 'GenRich' individuals will be separated from mere 'Naturals', and where the power brokers of society will all be genetically enhanced.

The idealistic and unrealistic façade of such fantasies is helpful in one regard: it uncovers the religious longings behind it: the deep longing for a better life, for redemption and salvation. Unfortunately, it is unhelpful in the extent to which they suggest that these longings can be found in biological manipulation, and that the hope of a better life emanates from genetic intervention.

11.1 A continuum from the known to the unknown

In order to get down from these heights of fantasy, consider the following continuum. Medicine A is found to cure disease A'. It is not known how medicine A works, but it does. The patient recovers from disease A', and no major problems are raised by anyone. Medicine B is effective in controlling and even curing disease B'. The way in which this medicine works is known, and this knowledge is important in determining who will and who will not benefit from its use. Medicine C cures disease C', and in this instance the medicine is gene-based and acts on a particular gene. The medicine modifies the protein causing the disease, since it acts by targeting this gene.

Even though there is a considerable distance scientifically between medicine A and medicine C the effectiveness of all three medicines means that the outcome for the patient is similar in all three cases. In view of this, it is unlikely that we will encounter any ethical or theological issues. Medicine C with its genetic rationale is no more problematic than medicine B, which in turn is no more problematic than medicine A. The degree of control and the sophistication of the technology have changed markedly in the move from A to C. In parallel with this, the efficiency and the effectiveness of the approaches have also changed. However, the control being exerted, even with C, is far from complete.

There is no way in which the integrity of the human person has been threatened by any of these treatment regimes. In each instance the central consideration is whether the treatment will benefit the patient. If medicine C, the gene-based medicine, assists the patient, whereas medicine A, the far more traditional and relatively ineffective approach, does not, use of medicine C is preferable to use of medicine A. Under these circumstances the role of genetics ethically and theologically is of subsidiary importance.

Imagine now a future world in which there is far more precise genetic control. Consider a patient with Alzheimer's disease (AD), when the protein deposition largely responsible for the dementia can be prevented using genetic tools. Very early cases of the disease can be prevented from developing further. This is routine medical treatment using a very advanced gene-based therapy. The patient has a disease, and this disease is cured. There are no religious quandaries since all that has changed is the precision of the tools at the disposal of the medical profession. The fact that these are genetic in nature is incidental.

But what about a more radical approach, in which the genetic tools are applied at the embryonic stage? In this case it is known that the embryo has a set of genes responsible for a disease (it could be breast cancer or even AD). Obviously, the embryo does not suffer from this disease, but the individual into which the embryo will develop will possibly or probably do so many years in the future. The state of genetic control is such that, instead of discarding the embryo (as discussed in chapter 5), gene therapy has reached a stage where this disease-causing gene can be replaced by a normal gene, without giving rise to deleterious side-effects. Consequently, the likelihood that this future individual will suffer from the disease in question is markedly decreased. Hypothetical, and perhaps unrealistic as this simple depiction is, it suggests that genetic tools may one day have far-reaching repercussions for patients without in any way threatening their status or dignity.

Let me now move into more threatening territory by envisaging a world where the genetic make-up of individuals is totally known and, hence, is open to being analysed by others. Genetic 'chips' are available, and these could be used to read our individual genetic make-up. Theoretically, everything that could be known about us genetically is open to scrutiny. Information is available about the functioning of our kidneys or brain, the chances of our manifesting a whole range of cancers or heart disease, and even our ability to cope with stress, or our proneness to depression.

Genetic knowledge of this order could enhance people's understanding of themselves and their world. For instance, instead of having to think vaguely about, say, cholesterol levels, which may or may not be that significant for particular individuals, people could have a far more precise means of knowing whether these levels should be taken seriously in individual cases. By our standards this would be a world of genetic foreknowledge. Forbidding as this may appear, there would still be an intimate connection between people's genes and the numerous environmental factors that have influenced genetic expression since the first few days of embryonic existence. A strong predisposition to develop stomach cancer is affected by dietary, neuroendocrine, external environmental, and attitudinal factors. It is a person, and not a set of genes, who develops stomach cancer. In other words, even in some future world of genetic foreknowledge, the crucial context will still be that of people in their wholeness, and not genes in some aseptic, depersonalised cellular compartments.

The fear this scenario raises for some people is the loss of privacy. If others can know what is going on within me (in my genes in this case), I can never keep anything to myself; I am always open to the prying eyes of others. There is no doubt this is a legitimate ethical concern, and stringent regulations would have to be in place to protect privacy, but this concern is a limited one. It does not have profound theological overtones.

Two principles emerge from this discussion. The first is that genetic interventions are no more going to transform the essence of what it means to be human than are many other interventions. One does not require sophisticated genetic technology to threaten human dignity—cruder methods are available, such as solitary confinement for long periods, torture, malnutrition, and rampant disease. The examples I have given come nowhere near the control required to effect fundamental changes in the human condition. Christians should reject hubris based on unsubstantiated claims.

The second principle is that we embrace humility in the face of genetic advance, and adopt a largely therapeutic framework (see chapter 4 for a discussion of the therapy-enhancement interface). This will help direct our gaze towards what can be realistically accomplished for the benefit of actual people. Within this framework, the guiding principle is the good of people, especially patients, with its commitment to improve the quality of the patient's life and possibly the replacement of illness by health.

Unfortunately, many will want to go further than this and seek to explain genetic interventions in far more probing terms than these. This is where genetic control enters the picture.

11.2 Genetic control and the person

Once in the genetic realm we meet oversimplifications galore. This is where we are introduced to gay genes, IQ genes, aggression genes, infidelity genes, God genes. Why not atheist genes, thin genes, depression genes, or poverty genes? Facetious as these suggestions may be, someone somewhere is probably proposing such genes even now. We are in the realm of total genetic control; everything can be 'explained' in genetic terms. This is based on the idea that there is a direct correlation between genes and disease, genes and behaviour, or even genes and belief. Choose your gene and you will produce the person of your desires. As we look to the future, we can imagine a time when people will be designed according to the whim of a human controller. Of course, this is light years from the truth, and yet the drive is there. Genes are at the basis of what we are, and therefore of what we would like our children to be. This is the ultimate in control—or so it is imagined.

Life is far from this simple, but even these vague prospects worry us, because even if they were half true they would undermine central elements within our responsibility as human beings. Do I have no choice about being aggressive or impulsive or short-tempered? On the other hand if I am loving and kind, is this a product of my genes rather than of me as a responsible individual? Are the fruits of the Spirit genetic in origin, and do they have nothing to do with the living Christ redirecting our lives and behaviour? Could it even be that the whole of my Christian journey amounts to nothing more than a genetic predisposition?

This is where theology and genetics come head to head, or so it might seem. This is because we gain the impression that everything can be explained away in genetic terms. We live according to certain basic genetic designs; modify those designs, and we become different people with different characteristics. Underlying possibilities like this is the spectre of some all-powerful genetic explanation, which presupposes that all our physical and mental characteristics are dependent upon single identifiable genes. Characteristic A is controlled by gene *A* and behaviour B is controlled by gene *B*. But this bears little semblance to what actually happens, where there are intimate relationships between most genes and a whole set of other interacting genes. On top of this, the expression of genes is controlled by environmental factors, so that even the presence of a gene for characteristic C usually does not inevitably lead to the appearance of that characteristic. The complexity of the interaction means that little is a foregone conclusion, except in a few well-known diseases where the disease in question (cystic fibrosis is a well-known example) will manifest itself whenever the gene is present. So often though, genes are switched on and off in response to a variety of pressures, both during development and later in cell life. Even the proteins produced by genes can themselves be subsequently modified.

It follows that concentrating on genes to the exclusion of other factors grossly oversimplifies the human condition. Human beings are far more than genes writ large; they are not gene machines. Any understanding of the human body, let alone the human person, has to incorporate far more than genetic explanations. This is not to deny that our character and personal identity have a genetic basis, but this is no more than a basis for what must be a much more far-reaching explanation of all that makes us what we are. Genetic factors are inevitably involved, even at the deepest levels of what makes us the people we are. But this in no way threatens the conception of a person as a rational being, capable of taking responsibility for ourselves as free agents. Neither does it detract from our ability to act as God's agents and stewards in his created order.

Human beings have a freedom that is constrained by biological and environmental circumstances and also by genetic make-up. This is valuable self-understanding, since it helps us appreciate our moral and spiritual limits, as well as our addictions and predispositions. We can also learn how God's grace can renew what we are as people, working through our physical bodies and genetic substratum.

In Christian terms we can say that humans are 'of the earth', they also recognise that God himself was incarnated to become one with humankind: to become flesh, with (among many other things) its genetic building blocks. These building blocks, however, are far from unalterable, since the environment affects everything to which they give rise. The environment extends down to the cellular level. In other words, genes should never be looked upon as isolated units, acting in predetermined fashion oblivious to a host of environmental influences. The implications of this are that genes are switched on and off indirectly as well as directly. Advertently or inadvertently, their functioning may be modified by the nature of the environment in which children grow up and function, and later in which adults function. None of us exists in a social vacuum, so that we (and our genes) are constantly being influenced by factors of all descriptions. Nothing is set in concrete, not even genes and their influence. Consider the following:

> Hannah is twenty years of age, and in our imagination let us sketch four ways in which she might have been brought up, remembering that the Hannah of our story commenced life with a particular set of genetic characteristics. Hannah 1 has been brought up in a loving home in an affluent neighbourhood; she has three siblings and has received an excellent education. Hannah 2 has also been brought up in a loving home, but her family are poor and her father dies when she was ten. They live on a barely satisfactory diet, there are three younger siblings, and Hannah 2 had to leave school at sixteen in order to help financially with the family. Hannah 3, like Hannah 1, was brought up in affluence, but there is constant strife in the family, and her father is abusive towards her mother as well as her. Hannah 3 is an only child and has had a good education. Hannah 4

is also an only child, is encouraged constantly to perform well and is pushed educationally in order to be the doctor her father wished he had been. She was sent away to boarding school at the age of ten.

There is little doubt that the hypothetical Hannahs of these scenarios (versions 1 to 4) will differ markedly by the age of twenty, even though genetically they would have been identical. Nevertheless, the contrasting environments in which they were reared and their different life experiences will ensure that the twenty-year-old we encounter will, in some respects, have only a limited amount in common. Of course they are recognisable as the same person, but they are far from identical. They are their own persons, moulded as they have been by their genes and their formative influences.

What is of crucial significance is the ability to be oneself and to relate productively to others within the human community. Relationships such as these emanate from our personhood, as those made in the image of a triune God. The manner is which humans are treated should always be viewed within the broader context provided by human relationships, and never simply within the much narrower framework of biological parameters. Any choices we make should be choices to benefit people, and not simply to enhance disconnected building blocks, whether genes, brains, or livers.

To argue like this is to argue for a person-centred model, and this is the model that governs every facet of my approach to genetics (and equally to neuroscience if I was discussing that). I regard it as a model that is consonant with biblical and theological imperatives. We are people made in the image of a personal triune God, and created to relate to each other within community as well as to God as creator and redeemer.

In terms of a person-centred model, it is acknowledged that we make choices for ourselves and on behalf of others, because people have to make choices. Some of these choices will not raise any genetic or technological issues and do not generally elicit vigorous ethical debate. However, others will, such as when genetic choices are made at the earliest stages of children's existence—probably when they were embryos. Once the notion of choice is raised in a genetic context, it introduces the possibility of design—choosing and, to a very limited extent, designing people (see chapter 4). However, it should be clear by this stage that any design within genetics will be of a far more limited and humble variety than so often encountered in these debates. It is far removed from the bravado and hubris associated with the picture of a factory production line of identical and preordained babies. The challenge is to determine how we do these things, and under what circumstances we do them, because this is where responsibility, judgment, and discernment come into play. We cannot do anything we like; we should not wish to be able to do anything we like. But we should do all we can to improve the quality of the lives of those around us, whether by using biological means or simply by treating them as beings of importance and as people who matter.

This, it seems to me, is where Christians should be contributing to this debate. If we consider that God is sovereign over all, he is sovereign over the genetic realm, just as he is over human life, human community, and the ecosphere. Divine grace and creativity are evident in all these realms, and human creativity is to follow suit. If we can say that God works through creation and, therefore, through what we describe as the natural world, there is no reason to say that he does not also work through the basic processes described by biology and, therefore, through genetic mechanisms (see chapter 9).

Humility is essential for rigorously assessing the merits of what can and cannot be accomplished by genetic science. Using the therapeutic and person-centred framework I have advocated, our eyes can be directed towards what can realistically be accomplished to benefit the patient. This is a far cry from the hubris sometimes encountered, but also from the anti-hubris that has become so caught up in the fear of extravagant claims that it has lost sight of the good that could be accomplished by utilising some of these technologies.

Nevertheless, there is a cautionary lesson here, and this is to beware of obsession with the normal, something that could be accentuated by any of the current biomedical technologies. The genetic realm is as limited as any other, and talk of designing wonderful new human beings is futile. On the other hand, the rejection of a modicum of limited and very cautious design is the outcome of a spirit of fear rather than a spirit of faithfulness. We are to do what is consistent with the nature and purposes of God, and are to assess all scientific developments by the benchmark of whether they appear to promote God's work in creation. Daunting as these tasks are, and inadequate as we are to tackle them, they are enriched when theological, scientific and ethical insights are brought to bear on them in an integrated fashion.

11.3 Does genetic manipulation stand in opposition to God's purposes?

Once again, though, we return to the recurring theme that there seems to be something inherently different about any form of genetic manipulation, even the therapeutically-based variety I am advocating. The feeling is that somehow fiddling with genes is an intrusion into the locus of what makes us human. Genes are different; some even refer to them, or at least DNA, as sacred. For some, the future of the human race is at stake; people are being so radically altered that we are losing the idea of what it means to be human. It may even be that in a few years time humans will be unrecognisable compared to what they are now. Such fears strike me as extreme and unfounded, and yet I have to admit that they encapsulate the theological as well as social concerns raised by any intrusion into the genetic make-up of human beings.

Inherent within these fears is the premise that the genetic realm is a sacred one that should remain untouched by mere humans. Alter people's bodies, at least to a limited extent, but leave genes well alone (these, of course, are an integral part of our bodies). The uncertainty that is implicit within genetic mechanisms and that lies at the core of normal human reproduction is regarded as being central to the maintenance of human dignity, in part perhaps because this is where God's influence reigns supreme. This leads to the stance that manipulation of this realm is deeply antithetical to Christian aspirations, putting as it does unwarranted control into human hands.

What we emerge with, then, is a clear illustration of science and theology pulling in opposite directions. And so, we are presented with a modern-day illustration of the well-worn 'science-religion warfare' metaphor. You can have genetic control or God's control, but not both. Which do you choose: to be a slave to secular science or a faithful follower of Christ? In my view, this choice is disastrous and totally unwarranted.

Until recent times Christians, including Christians in the health professions, have not hesitated to do all they can to prevent and cure illness. Conventionally this is done by manipulating the results of genetic errors, using traditional medical approaches that are forms of control.

Underlying all such niceties is a more fundamental query, and this is whether or not we are prepared to accept the random genetic combinations that sometimes turn up. The answer is 'no'. We have not been prepared to go down the road of genetic fatalism. Illness is illness, and is to be overcome if at all possible, whatever its causes. There is no difference in principle between the genetic lottery, the accident lottery or the environmental lottery. There are chance elements in all three, and all three may have dire repercussions for the character of human life. We either tackle all three, or we ignore all three.

In principle, there is nothing sacrilegious about modifying DNA or any processes at the commencement of human life; they have the potential for extending the work of God, as long as the modification is guided by the well-being of humans. Such creativity accords with God's creative activity in nature.

This is not *carte blanche* for carrying out every modification imaginable at the genetic level, any more than it would be at any other level. Discernment is always required, and a weighing of possibilities is always called for. This is not an argument that everyone should be born 'normal', since obsession with the normal is itself a stumbling block. There is no ideal in human existence, and there is no genetic ideal to be approximated. Genetically, we are all flawed in various ways, and the interaction between combinations of genes that seem to be beneficial and those that seem to be deleterious is intimate and complex. To look for a genetically perfect human ideal is not only to treat humans as unchanging, but to ignore our human creatureliness and the randomness of all new genetic combinations. A Christian perspective is far more realistic than this, with its concern for the weak and disadvantaged, the unlovely and the impoverished, the outsiders and the downtrodden.

11.4 Is Armageddon inevitable?

If we decide to opt for knowledge over ignorance, a choice between human embryos based upon genetic considerations may have to be made in some cases. At a more general level, research on human embryos raises similar issues, where the anticipated outcome of the research, albeit some distance into the future, is improvement of human health (see chapter 5). The general thrust of acting as God's stewards comes into play here as well, since there are two possible courses of action, both of which have problematic elements. We may seek a definitive answer to the question of when human life (or personhood) begins, and the answer with which we emerge may preclude any ventures involving embryos. Alternatively, if our focus is placed not upon the embryo alone, but upon the choice that has to be made—between the interests of early embryos and that of children and subsequently adults who will have a potentially serious genetic condition—the nature of the ethical decision-making will have changed. This is where Christians (as well as others within the community) reach different conclusions, since explicit biblical teaching is unavailable. Equally sincere Christians arrive at different conclusions depending upon the respective emphases placed upon the embryo in isolation and the embryo within the broader human community.

Simple solutions will probably bypass this choice, since they will concentrate on one party or one interest, out of all those directly or indirectly affected. In order to do justice to a range of theological directives, a number of guiding principles will have to be consulted and balanced. These will not provide definitive answers, but they will hopefully enable us to construct a helpful forum within which to debate the respective merits of contending forces.

The first directive is that we are to restore the material world: to improve it, care for it, and cure those with distressing conditions. Inevitably, our attention is on human beings in need of medical help and assistance. Any scientific measures that might realistically be able to alleviate serious illnesses, under normal circumstances should be pursued. This should be within the bounds of a balanced life-style and broad overall interests.

The second directive that comes into play in the genetic area is to ask whether some of these medical conditions can best be tackled at the embryonic stage, later on in foetal life, or in postnatal life. In searching for an answer we will be guided by the scientific and clinical evidence. At any particular time, one stage may be preferable to another on account of the level of clinical understanding and/or moral preferences. What is in the best interests of the patient now and in the future?

Christians will be alive to a third directive, and this is one's relationship to God, the bedrock for all considerations such as these. Couples contending with invidious genetic conditions, like cystic fibrosis in their family, should be guided in all their decisions by their dependence upon God. This will help them come to terms with the agonies and trauma of the ambivalence implicit within their moral decision-making. Where there are no 'correct' answers, there are answers that demonstrate faithfulness to one's relationship to God and one's position within a community of God's people.

As science encroaches increasingly on realms that once lay outside human control, one has to ask whether the sphere of God's control is being eroded. In other words, do we wish to confine God's domain to areas of life where there is little, if any, human control? Indeed, is there an inverse relationship between divine and human control? Questions like these are especially poignant in the genetic area, since genetic modification appears to have creative overtones. If we argue that the mandate to act as good stewards of God's creation is a limited mandate, in that it excludes the genetic realm, it behoves us to establish what those God-ordained limits are.

Faced by these possibilities, I conclude that God is sovereign over the genetic realm, just as he is over all aspects of human life, with the result that genetic modification brought about by humans has the potential for extending the work of God. This has its dangers and its pitfalls, since appallingly injudicious choices can be made. However, if we refuse to go down this path we will end with the appalling paradox of confining God's activity to an ever-shrinking realm of ever-increasing irrelevance.

12

The First Month of Life

In this chapter we make a transition from the esoteric world of genes and the embryo to real babies. We leave the world of 'may be' and 'what if' and enter the world of new human beings with all their beguiling attractiveness, apparent innocence, and occasionally overbearing demands. Here it is clear that we have 'one of us', no matter how helpless and dependent they initially are. The transition from the prenatal foetus to the postnatal baby is a gradual one, both biologically and ethically. Nevertheless, the birth of a baby, with all the responsibilities that come with it, represents a dramatic event. The vulnerability of this event for the baby itself (and sometimes the mother) continues for some time and it is the first month that is especially significant medically.

12.1 A world of disparity and inequity

We love babies: cuddly, smiling babies. But it is not so simple when there are major problems. We live in a world, which is full of death, pain, and suffering, and also disparity and inequity.

The neonatal period is defined as the first twenty-eight days of life. The first of these four weeks is the most dangerous time in any individual's life; globally two thirds of neonatal deaths occur in that one week, making up twenty-two per cent of all childhood deaths. The whole of the neonatal period accounts for about thirty-six per cent of all such deaths. However, these figures by themselves provide no clue about the maldistribution of neonatal deaths worldwide, since ninety-eight to ninety-nine per cent of these deaths occur in impoverished countries (the mortality rate for babies in sub-Saharan Africa is more than twelve times that of the United Kingdom). What this tells us is that deaths are regularly occurring that could be prevented were adequate health care and nutritional regimes available.

The major direct causes of neonatal deaths globally are infections (thirty-six per cent), premature birth (twenty-eight per cent), and asphyxia (twenty-three per cent). A baby in a low-resource, high mortality country is eleven times more likely to die of infection than a baby in a rich, low mortality country. Neonatal tetanus, which has been virtually unseen in rich countries for a century, kills half a million babies each year. Around sixty to eighty per cent of neonatal deaths are found in low-birthweight babies, although many of them could be saved by simply providing basic warmth and feeding. Every year in Africa alone more than a million babies die in the first month of life.

More than half of women in Africa and South Asia give birth at home without the presence of a skilled attendant. Not surprisingly, countries with the highest neonatal mortality rates are also generally found to have the lowest skilled attendance and institutional delivery rates.

In the past death rates in the first week of life in the developed world were far higher than they are today. Due to a greater standard of general public health and good nutrition most babies now survive. However, poor public health and malnutrition are still rampant throughout much of the world resulting in many preventable deaths, such as would have been commonplace in the developed world in the past. We can easily forget how recent it was that neonatal deaths, due to poor sanitation and malnutrition, were routine. Along with this, the majority of babies born never made it to adulthood. This required families to have many children to ensure that some actually made it through the perils of childhood and into adulthood. This is a world that is foreign to those of us living in developed countries in the twenty-first century, where the expectation is that all babies born will survive to adulthood. Sometimes of course this does not happen, and then the tragedy of the death of a child strikes us far more forcibly than it would have one hundred or so years ago.

And yet we live in a divided world, since the historical reality of today's developed societies is the present reality in so many parts of the world. How can this be? This is where the subject matter of this chapter deviates so markedly from that of many of the previous ones. The issues that emerged in those chapters are ones that confront the whole of humanity, even if discussion of them is currently confined to a limited number of countries. However, with the move to this chapter we enter a world of gross disparity; we know what could be done to prevent millions of deaths, and yet this is not done. The issues involved are frequently complex socio-political ones, and it is not my role to unravel them. The thrust of this chapter is to point out that here we are confronted by fundamental ethical and theological queries. How can those of us in the developed world continue when we are aware of these appalling inequalities and injustices? In Christian terms one has to ask what it means to talk about the sacredness of human life or the inviolability of human beings when faced by the unnecessary deaths each year (strictly speaking every day) of millions of the youngest of our fellow beings. If human beings have an inalienable dignity, surely we cannot sit by while these totally unnecessary deaths occur.

In raising these queries, I am not overlooking the undoubtedly complex interplay of political and economic factors, nor of the role of corruption and internecine struggles in all too many societies. These, too, raise immense theological challenges. Nevertheless, we would be theologically naive and brutally self-centred to ignore the plight of the weak and defenceless, by continuing unthinkingly in our affluence without lending as much as a helping hand to those whose dignity is demeaned by a lack of the most basic of medical resources.

Resource issues are not confined to babies and the neonatal period, but they come to a head here.

12.2 Premature babies

The disparities noted above affect babies that, under other circumstances, would have done well. Medically, far more problems arise when babies are born prematurely, problems that are accentuated when there are inadequate provisions to care for them. Premature babies are those born earlier than thirty-seven weeks' gestation, and very premature babies at less than thirty-three weeks. Extremely premature babies are those born at twenty-three weeks' gestation, and beyond. Babies born earlier than twenty-two weeks may have a heartbeat or pulse, but rarely survive. Those born before twenty weeks' gestation constitute a 'miscarriage'.

In the United Kingdom about 6,000 babies are born very prematurely at less than thirty-three weeks' gestation each year. Also in the United Kingdom about 2,400 babies die in the first four weeks of life. Alongside these figures it is worth noting that in the United Kingdom 2,800 abortions a year are performed after twenty weeks' gestation, with 100 at twenty-four weeks and over.

In recent years survival rates for premature babies have increased due to the medical technology now available, in advanced societies. In these societies, more than ninety-six per cent of babies survive at twenty-eight weeks; fifty per cent at twenty-four weeks; and two per cent at twenty-two weeks. These, of course, are overall figures, applying to specialised centres within these societies. The success rates vary considerably between centres, and the ability and preparedness to undertake aggressive treatment on extremely premature babies vary widely. Variations also occur between countries. For instance, in the Netherlands no baby born earlier than twenty-five weeks will receive intensive care. In countries like the United Kingdom, while not specifying a time frame, the reality is that aggressive treatment is confined to babies twenty-three weeks or older. The decision whether to opt for intensive care treatment is usually made by the doctors and parents together. However, legislation in the US forces doctors to do all they can to ensure that a baby survives, no matter what quality of life the child might be left with.

Headlines emphasise babies who survive against all the odds. Unfortunately, they tend to pay far less attention to those who survive but are left with numerous medical problems. This is the problem of morbidity, a problem that is severe enough clinically but in my estimation is even more demanding theologically.

In the 1970s less than twenty per cent of babies born before twenty-eight weeks of gestation survived. However, with improvements in medical care, about eighty per cent of these will survive today in the United Kingdom. At twenty-three weeks a baby may weigh about 500 grams, and with full intensive care approximately fifty per cent of these babies survive, although many of these will have long-term developmental problems.

The latest research on premature babies comes from the EPICure study following babies born in the United Kingdom at or before twenty-five weeks' gestation to two-and-a-half and six years of age. At two-and-a-half, fifty per cent of the children have no disability, twenty-five per cent have some form of disability, and twenty-five per cent have a severe disability. At six years of age learning disabilities can be detected more accurately, and the results show that twenty per cent of the children show no disabilities and thirty-four per cent have mild impairments such as a squint or low to normal cognitive scores. At this age twenty-four per cent have moderate disabilities, such as cognitive scores in the special needs range and visual or hearing impairment, while the remaining twenty-two per cent have severe disabilities such as very low cognitive scores, severe cerebral palsy, blindness or profound deafness.

One manifestation of the neurological problems is lower IQs. While one would not wish to place too much emphasis on IQ, their lower levels point towards generalised neurological deficits. Studies in the US have found that thirty-eight per cent of children born prematurely have IQs below eighty-five, as opposed to fourteen per cent of normal birth weight children. Furthermore, twenty-one per cent have asthma, compared to nine per cent of those with normal birth weight. While neurological problems may persist, pulmonary problems are commonly resolved within a few months after discharge. Some babies go home with oxygen tanks to assist their breathing, but almost all of these babies have been weaned off them by their first year. Although a significant proportion (around fifty per cent) of premature babies will generally develop normally and be able to keep up with their peers, even with behavioural and learning disorders, the risk of moderate to severe disabilities is about equal.

The issues encountered in the more severe cases can be illustrated by what became a much publicised instance a few years ago in the United Kingdom. This concerns the tragic case of Charlotte Wyatt, who was born at twenty-six weeks weighing 458 grams (1 lb). Her body was the length of a ballpoint pen. Her organs were undeveloped and she had to be resuscitated three times. At nineteen months of age, she had serious brain, kidney, and lung damage, was incapable of voluntary movement or response, and was fed through a tube and had a constant supply of oxygen. It was considered that she would never be able to leave hospital.

Doctors argued that she could feel nothing other than continual pain, and so they kept her sedated to relieve her distress. They went to court to seek permission not to put her on a ventilator next time she developed breathing difficulties. Against this, Charlotte's parents wanted to keep her alive at all costs. However, a judge renewed a court order allowing doctors to let Charlotte die if she stopped breathing. He said 'futile aggressive treatment' would not be in Charlotte's best interests. The Wyatts, who are Christians, went to the Court of Appeal.

By the age of three years, she was able to respond and smile, and the court order was lifted. To the amazement of the medical professionals involved, Charlotte did far better than had been expected. Tragically though, her family situation deteriorated to such an extent that, when finally able to leave hospital, she had to be placed in foster care.

Before considering the implications of an extreme case such as this one, it is important to bear in mind that neonatal care is based on the premise that every baby deserves the very best care, medical treatment, and protection from harm that can be provided. This stems from the foundational principles that every baby, no matter how ill and medically compromised, is a unique person and is to be respected and viewed as having very considerable value. But it does not follow from these that aggressive treatment and intensive care are to be employed in every instance. The underlying question is whether the baby will benefit from this medical treatment, and whether there is some reasonable prospect of recovery. This is quite different from prolonging life for its own sake. Of course, these are matters of judgment, since the burdens and benefits of intensive medical treatment have to be weighed up by both the medical professionals looking after the sick baby and the baby's parents, and all will not come to the same conclusion.

The Charlotte Wyatt illustration has within it many of the appalling ethical dilemmas sometimes encountered in the most extreme cases of prematurity. To say that the ethical issues are complex is a dramatic understatement. The availability of highly sophisticated technology is a prerequisite for any move in the direction of aggressive treatment. After all, if it is not available, no choices have to be made—the babies will die. This is the situation in many places in Western societies and almost universally elsewhere. So one cannot get away from inequalities in this area. Only a very small percentage of extremely premature babies have any chance of surviving, let alone surviving well. But when should aggressive treatment be used in any particular case? As discussed above, these revolve around the extent to which it is or is not considered to be justified in relation to each baby. This is going to be a decision based on both medical criteria and a person's world-view. The two are difficult to separate. It has been proposed by John Wyatt, a neonatal paediatrician and Christian, that someone committed to the dignity and worth of all life, including that of severely compromised newborns, will not aim to make value of life decisions, in which they decide which life is worthwhile and which life is futile. But they will make treatment decisions, deciding which treatment is worthwhile and which is futile. On occasion this may incline them towards aggressive treatment that would not be undertaken by someone for whom severe incapacity is an indication that life will not be worth living. But aggressive treatment will not be viewed as an inevitable option.

The distinction between these two may be a very thin one, and on occasion only paediatric practitioners may be in a position to distinguish between them. But it is worth holding on to, since it points to an important Christian precept: that we have to use our abilities and expertise to make crucial ethical distinctions. In this instance, deciding when continued treatment will jeopardise the dignity of the patient rather than enhance it. One also has to be aware of the possibility that nurses and doctors caring for premature infants may be wrong in their predictions as to which babies will or will not survive.

In spite of these problems, professional bodies such as the Royal College of Paediatrics and Child Health in the United Kingdom have proposed guidelines on withholding or withdrawing life sustaining treatment in children. These guidelines recognise that technological advance has led to the situation whereby a life-sustaining treatment may be available even though that treatment is unable to produce real benefit to the patient and/or may cause prolonged suffering for children and their families. The College's report contains five general situations where withholding or withdrawal of curative medical treatment might be considered in cases:

- of brain death, where artificial ventilation and intensive care are futile;
- of persistent vegetative state, where the child is unable to relate to the outside world;
- of severe disease, where treatment may delay death but is unable to alleviate suffering (the 'no chance' situation);
- where survival would leave the child with severe mental or physical impairment and he or she will never be capable of choice (the 'no purpose' situation);
- of progressive and irreversible illness, where the child and family decide that further treatment is more than they can bear (the 'unbearable' situation).

A 2006 report by the Nuffield Council of Bioethics has suggested prohibiting active killing of infants, no matter how serious their condition, but has set guidelines for the treatment of premature babies born at various weeks' gestation. The Council recommendations are as follows: babies born before twenty-two weeks' gestation should be given only palliative care, as it is extremely rare for them to survive; the normal practice for babies born between twenty-two and twenty-three weeks should be not to give intensive care, unless the parents request it and the doctors agree; for babies born between twenty-three and twenty-four weeks, the parents should have the final say on treatment; the normal practice for babies born between twenty-four and twenty-five weeks should be to give intensive care, unless the doctors and parents agree this would be futile; beyond twenty-five weeks' gestation, intensive care should normally be given. The report stresses that full consultation and joint decision-making between parents and clinicians is essential. Some groups have criticised the report for its broad statements and stringent cut-off points.

Such guidelines indicate the general direction in which professional thinking is moving, and they can be incorporated within the perspective of Christians. A Christian bias is to be in favour of continued existence, and of providing infants with as much of a quality future as possible—a future enshrined in love and warmth, a future with as many prospects as possible of interacting with others and of enjoying life as a gift from God. All these are possible even in the face of considerable deficiencies. However, there are limits. A grossly deformed infant may have no further potential for human relationships. It can be argued that if the infant's potential is nonexistent and would be utterly submerged and underdeveloped in the mere struggle to survive, then that life has achieved its potential. This acknowledges that our technological wizardry has limits, and that caring for the dying is preferable to futile attempts at curing the incurable.

A Christian stance is built upon a foundation provided by the humans-as-equals perspective, but, in order to develop this stance, technically-based distinctions will sometimes have to be made. Approaches such as these are attempting to provide a means of distinguishing between damaged infants it is worth treating and those it may not be. Medical intervention may not be the most ethical course of action if treatment is deemed futile, in fact, it can become abusive rather than restorative. While as Christians we are called to value life in even its weakest stages, this does not necessarily entail always taking heroic measures to prolong life. Inevitably, considerable value judgments, as well as technical considerations, are bound up in such decisions, and professionals as well as Christians will vary in their emphases.

Resource costs are as much of an ethical issue as are any of the other considerations, since money spent here cannot be spent elsewhere. This is always an exceedingly demanding area, since invidious choices are being made. The choice in this instance is made more difficult by the inevitably emotive and deeply human responses generated by vulnerable sick babies. Nevertheless, these decisions have to be taken into the resource calculation.

12.3 Rescuing newborns

Far more discussion has occurred in both general ethical and theological circles on the status of the embryo and foetus, than on that of the infant. In recent times it has been generally accepted that, once a baby is born, it is to be given all the protection afforded any other postnatal human. However, as we have seen the ethical complexities are formidable when dealing with premature babies.

What principles apply when dealing with babies suffering from abnormalities? This is where quality of life considerations enter the picture more than they do with premature babies. Hence, world-view perspectives may become more prominent as a background to decision-making. There may also be different categories of abnormality. For instance, one suggestion is that three categories can be recognised: w here newborns should receive no treatment (such as an anencephalic), where there should be mandatory treatment (Down syndrome infants with, say, oesophageal or duodenal atresia), and marginal situations where treatment is optional (considerable mental retardation and/or severe physical handicap). In order to take this further, I shall refer to one case study, based on a well-known instance involving Down syndrome (this is an extension of case 5, chapter 1).

> Gavin was born with Down syndrome and oesophageal atresia. His parents refuse to consent to the surgical procedure necessary to correct the abnormality of the oesophagus, even though it is a straightforward operation. The obstetrician supports the parents in their decision, while the paediatrician disagrees. The ensuing conflict goes to court, the outcome of which is refusal to order the surgery necessary to correct the oesophageal malformation. As a result, Gavin who was unable to feed, died five days after birth.
>
> The obstetrician in this case considered that the chances for successful surgery were about even, that other physical defects such as congenital heart disease were probably present and would subsequently have to be surgically corrected, and that the child would be severely retarded. The paediatrician, on the other hand, considered that the likelihood of successful surgery was close to ninety per cent, that there was no evidence of congenital heart disease, and that it was impossible to determine the severity of the mental retardation. Substantial as the clinical conflict was, there was also moral conflict.

With this case in mind, think about the birth of two other babies:

> Lily was born without Down syndrome, but with oesophageal atresia. Consent to operate was given and Lily survived. The second baby, Sophie was born with Down syndrome but without any life-threatening malformation of the oesophagus or any other organ. No operation was required and Sophie lived.

The only difference between Lily and Gavin is that Gavin had Down syndrome, a difference that also signifies the boundary between life and death. The only distinction between Sophie and Gavin is that Gavin had oesophageal atresia in addition to Down syndrome. Once again, this single difference is the critical factor between life and death. The crucial role is played by the Down syndrome and not by the malformed oesophagus. The issue, therefore, is what treatment is appropriate for Down syndrome infants.

An infant with Down syndrome can be deliberately neglected only if its loss will be of no moral consequence. If it is considered to be a human of equal value to others, to be accorded the respect we give to other humans, because it is a being of dignity, it cannot be peremptorily neglected. Over against this is the well-known position of secular utilitarians like Peter Singer for whom its loss has no negative moral connotations, any more than would the loss of a stray dog. But this no longer holds once infants are recognised as part of the human community. For me, an infant with Down syndrome is just as much part of this moral community as is a healthy infant. Very challenging ethical decisions will sometimes have to be taken regarding treatment options, but these should be on the basis of the legitimacy of treatment. This shifts the bias towards the welfare of the endangered infant, and away from its destruction. If intervention is justified in a normal infant, why should it be denied to an infant with Down syndrome?

A traditional medical ethos affirms human life, setting out to benefit the sick, to protect and nurture health, to maintain and restore a measure of physical well-being, to care for those in need, and to cure as far as is possible. Using this approach all reasonable efforts will be expended on a Down syndrome infant. We are to care for neonates and infants with deformities, doing everything possible to provide for their physical, emotional, moral and spiritual needs, for the simple reason that they are people like ourselves.

On the other hand, a market-place model, in which medicine embodies a set of technologies and skills, may or may not lead to treatment of the infant with Down syndrome. In the market-place environment, an operation is or is not performed depending on what the client demands, regardless of the consequences for the client or the client's offspring. The imperilled newborn is viewed as the property of parents to be disposed of as they wish, on the ground that infants exist for the parents' happiness. This perspective lends itself to demands for ideal children; normal, healthy infants who fit neatly into our ideal of the good life. Down syndrome infants with congenital abnormalities fail this test, and are allowed to die because of their lack of perfection. In such situations, it may be considered preferable to start again. This is no theoretical statement in our society, since the number of infants born with Down syndrome has declined dramatically over the past few years (by around eight per cent), even though the number expected has increased (by around fifty per cent) as the number of older mothers rises. In the US, the estimated number of children born with Down syndrome is about half that predicted based on maternal age. It is estimated that eighty to ninety per cent of women whose foetuses test positive for Down syndrome choose to terminate the pregnancy. This is a salutary reminder of how far our societies have come in very recent times.

Responses of this nature are understandable in societies where so much can be controlled and where so little assistance may be given to parents struggling with deformed children (and adults). An ethic of perfectionism stands against an ethic of trust, one that incorporates hope, care and nurture. Perfection and sinlessness of this order have no place in an inherently imperfect and sinful world. Such goals are resolutely at odds with any Christian perspective, which is more at home with the ethos of integration and its overtones of welcoming children without celebrating or romanticising their condition. Such an attitude is biased towards equal treatment for infants, no matter what their condition.

These pointers provide no easy answers to any ethical problems. Neither do they condemn those involved in the decision-making over

Gavin, or those who have made similar decisions over many other infants in similar predicaments. But they are reminders of a way that would seem to be more in accordance with the Christian way, with its tradition of accepting society's outcasts and caring for those in need, even though it does not provide ready-made answers.

12.4 Confronting uneasy truths

It would be easy to leave the chapter at this juncture, and yet in this instance this seems unsatisfactory. There are two matters I would like to underline, matters to which I have no ready answer or even response.

The first are the figures with which I commenced the chapter. The disparity in life expectancy in different parts of the world is so great as to be catastrophic. Bioethical debate concentrates on the earliest stages in human existence: the significance of fertilisation, the blastocyst, the primitive streak, and thus the status of the embryo even prior to implantation. Concern focuses on whether these youngest of embryos can ever be justifiably used for any ends other than those of generating new human life. And yet once human beings have been born, our focus appears to dim and we turn a blind eye while millions of these postnatal humans (mainly neonates) die needlessly before our very eyes. How can we expend so much energy on claiming that we value very early prenates so highly, but pay so little attention to neonates? This surely is a travesty of decision-making that makes a mockery of our much vaunted ethical and theological systems.

The second uneasy truth has quite a different character. Pregnant women and their partners love having CDs and DVDs of scans of their foetuses. It is exciting looking at their head, face, lips, spinal cord, heart, kidneys and limbs. And look at those movements; they even suck their thumbs. And who can deny the woman and her partner this joy? And yet the purpose of these scans is not entertainment; it is diagnostic. When everything seems normal and healthy, they are a wonderful memento of their child-to-be. But what if something is amiss? How prepared are they to come to terms with this? What decisions might have to be made very rapidly and possibly with out any preparation?

The scans are routine; they have become an essential ingredient in the experiences of the parents-to-be, but do they also signify a consumerist, perfection-directed culture? Are they part of a culture that wants perfect children, and that will eliminate the imperfect without too much thought in most instances? To what extent are Christian parents-to-be prepared for the scanning culture, or has this become an integral feature of Christian expectations as well? This, too, requires serious thought and analysis.

Section 3

Coping with Life

13

Dilemmas of the Mind

Mental illness is often misunderstood by society at large, so much so that the stigma associated with those suffering from mental illness is difficult to avoid. It is not hard to understand why this is so. After all it is easy to empathise with Charles who has failing kidneys, or Ella who has secondaries from breast cancer. In both instances, it is as if something is happening to them. Charles and Ella remain the same people we have always known, apart from the illnesses that may be destroying them. We readily sympathise with them and feel one with them in their suffering. But what about Ryan who is mentally ill? He is moody. Sometimes he spends his time condemning his wife who is doing everything she can to hold the family together. But nothing she does is good enough; it seems that he would be better off without her. We are embarrassed when we visit him, because of this and also because he swears repeatedly and talks volubly about the inadequacies of his wife. All semblance of his Christian faith seems to have disappeared, and he lives as though he has no hope of any description. We know he is ill, but we think it would be so much easier if the organ affected was his heart or liver, and not his brain.

Herein lies the core of the problem. Our brains make us the sort of people we are; they are more closely associated with our personalities, beliefs, attitudes, hopes and aspirations than is any other part of us. And so when they go wrong, we function differently than we have previously. We may be unable to respond in normal ways; we may lose hope and become deeply depressed; our ability to set goals may go. If we are people of faith, our faith may suffer, the central facet for what made us the people everyone knew us to be. No wonder mental illness takes us into a world of darkness and profound perplexity. And no wonder Christians in particular find it especially difficult to handle, since the certainties of their faith may be threatened and shattered.

No groups of people are completely protected from the forays of mental illness, no matter how spiritual they are. In other words, Christians are affected, just like those who lack any belief system. Whether or not religious faith makes a difference is a moot point. What is clear is that Christians as a population are afflicted, just as they are by all other diseases. To ignore this is nothing less than tragic. However, for once this is not a new phenomenon. Many pillars of the faith have suffered in this way throughout history. Before turning to case studies let us consider some basic issues underlying mental illness.

13.1 A geography of mental illness

Mental illnesses cover a range of conditions, of which the major ones are depression, manic-depressive illness, phobias, eating disorders (anorexia nervosa and bulimia nervosa) and schizophrenia. While it is relatively straight-forward sketching the major conditions in this way, the boundaries between them are far from clear-cut. The result is that patients with the same symptoms may receive different diagnoses. By its very nature, psychiatry is an inexact discipline, and conceptions of the various conditions change over time. Further, a particular diagnosis may not be associated with just one generally agreed form of treatment.[1]

Descriptions of two of these conditions will suffice for our purposes in this book. Manic-depressive illness, or bipolar disorder, refers to extreme swings of mood, with marked depression and elevated mood occurring at different times in the same patient. During a manic phase patients may have enormous drive, initiative and enthusiasm, and may require little sleep. They may talk endlessly, and may even have delusions of grandeur. Alternating with these episodes are depressive ones in which patients sink to great depths of despair and inertia. Both phases are pathological, being extensions of anything normally encountered. Those suffering from this condition are often difficult to live with or relate to, although if

1. In this section I am indebted to the discussion in Robert Miller, *Straight Talking about Mental Illness, second edition* (Christchurch: Schizophrenia Fellowship of New Zealand, 2000).

the condition is not severe this may not be the case. Some sufferers may be very creative, with Van Gogh quoted as such a person. The major treatment is lithium, a regime that has been used for many years.

The second condition I shall touch on is schizophrenia, one of the most feared mental conditions and one of the most stigmatised. This generally starts between the ages of seventeen and twenty-five years, a crucial time for intellectual and personality development. It is characterised by delusions and hallucinations, and initially tends to consist of episodes of severe illness, the acute phases of the illness. Recovery from these is possible, but as the episodes increase the patient tends to become permanently impaired. In the light of this, it is very important that the condition is diagnosed as early as possible, with treatment started immediately. If this is accomplished, the chance of returning the individual to relatively normal existence, albeit with continued treatment, markedly increases. Anti-psychotic drugs are the mainstay of treatment.

The long-term prognosis for people diagnosed with schizophrenia is, therefore, varied. Some make a complete recovery. Others may need to take medication for much of their lives, but make a reasonable recovery and lead lives more or less unhindered by their illness. The rest, however, will experience long-term difficulty and disability in relation to their illness.

Fear surrounding schizophrenia has been fuelled by the media portrayal of the link between violence and schizophrenia. While it is true that there is a statistically greater risk of violence from individuals with schizophrenia, this is the case when other factors are also present: substance abuse and acute psychotic symptoms.

Mental illnesses are far more common than often appreciated. Depression has the highest incidence, with around nine per cent of males and sixteen per cent of females afflicted at some time during their lives. The incidence of manic depressive illness is around 0.5% in males and 0.9% in females, with schizophrenia at 0.3% in males and 0.5% in females. When drug and alcohol abuse are included, the figures rise considerably.

Although the exact cause of most mental illnesses is not known, it is becoming clear through research that many of these conditions are caused by a combination of genetic, biological, psychological, and environmental factors. One thing is for sure—mental illness is not the result of personal weakness, a character defect or poor upbringing, and recovery from a mental illness is not simply a matter of will and self-discipline.

- *Genetic factors*: mental illness often runs in families. This implies that mental illness may be genetically inherited. However, the presence of mental illness within a family group does not mean all members of that family will suffer from it. Hereditary factors simply increase the likelihood of getting the condition. Many mental conditions are multi-factorial, that is, many genes may be involved, along with a host of other factors. Therefore a person inherits a susceptibility to a mental disorder and not the disorder itself. The latter occurs as a result of the interaction of these genes with factors such as psychological trauma and environmental stressors.

- *Biological factors*: links have been made between an abnormal balance of neurotransmitters in the brain and some mental illnesses. If neurotransmitters are found either in excessive or inadequate amounts, messages may not make it through the brain correctly, leading to symptoms of mental illness. Furthermore, different mental illnesses have been linked to brain injuries or defects in particular areas of the brain.

- *Psychological stress*: psychological stress can trigger some mental illnesses. Some examples of such stresses are: trauma experienced as a child, such as severe physical, emotional or sexual abuse; the death of a loved one; the demise of a relationship; alcohol or substance abuse.

What we are dealing with are illnesses. People suffering from them are not bad or evil, any more than someone suffering from a lung condition is bad or evil. While lifestyle may have repercussions for our state of health, in that heavy smoking for long periods of time may well have implications for the state of our lungs, there are other precipitating factors that will influence the appearance and severity of the disease in question. Some people develop lung cancer without ever smoking. The same is true for these mental illnesses. And yet many people still find this a difficult message to comprehend. Consider then the following cases.

13.2 Case studies

William Cowper, a leading poet and hymn writer, has long been recognised as suffering from depression. Born in 1731, he was the fourth of six children, only two of them surviving into adulthood. His mother's death when he was six years old had a devastating and far-reaching impact on him. Shortly after his mother's death William was sent away to boarding school. There he was severely bullied until the pupil responsible for the bullying was removed from the school. After such a difficult time at boarding school, and also suffering from problems with his eyes, he later flourished at school.

William's father wanted him to be a lawyer and he was admitted to the bar in 1754. In the year prior to this Cowper suffered his first bout of depression. His first severe depressive breakdown occurred in 1763. After a number of attempts to commit suicide he was moved to the St. Albans asylum, a private nursing home run by a Christian. It was while he was at St Albans that Cowper himself became a Christian. Thereafter he moved house on a number of occasions, had a number of relationships, and lived with or close to various households, one of special significance being that of John Newton, alongside whom he served in a parish in Olney. Here he wrote two volumes of his poetry and also his famous hymn containing the words:

> God moves in a mysterious way
> His wonders to perform;
> He plants His footsteps in the sea,
> And rides upon the storm.

Cowper died 'of a worn out constitution' on 25 April 1800. A year previously he wrote the poem 'The Castaway', concluding with the words:

No voice divine the storm allay'd,
No light propitious shone;
When, snatch'd from all effectual aid,
We perish'd, each alone:
But I beneath a rougher sea,
And whelm'd in deeper gulfs than he.

Cowper suffered from depressive episodes in 1753, 1763, 1773, 1787 and 1794. Although these were spaced years apart, he spent much of his life under the shadow of despair. It is noteworthy that each of his depressive episodes was preceded by some traumatic event in his life, a common strand running through each of them appearing to be his inability to cope with loss or change. Gaius Davies, a Christian psychiatrist, writes that Cowper 'shows what grace can do to a man's personality, and also what it sometimes appears not to be able to do. By this I mean that his experience points to a need for an honest explanation of non-healing, and the suffering that can go on and on.'[2]

Those who suffer from mental illness should be viewed with enormous compassion and understanding. Unfortunately, this has not always been the case. Christians in particular have sometimes, perhaps often, failed to do so. Some Christians have been tempted to view all mental illness as signs of demon possession, telling those who suffer that all that is needed is for the demons to be removed. Or those with depression are looked upon as failing to live up to Christian standards, in that they are failing to rely upon the Holy Spirit. But how can this be when the basic failure is to be found in disrupted neurotransmitter levels in the brain? For many suffering from chronic mental illness it is only with medication that their condition can become manageable.

Much closer to the present day is the story of Cathy Wield, who stands as a modern example of a Christian who has suffered extreme anguish due to depression. Her story is an extreme one, perplexing, full of anguish and despair, but with an unexpected positive outcome. While it raises far more questions than it answers, its

---

2. Gaius Davies, *Genius, Grief and Grace: A Doctor looks as Suffering and Success* (Fearn, Scotland: Christian Focus Publications, 2001), 94.

enigma provides a rare and valuable insight into the life and struggles of a Christian suffering from severe depression. She writes:

> My life journey took me through a single, but continuous, seven-year episode. It was a terrible nightmare of torture and imprisonment. I am one of the fortunate ones to have survived and recovered.[3]

As a mother of four children she was working as a junior doctor when she suddenly found herself feeling very down and realised she was suffering from depression. What followed were seven years of extreme mental anguish (1994–2001), which no amount of medication or therapy could touch. Only repeated bouts of ECT (electro shock therapy) made any difference, but this was always short-lived. During those seven years she was admitted to five different hospitals, under the care of seven consultant psychiatrists; she was put on thirteen different classes of drugs, with psychotherapy at least once a week. For two out of the four years she was in hospital, she was there on enforced detention, since she was a danger to herself.

Five years after she was first diagnosed with severe depression, Cathy Wield was referred for NMD (neurosurgery for mental disorder), where discrete lesions are made in one part of the brain. This surgery took place eighteen months later. Eight days after the operation Cathy's depression suddenly lifted:

> I believed that God had stepped in and his healing touch had been upon me. No one could give me any medical explanation for what had happened, but whatever anyone believes, there is no doubt that something truly remarkable had put me back into life without the need for any of the extensive rehabilitation programme which had been planned.[4]

---

3. Cathy Wield, *Life After Darkness: A Doctor's Journey through Severe Depression* (Oxford: Radcliffe, 2006), xv.
4. *Ibid,* 185.

There are no simple answers in this case, neither medical nor spiritual. Seven years of her life were totally lost; family life went on without her. The extreme severity of Cathy's depression is unusual, and yet even here there is hope in the midst of grave suffering. It also compellingly illustrates that doing something to the brain can have major consequences for good in a person's mental state. The brain and the mind are not separate compartments.

13.3 Thinking again about mental disease

We have already encountered situations where mental illnesses can be alleviated by the use of drugs that act on the brain. One such is the well known pyschopharmaceutical, Prozac. This affects the activity of a particular neurotransmitter substance in the brain, serotonin. These drugs generally act in the emotional centres of the brain, and so influence emotional responses, making people more outgoing and combating depression and anxiety disorders. Consider the following:

> Helen wanted to die in spite of a great deal of prayer and spiritual counselling, which appeared to be of only limited value. After a considerable amount of cajoling she took a course of Prozac, and to everyone's surprise she began to feel normal. What this meant for her was that she could once again experience God in ways she dimly remembered from the time years ago before the onset of her depressive episodes. She felt she was normal again.
>
> And then there was George, whose life was dominated by severe depression and outbursts of anger. He resented the anger since he felt this was not the way he should react, and yet he was unable to act in more moderate ways. It was as though the anger came from outside him. Following a number of weeks on Prozac he was transformed and felt just as he had years previously when he became a Christian.

For people such as Helen and George medication is a fact of life, allowing them to experience normality, with its highs and lows. This suggests that even people who are deeply committed to God may have no hope of a normal life without this sort of assistance. But is this the way things should be? Why do drugs work when prayer and counselling appear to have failed?

Answers to these questions are not hard to find if we accept that we are dealing with illness. For most people drugs are appropriate when faced with severe pain, or a dysfunctional heart, or arthritis. Why not for a dysfunctional brain which manifests itself in mental aberrations? There is an inextricable link between the biochemistry of the brain, who we are as persons, and how we relate to each other and to God. Certain brain regions are associated with certain functions, like goal attainment and anxiety, consequently, emotional and mental health requires appropriate functioning of such brain regions and their connections. There is, to some degree, a neural basis for emotional well-being, and so when aberrations occur, the appropriate neural systems need to be targetted.

In these terms Prozac may allow an individual to achieve freedom from emotional dysfunction and specific psychological disorders, thereby enhancing that individual's ability to be the sort of person he or she really is. This becomes important for an individual whose actions stem, not from understanding, but from compulsion or as a means of dealing with feelings of guilt or failure. To the extent that the latter emanate from emotional affliction, it is apropriate that they are tackled in whatever way is best, including possibly the use of Prozac-like drugs.

Prozac may have a role in healing emotional afflictions because we are persons who are part of God's physical creation, a creation that is maladaptive and in need of redemption. Prozac provides a limited means of redressing brain systems that have been warped by many forms of maladaptation, and which by itself is one means of effecting short-term restoration.

Nevertheless, there is a proviso, and this is that drug-based approaches to emotional illness constitute a direct means of modifying the brain's, and hence the individual's, responses. Modifications of this nature are not without their dangers, and leave untouched social, community, and spiritual problems. Consequently, long-term solutions need to take account of this broader relational context within which the indivdiual is seeking to live, since these indirectly influence neural and mental functioning.

So far I have confined my attention to relatively severe mental illness. But what about less severe situations, where it may be difficult to determine whether we are actually dealing with the abnormal? While clinical depression, such as I have described above, is a recognised clinical entity, what are we to make of low-grade depression? Is there any virtue in living with this, if it can be removed? Similarly, should we treat hyperactivity in children who appear to some to be stretching the bounds of normal behaviour patterns? Are they mentally ill or is their behaviour simply difficult to control? Does Ritalin administration have a role as part of a genuine therapeutic regime or is it an easy way out for overstretched teachers and fraught parents? What we have here are instances of treading a fine line between the normal and the pathological. But which is which?

There is never a simple answer to these questions; mental illness always brings us face-to-face with murky borders. This murkiness becomes more significant when we have at our disposal an array of drugs that can directly interfere with how people's brains function. We have to be ultra careful that we only alter an individual's brain with psychopharmaceuticals when all else has failed. To use these remedies as a front-line measure is fraught with danger.

Consequently, any modification of the brain utilising psychopharmaceuticals or behaviour therapy should be controlled by the welfare of the people concerned, and not simply aimed at enabling them to conform to the mores of society. What is more, people live within communities and societies, and help may stem principally from effecting improvements to the social structures around them. Direct assaults upon their brains may be inappropriate. But no matter how we argue these points, perplexing situations remain, where people's actions appear to be unnervingly controlled by the organisation of their brains. Consider these examples.

When the brains of depressed subjects who have committed suicide are examined, it is invariably found that there is a reduction in serotonin, one of the brain's neurotransmitters we have encountered previously, a deficiency in which can lead to a predisposition to impulsive and aggressive behaviour. In some extreme situations this may precipitate not only suicidal thoughts, but the likelihood of acting on them.

Studies of depressed patients have shown a variety of abnormalities in their brains, including a decreased volume of one brain region (the anterior cingulate) and abnormal activity in a neural circuit involving the anterior cingulate and the amygdala. However, it has been far from clear whether these abnormalities precede or are caused by the depressed state (a common situation with findings of brain abnormalities).

Are these individuals genetically determined to become depressed, or is something else required to precipitate depression? The general opinion is that it is the latter and that something else is required, namely, environmental factors. For instance, carriers of the high-risk gene may never develop depression unless they are exposed to stressful and traumatic events, especially in early life. Additional genes may also contribute to susceptibility to mental illness.

One recent study seems to show that depression-like changes in the cingulate-amygdala circuit are present in healthy carriers of a high-risk gene. In other words, these individuals who have a genetic vulnerability to depression demonstrate brain abnormalities even though they do not show signs of clinical depression.

These data can be viewed from different perspectives. One approach is to conclude that individuals with such abnormalities have little hope of escaping depression or suicide attempts. However, most researchers see the situation as more complex than this, since these abnormalities do not exist in isolation, but are found alongside other abnormalities in the brain and also precipitating social factors. It cannot be determined which comes first—the abnormality or the other factors. Are people at risk of becoming depressed normal or abnormal? The answer appears to be that they are normal, and that what we recognise as depression is a result of myriad factors, some biological but the remainder non-biological.

13.4 Mental illness and society

From the above we can conclude that mental illness has a biological component, that affects the functioning of the brain. However, this is never to be seen in isolation. There is no doubt that Cowper was prone to severe bouts of depression. However, had his childhood been more benign than it was, had he lived a more settled life, had he been able to marry one of the women who meant so much to him, his depression may have played a far less prominent role in his life than it did. Of course, we can never be certain but we can speculate. There were also demands placed upon Cathy Wield as a young professional mother with four children that may have precipitated the depression to which she was undoubtedly subject. Once again this is speculation, but family and social pressures play a crucial role in making us the people we are. Similarly with the suicide victims, brain abnormalities may be present (in some cases anyway) and yet these by themselves are insufficient without the presence of environmental factors.

Simple conclusions based on brain features alone are unlikely to be helpful. Decisions concerning the bounds of normality are not decided solely on the basis of biological criteria; they incorporate environmental, social, philosophical and theological considerations as well. However, the answer is not to ignore brain differences, but to accept that the neural data constitute one crucial ingredient in determining which approaches may be of greatest assistance to people in need.

As embodied individuals, all human beings function within limits that are both biological and social in character. Some are far more prone to mental illness than are others. But none of us is totally immune. An awareness of those situations that may precipitate mental crises is an immense help if we are to avoid them. By the same token the use of appropriate measures, from drugs to counselling, to help individuals cope with mental pressures is equally crucial. Both approaches signal the importance of community and community relationships when responding to mental illness.

14

When Organs Wear Out

One of the most dramatic breakthroughs in modern medicine has been the success of organ transplantation. The ability to overcome rejection of a foreign organ has led to a whole new area within medicine, one that has given many people a second chance at living a good quality life. Unfortunately, this success has not been without its problems, due to the reluctance of people to allow their organs or the organs of their loved ones to be removed at death. The result is a huge backlog of patients waiting for organs, knowing in many cases that they will never come. The tragedy is that each year the gap between the number of available organs and the patients on the waiting list increases. For example, in New Zealand between 1997 and 2001, 368 people received a kidney transplant while 1,550 remained on the waiting list. This situation is repeated in one country after another. Mortality rates while waiting for a heart, liver or lung transplant range from fifteen to thirty per cent.

Why this reluctance on the part of people, since surveys have shown considerable support for organ donation programs? The reasons adduced include: a need to respect the dead and maintain the integrity of the body after death, a feeling that transplantation is contrary to nature, and on some occasions mistrust of the medical establishment. Some of these feelings are associated with particular religious and cultural beliefs. The situation is aggravated by an unwillingness to abide by the consent of the recently deceased if living family members are opposed to the removal of organs.

Because of this widespread reluctance, people are dying when their lives could be saved. One could say that people are putting respect for the dead body (their own and others) ahead of respect for the dying. Instead of doing good to assist others, large numbers of people are putting their own interests ahead of the interests of others. While this is to oversimplify the dynamics of the consent process and of the role of altruism within it, it pinpoints a tragic state of affairs, due in part to the attitude of people but also to organ retrieval systems unable to cope with the demands placed upon them. Additionally, it may be that many people are unwilling to face up to the reality of their own death to make informed decisions about what should happen to their bodies when they do eventually die.

Unfortunately, the high profile scandals in hospitals, where organs have been taken illicitly from the dead to be used in research or in treatment, have seriously damaged the reputation of the whole organ donation area.

In the United Kingdom children's organs were removed at post mortem at the Bristol Royal Infirmary and the Alder Hey Children's Hospital in Liverpool; they were retained without consent from the next of kin. This commenced as far back as 1948, but intensified between 1988 and 1995, when it became standard practice to remove organs from all children and retain them indefinitely with the stated intention of carrying out research on them. However, little research was ever done, making the unethical removal of organs doubly tragic. In Australia, at the Institute of Forensic Medicine in New South Wales, long bones and joints were removed from adult cadavers for research purposes, which in most instances involved serious studies. However, the initial obtaining of the material lacked consent. In addition, some bodies were misused: one was struck on the head with a hammer, another was scalded, and others were stabbed. There had been no informed consent for any of these procedures. In New Zealand, in 2002, it was revealed publicly that Green Lane Hospital in Auckland had been retaining children's hearts following post mortem examinations without parental consent, or indeed knowledge. The studies in which these had been used were very helpful clinically, although no consent had been sought.

In the US scandals over the misappropriation of body parts are all too common, due perhaps to the lack of centralised policies and controls over the use and disposal of cadavers. They have involved Anatomy departments, tissue banks, biotechnology companies, and crematoria. While money-making ventures underlie many of the American cases, the rationale behind the retention of organs and tissues in the other cases was research, teaching, and clinical work. Unfortunately, informed consent for their use in certain ways and for designated purposes has been lacking.

14.1 Why bother about dead bodies?

Although the main focus of this chapter is organ transplantation, it should already have become evident that the ethical issues surrounding organ transplantations stem from the way in which societies treat the dead body. It may be too obvious to state that there would be no ethical issues if we considered that dead bodies had no value; if we thought we could do what we liked with them. If that was the case we could take organs from anyone who had died without seeking permission.

Most societies do not think in this way, and have not done so for very many years. Of course this position has only been arrived at gradually, and there have been many vagaries on the way. In the Europe of two hundred years ago there were nefarious means of obtaining human cadavers for dissection in medical schools; the use of executed criminals, stealing the bodies of the recently deceased, murder, and then the very widespread use of unclaimed bodies (those without relatives to claim their bodies) were all rife. Some of these measures were legal, while others were decidedly illegal, and some of these still exist today in some countries. It is only very recently that it has begun to be realised that the manner in which these issues are approached determines the manner in which the donation of organs for transplantation purposes is approached.

How we think about and treat the dead body is foundational for ethical analysis in this whole area. The manner in which we respond to the dead human body stems from what we think it means to be human, since there are many links between the way in which we treat the living and the way in which we treat the dead. This leads to the view that dead human bodies are to be respected in some way, and therefore we cannot do whatever we like with and to them. Once this is conceded, we begin to understand that the cadaver has *intrinsic* value: it is an end in itself. A person and their body are practically inseparable, and the intrinsic value of a living person (shown especially in their autonomy) is bestowed upon the cadaver at death. Alongside this, is the cadaver's *instrumental* value: it can be used as a means to an end. It is associated with memories and responses, in that as we remember a person who has died, we respect the person who *was*. All that remains of the person is the corpse, and yet our respect for that person and for the memory of that person leads to respect for the person's remains. One of the outcomes of these insights is that we respect a person-now-dead when we take note of that person's wishes when still alive.

How do these thoughts help us to approach organ donation? They bring out the importance of a person's autonomy, and therefore of their free and informed decision to allow their bodies to serve as the source of transplanted organs. They are *giving* the thing that is more closely identified than anything else with what they are and represent. Inherent within this is the related value of altruism, with its message that it is better to give than to receive. The *giving* of one's body is preferable to coercion.

Against this background it follows that cadavers can be abused. But what does this encompass? This is not a new question, even though its dimensions have changed substantially over recent decades. One only has to think of the minor prophets in the Old Testament, all of whom were deeply concerned with justice within their societies. Of these, Amos specifically separated out for condemnation the crimes of one group of people who, not content with marauding, pillaging, and killing, directed their venom at the body of one of their enemies. Having killed a particular king, they burnt his bones to ash (in those times this was a hideously denigrating practice unlike today where cremation is widely accepted) since killing him by itself was considered to be inadequate. Their hatred could only be assuaged by desecrating his dead body, thereby undermining his integrity as an individual. In its negative way, this highlights a crucial strand in Hebraic thinking: the importance of the dead body. This is an emphasis that persists in present day society, even though the reasoning behind it and its practical repercussions may prove elusive.

Central to present-day thinking is the centrality of informed consent on the part of the person concerned when still alive, and/or of close family at the time of death. When this is in place, the giving of one's body or organs is an act of altruism. This is why organs will only be removed for transplantation purposes when it is known that the dying person has agreed to this via an organ donation card or the like, and when close family agree to it. In many countries close family members can actually override the deceased person's wishes, a very contentious ethical position. Regardless of the pros and cons of this stance, what emerges so clearly is that informed consent is the lynch pin of ethical behaviour. The converse of this, unethical behaviour, occurs when organs or body parts are removed in the absence of consent, or are used in ways that were not approved by the people concerned.

14.2 Organ transplantation: scientific and clinical developments

Kidney transplantation was performed sporadically during the first half of the twentieth century, but it was only in the late 1940s that planned programs for human organ transplantation commenced. In the face of pessimistic warnings from both scientists and other clinicians, some clinicians began kidney transplantation in non-immunosuppressed human patients at that time. Even the outstanding biologist and Nobel prize winner Peter Medawar claimed that human allotransplantation would never prove viable because the roots of individuality were so deep and impenetrable. However, major developments in the understanding of skin grafting and acquired immunological tolerance, along with surgical developments in transplantation, led to the first successful kidney transplantation in 1954. This was performed in the US, and recipient and donor were identical twin brothers, thus bypassing the problem of biological incompatibility.

Major developments in the use of genetically unrelated transplants had to await the introduction of immunosuppressive drugs in the late 1950s, leading to the first successful unrelated cadaveric transplant in 1962. By 1965, one-year survival rates of grafted kidneys from living related donors approached eighty per cent, with survival rates of kidneys from cadavers approaching sixty-five per cent. As shown in the table, further developments have improved these rates, and have led to a general acceptance of cadaveric kidney transplants. Well over 250,000 human kidney transplants have been performed worldwide.

The transplantation of other organs followed in the wake of the success with kidneys. The first heart transplant was performed in South Africa in 1967, and while this was followed by a bleak period in transplantation, cardiac transplantation later became a recognised form of treatment. Worldwide a total in excess of 27,000 cardiac transplant procedures have been carried out. Transplants of other organs, including single and double lung transplants, heart-lung transplants, and transplants of the pancreas and liver have also been successfully undertaken. In New Zealand between 1999 and 2004 approximately eighty-six per cent of grafts and ninety-two per cent of patients survived two years after kidney transplant, during the same time period in Australia approximately eighty-eight per cent of grafts and ninety-two per cent of patients survived after kidney transplant.

The following statistics are patient survival rates from the US for the years from 1997 to 2004:

	One-year Survival Rate		*Five-year Survival Rate*	
Donated Organ	Cadaver	Living Donor	Cadaver	Living Donor
Kidney	94.5%	97.9%	82.0%	90.2%
Liver	86.3%	90.3%	72.1%	77.7%
Lung	83.3%	85.8%	47.3%	35.7%

Besides organs, certain tissues can be transplanted, most commonly blood and bone marrow, but also dura mater, one of three meningeal layers that surround the brain and spinal cord, corneas, tendons and ligaments, and most recently, whole bones.

14.3 When should organs be taken from dead bodies?

Discussion about consent introduces two diametrically opposite notions: opt-in and opt-out. Of these two, opt-in systems (informed consent) have predominated in most Western societies until recent years, with their stipulation that consent is explicitly required for organs to be removed for transplantation purposes. In contrast, in the opt-out position (presumed consent) consent is assumed to have been given, unless people have expressly stated their opposition to this possibility during life.

Regardless of which position is adopted, the notion of consent is not neglected, due to the fundamental ethical requirement to respect individual freedom of choice and self-determination. In the case of cadaveric organ transplantation, the opt-in position suggests that this is best provided by the donor when still alive. If consent has not been provided in this manner, it may be possible for the dead person's family to provide it on their behalf.

The strength of the opt-in policy is its recognition of the importance of the integrity of the dead body, which is to remain intact unless specific consent is given to interfere with this integrity. A drawback of the opt-in position is its focus on the deceased's wishes to the exclusion of all others with interests in the transplantation. These include the deceased's next of kin, as well as potential recipients and their families. Less obviously, it also includes society in general, since society is obliged to shoulder the economic burden of those with conditions such as kidney failure and end-stage heart disease and who could potentially benefit from transplants. If our moral gaze is focused exclusively on the deceased, these sets of interrelationships and possibly competing interests may be overlooked.

One of the on-going problems with an opt-in system is the lack of a centralised record-keeping data base. In those countries where these have been introduced, and where they are efficiently administered, there has been an increase in the rate of organ donations. However, these are not easily administered on account of the complexity of the issues, and they have to include sensitive education of the public about how the dying will be treated.

The presumed consent (opt-out) policy operates in many countries including Belgium, Austria, Denmark, Switzerland, Israel, Singapore, and in some states in the US. Under an opt-out system an individual is presumed to consent to being an organ donor, unless he or she specifically refuses. In order to opt out under this system, people have to carry a 'non-organ donor' card. In France, for instance, the presumption is that all mentally competent adults are organ donors, unless they have registered prior exclusion from the policy: similarly, parental consent for removal of organs from children is presumed. Some arguments about this option regard it as having a coercive element, with the possibility that it discriminates against dissenters.

The obvious advantage of the opt-out system is that far more organs become available for retrieval and subsequent transplantation.

This is a pragmatic argument, and it is both the strength and the rationale of this system. However, presumed consent overturns people's right to make decisions about their priorities regarding their own dead body, thereby undermining individual self-determination.

Proponents of an opt-out system argue that the value of self-determination must be balanced by another value, that of maximising overall well-being or benefit. This is the lives saved that would have been lost under the standard voluntary system, simply because the opt-out policy makes more organs available for transplantation. This throws the spotlight on the tension between individual self-determination (of a person now dead) and the enhanced prospect of salvaging the lives of other human beings.

In between these two options there are other, intermediate ones. One such intermediate position is the policy of required request. According to this, hospital administrators or physicians are legally responsible for ensuring that the next of kin or legal guardians are asked about their willingness to donate the deceased's organs and tissues after death. A related proposal is a policy of mandated choice under which individuals would be required to declare their preference either for or against becoming an organ donor at a nominated time, such as the renewal of drivers' licenses, or when income tax forms are filed. Additional possibilities are based on compensation for the donor's family. Some go so far as to want to legalise selling of organs. This extends what occurs now in some societies where there is payment for gametes, blood and breast milk.

If we go far down some of these paths we will end up viewing human organs (and even human bodies) as commodities. This raises substantial ethical quibbles, since once bodies and body parts can be bought and sold, one has to question what is left of human dignity. In what ways does the human body differ from a motor car or house? Once human body parts are treated like inanimate objects, there is no room for values like altruism and goodwill, even if the intention is the saving of human lives.

What emerges from this discussion is that problems connected with the supply of organs appear to stem not solely from a narrow ethical focus on opt-in or opt-out schemes. They have to be seen against the priority societies as a whole place on organ transplantation. Improving the efficiency of central distribution systems may help alleviate many of the perceived failings of an opt-in scheme, while maintaining altruism as the ethical bedrock of donation.

14.4 Organ transplantation in infants: using anencephalics

In December 2006 in the US there were approximately 238 children on the waiting list in need of heart transplants, and a further twenty were in need of a heart and lung transplant. Around 769 paediatric patients needed new kidneys and sixty-five were in need of a new liver. Approximately 240 children on the transplant waiting list die every year.

An additional problem with young children requiring organs for transplantation is the small size of their bodies, and therefore the small size of any organs that will fit into them. In one way this is a very obvious problem, and yet it brings with it extremely challenging ethical issues. The organs will also have to come from those with small bodies, that is, other children. But having stated the obvious, what is the nature of the consent that can be obtained from children, realising that removal of an organ from a dying child is an act that will help someone else and not the dying child? In other words, it is not in the interests of the child from whom the organ is to come.

There is also another significant difference between organ donations from adults and children. The majority of adult organ donations are from previously healthy people who suffer a stroke. By contrast, relatively few infants and young children become donors in this manner. Age also makes a difference in the sense that adults (even older teenagers and those in their twenties) have had an opportunity to experience life and make something of it for themselves, whereas this is not the case with young children. This is particularly the case with one source of children's organs that is discussed in the ethics literature, namely, anencephalics.

In anencephaly major portions of the brain, skull and scalp are congenitally absent due to a disruption in the process of development. Although most anencephalic infants are stillborn, in which case the use of their organs for transplantation is not feasible, approximately twenty-five to fourty-five per cent are live births. In most instances, these infants will die within a few hours or days of birth, but during this brief period residual brainstem function makes possible activities such as sucking and swallowing, crying, withdrawal from noxious stimuli, and the presence of normal wake/sleep cycles. More significantly, circulatory and respiratory systems function naturally.

The vast demand for suitable transplants has been put forward as one justification for using anencephalic infants as organ donors. It is a way of meeting demand, but this on its own does not constitute a good ethical defence of the procedure. A second reason is that, by donating the organs of their anencephalic infant, parents may feel that their child's life has had meaning, with the donation helping to alleviate some of their anguish. But this may negatively influence the grieving process. A further reason is that these infants are beyond suffering, cannot be harmed and, hence, have no interests in how they are treated. True as this may be, in part at least, by itself it amounts to nothing less than using the body of one to serve the purposes of another. There are additional reasons that depend upon definitions of brain death (see chapter 15), suggesting that anencephalics with their non-functioning cerebral hemispheres are brain dead.

In the end what is of crucial importance is the viewpoint of the parents, recognising as it does the close relationship between the mother and anencephalic foetus/infant. The wish on their part to maintain a pregnancy to term, with the prospect of donating the infant's organs, constitutes substantial justification for their use in this manner. However, the difficulties touched on above are very considerable, and mean that in practice only a limited number of anencephalics will become available for donation purposes.

14.5 Organs from living donors

The discussion up to this juncture has ignored one potential source of organs for transplantation, and this is living donors. Why should people not donate one of their own organs to someone in need? And if you can give an organ to someone else, why not sell one if you are hard up? In practice these questions will usually be confined to those organs of which we have two, generally a kidney. Consider the following:

> Jacob is thirty-five years of age, and is in renal failure. He has been on renal dialysis for two years, and his quality of life is very severely compromised. The chances of his getting a kidney from a cadaver are slim, and neither he nor his family wants him to live this very restricted type of life for another five or more years. And so his wife, siblings and very close friends decide that they will investigate whether any one of them could become a donor. They know their kidney would have to be compatible with his body, and so they are prepared to put themselves through the necessary tests to see if any one of them could serve as a donor. It emerges eventually that Amy, Jacob's younger sister is compatible. She consents to the operation and one of her kidneys is removed and donated to Jacob. Both recover without any side-effects, and very shortly after the operation Jacob once more begins to feel as he did a few years previously before the onset of the kidney disease. There is every likelihood that Jacob has many years of high quality life ahead of him. The same goes for Amy.

This is an illustration of altruistic organ donation. There is no hint here of coercion (if there was it would be unethical) and Amy is sacrificing one of her kidneys, knowing that it may have negative consequences for her, but also knowing that the chances of this happening are small. She is going into this with her eyes open, having had the risks and side-effects very clearly explained. There is no talk of any money changing hands, since what is taking place is one person aiding another within a well-defined caring community. The element running through the transaction is love.

There has been widespread acceptance that a patient's relatives may donate a kidney for altruistic reasons. They are volunteers, and may well consider it a privilege to do this for a loved one. Donations to patients other than relatives are also approved, provided that donors are fully informed of the risks, free of coercion, and give their fully informed consent to the donation. The benefits to both the donor and recipient must be seen to outweigh the risks associated with the donation. There appear to be no ethical reasons against this, and perhaps the altruism and risk-taking involved are to be encouraged. Turn now to a contrasting scenario:

> Ali was desperate. Due to lack of rain his family had borrowed money. Now they owed more than $5,000 and he knew that there was no way they could ever repay the money. One day he heard about a man who had been at the market, the rumours were he was offering money, lots of money, for something called a kidney. Ali decided that he would find out more and went to find this man. This man said that every person had two kidneys and that the body only used one, the other just slept, and so the doctors would take out the kidney he was not using and would give it to someone who was dying because their kidneys did not work. Ali was also told he would be given $6,000 for his kidney. After thinking for a while Ali agreed to donate his kidney.
>
> He woke up in excruciating pain and two days later was sent home. He was given $3,000 and was told that he would be given no more because there were lots of kidneys and people were no longer willing to pay so much. A couple of years later Ali still has pain from his surgery and has never seen a doctor.

This fictional story may seem to be an exaggeration of the truth, but for a family in financial strife kidney donation can appear to be an easy way out of their difficulties. What often appears to be an enormous sum of money to the donor is often only a small fraction of what the recipient pays. A donor in Pakistan can receive $1,250 to $2,500 for their kidney, while the recipient pays $6,000 to $12,000. Often the donor is left with no follow-up medical care and they can be left with debilitating side effects.

The purchase of kidneys from living donors, for transplantation, appears to be almost commonplace in some societies, despite the trade in human organs being illegal in almost all countries. Mostly the sellers are poor and healthy, whereas the purchasers are rich and unhealthy. The reaction of many public figures to this trade in human kidneys has been one of moral outrage, stemming principally from the notion that it is unethical to sell parts of the human body for money.

On the other hand, some writers have argued that organ donation for money is not inherently wrong, especially if the money is to be used to buy education or health care for a close relative. In this case, it is argued that the motives are altruistic, being ones of concern and care for others. In terms of a marketplace philosophy, the selling of organs may also serve to recirculate cash from the haves to the have-nots. However, treating the body and its parts as commodities threatens the dignity of the human person.

The one factor in this debate that is ethically unacceptable is exploitation. This is implicit in a marketplace situation, and yet once again the question is: who is exploiting whom? There may be emotional exploitation of a reluctant donor by family members, financial exploitation of a reluctant donor by relatives or a broker, or various forms of exploitation by the medical profession and intermediaries. These are dangers in any form of brokerage for profit, especially where the financial stakes are high.

Despite these dangers, an increasing number of people are proposing a legal trade in organs from live donors, on the basis that a legal trade can be regulated, whereas the black market cannot. However, the ethical principle that one should not sell one's organs applies whether the market is regulated or not. It has even been proposed that prisoners could save themselves from death row or be eligible for reduced sentences by donating kidneys for transplantation. This illustrates just how open to exploitation a relaxing of attitudes or laws regarding the trade in human organs would be.

The shortage of organs is a tragedy. However, attempts at alleviating it for those who are rich by exploiting those who are poor plumbs the depths of unethical behaviour. While altruistic donation of a kidney to a close relative or friend illustrates the 'good' that can be associated with living donation, removing (and sometimes stealing) a kidney from a healthy, impoverished individual illustrates the 'evil' of commercial exploitation. This underlines the ethical tensions encountered whenever live donors are used.

15

When is a Person *Really* Dead?

It must seem strange having a chapter with this title in a book like this. What has this topic to do with the practical sort of bioethics found in the other chapters? Not only this: isn't the answer obvious? We are dead when we stop breathing. There is no doubt this answer suffices in most instances, but things are not so clear-cut when someone is being kept alive on a respirator. Under these circumstances the lungs and heart may continue to function for a very long time, until the mechanical support is turned off. But what about when an individual is kept functioning in this way so that the surgeon can remove an organ for transplantation to someone else (see chapter 14)? When can this be done? What criteria do we possess for indicating that the individual is indeed dead? When the heart continues to beat artificially we have to turn to the brain for a determination of death. After all, the removal of vital organs like the heart from individuals who are not dead is unethical. One might phrase this in much stronger language and call it murder. Potential donors have to be protected as much as anyone else.

Hence, to ask the question 'when can potential donors be said to be dead?' becomes 'when are their brains dead?'. When can they be classed as cadavers? One writer has asked whether transplantation is a matter of stealing organs from living persons, or of salvaging organs from the still-living bodies of the dead? Brain death raises perplexing issues, since it enables us to talk about an individual with a living body (that is, all the body except for the brain) in the absence of a living brain. This is due to the technological ability that is now available to sustain brain dead patients when their bodies are biologically living. This, in turn, introduces a distinction between biological life and personal life, that is, the recognition that an individual may be breathing and functioning at a basic biological level but is unable to function as a thinking, reasoning, and responding individual, the sorts of functions normally associated with a human person. This is a fascinating philosophical quandary, accompanying which is a very practical ethical dimension, namely, the need to decide whether the continued provision of health care for such patients serves any useful purpose.

15.1 Knowing when someone has died

Brain death was described as far back as 1959, with the description of a condition called coma *dépassé* (a state beyond coma). The patients classified in this way were in very deep coma and were breathing with the assistance of a ventilator. Since they lacked reflexes and electrophysiological brain activity, it was concluded that these patients had suffered permanent loss of brain function. On postmortem examination it was found that there was extensive destruction of their brains.

As this concept of brain death has been developed, two definitions have emerged. The longer standing and more generally accepted definition is referred to as whole brain death. As its name suggests, this refers to death of all parts of the brain: the cerebral hemispheres (the brain's higher centres responsible for thinking and emotions) and the brainstem (the lower part of the brain that enables us to breathe and carry out the basic functions needed to keep us alive). Over more recent years a second definition has entered the picture, higher brain death, applying to death of the cerebral hemispheres even when the brainstem continues to function. An individual in this state is incapable of thinking and responding, but can still breathe. As we shall see, this is far more controversial than whole brain death, and raises even more problematic issues. However, discussion of it is unavoidable, since its clinical manifestation is the persistent vegetative state (PVS). Coma is not brain death, but applies instead to a transitory state with the patient either moving into a PVS, higher level of awareness, or total brain death.

The whole brain definition of death is a biological concept. What this means is that one could describe a dog or sheep as being dead in this sense—with the death of the brain the dog or sheep is dead, so is the human being. The alternative definition, the higher brain definition, in which there is destruction of the cerebral hemispheres alone, is a personalist concept. All that characterises human beings as persons has been lost. This includes the capacity for consciousness and the ability to think, feel and be aware of others. This definition makes sense for human beings but does not make any sense for dogs or sheep, since we do not consider that they are persons. Consequently, loss of the cerebral hemispheres is especially important for human beings, since in the absence of functioning cerebral hemispheres we are unable to act or react as normal people, we are unable to have any intentions or goals or interests. How do we encounter this in the clinic? This is where the PVS enters the picture.

15.2 Persistent vegetative state (PVS)

Discussions about PVS are dominated by well-known real-life scenarios that have hit the headlines and in some instances have made legal history. They have also been the subject of intense ethical debate.

> At the age of twenty-one Karen Ann Quinlan had a cardiopulmonary arrest following an accidental ingestion of a combination of prescription sedatives and alcohol. It was soon clear that she was in a PVS and eventually her parents requested that 'extraordinary' treatment, in particular, mechanical ventilation, be discontinued, since in their eyes her condition was hopeless. The doctors refused this request and her parents took the case to the US Supreme Court. The Quinlans eventually won the case, and the ventilator was removed. However, Karen began breathing for herself and was transferred to a nursing home where she remained in a PVS for another nine years, before dying of an overwhelming infection. Over the ten-year period, Karen never regained consciousness, but the episode led to a debate about the appropriateness of life-sustaining treatment in patients who are in a PVS, and this in turn led to the development of medico-legal guidelines in the US for the care of such patients.

> In 1989, 17-year-old Tony Bland attended a soccer match at Hillsborough Stadium in Sheffield. During the match the

> crowd surged against a locked gate, killing ninety-five people and injuring 200. Tony was among those crushed and after some minutes of oxygen deprivation, he was left in a PVS. For three and a half years he was fed through a nasogastric tube until the British High Court, the Court of Appeal and five Law Lords ruled that it would not be unlawful to withdraw artificial feeding and hydration. In March 1993, doctors stopped the hydration, nutrition, and drug treatment, and Tony Bland died nine days later.
>
> Far more recently, there was the infamous case of Terri Schiavo who, after a cardiac arrest, was in a coma for two months. This proceeded into a PVS, in which she remained for fifteen years. The battle between her parents and her husband around whether to remove her feeding tube centred on differing views of whether or not she was 'alive' and still herself, even though she was in a PVS. Her parents also argued that she had been misdiagnosed and that she was not in a PVS but rather a minimally conscious state. Politicians also entered the fray, as Schiavo's plight became a 'right-to-life issue'. Eventually her feeding tube was removed and she died. The postmortem revealed that she had been in a PVS.

Emotive and public as are cases like these, serious thinking has been going on around PVS for a number of years. On the clinical side, a major task force produced criteria for the diagnosis of PVS in 1994. These include:

- no evidence of awareness of self or environment and an inability to interact with others;
- no evidence of sustained, reproducible, purposeful, or voluntary behavioural responses to visual, auditory, tactile, or noxious stimuli;
- no evidence of language comprehension or expression;
- intermittent wakefulness manifested by the presence of sleep-wake cycles;

- sufficiently preserved hypothalamic and brainstem autonomic functions to permit survival with medical and nursing care;
- bowel and bladder incontinence;
- variably preserved cranial-nerve and spinal reflexes.

Patients in a PVS are distinguished by an irregular, cyclic state of sleeping and waking, unaccompanied by any self-awareness or recognition of external stimuli. They may move their trunk or limbs in meaningless ways, and may occasionally smile, or shed tears. They may even utter grunts or scream. There are motor activities, but no evidence of psychological awareness or any apparent capacity to engage in learned behaviour. Most vegetative patients retain good to normal reflexive regulation of vision and eye movement, but they lack any ability to track moving objects with their eyes. In most patients the gag, cough, suck and swallow reflexes are preserved, and gastrointestinal functions remain nearly normal.

Patients in a PVS commonly survive for five, ten, or twenty years, with the longest reported survival without recovery being over thirty-seven years. Injuries constitute a major cause of the vegetative state, and these in turn may be traumatic (such as road accidents) or non-traumatic in nature (for example, strokes, infection, and tumours). The pathological features of PVS vary from individual to individual, depending on the interval between brain injury and death. There is death of groups of nerve cells within the cerebral hemispheres.

The termination of all forms of life-sustaining medical treatment, including hydration and nutrition, in adult PVS patients is accepted by a variety of medical societies and interdisciplinary bodies. The patient must have been in this state for a minimum of six or twelve months (the agreed intervals vary in different places), and there must be agreement between the health professionals and close family members that their loved one will never return to a functioning and responding condition. However, there are those who consider that the withdrawal of life-sustaining measures is akin to euthanasia or even murder. When artificial nutrition and hydration are withdrawn, PVS patients usually die within ten to fourteen days. The immediate cause of death is dehydration and electrolyte imbalance (not malnutrition). Other patients die from pneumonia, or from heart or kidney failure. Because of the extent of brain damage, they are not thought to experience pain or suffering.

It is noteworthy that the P in PVS stands for persistent and not permanent. Is this of any significance? There have been a number of studies that have claimed to find recovery of patients from a PVS many years after its onset. In one a number of patients 'recovered', two of them well enough to care for themselves in most aspects of daily living. In another retrospective review of forty-three individuals in a PVS it was noted that eleven 'recovered', ten to the extent that they regained the capacity to communicate their needs to others. In the light of data like this, some have formed the view that PVS is neither a permanent nor irreversible condition. They consider that even patients with profound brain damage should be offered the opportunity of rehabilitation regimes. Others disagree on the grounds that we do not act in this manner in other 'hopeless' cases of serious disease where ventilation is withdrawn. Not only this, instances of recovery are few and far between.

Any move towards a higher brain definition of death, and therefore cessation of treatment (including artificial nutrition and hydration) in PVS patients after an appropriate length of time, is based on the premise that the patient is dead even though his or her body is still alive. The consequences of this position are startling in their novelty and starkness. Think about Miriam, someone whom we know well (case 4, chapter 1):

> Miriam is in a PVS. It is now seven months since the car accident that resulted in severe damage to the higher centres of her brain. Since the accident she has been sustained by excellent nursing, by artificial feeding, and by treating infections as they arise. In normal clinical terms the chances of recovery to any sort of meaningful human existence are nil. She could continue in this state for many years. There is ethical ambivalence on the merits of continuing to keep her alive in the knowledge that she will never again manifest any of the marks of human personhood. The medical and nursing staff want all forms

of artificial assistance discontinued; her parents wish it to be continued indefinitely.

Is Miriam alive or dead? In one sense this is an unhelpful question, since the answer is obvious: she is alive. But is she alive in a way that she (or we) would wish? She will never again be able to speak to us, even if she remains in this state for a further twenty years. Miriam was twenty-four years of age at the time of the accident; when she is fourty-four she will not have learned anything or responded to anything over those twenty years. Our memories of her will be those of a twenty-four-year-old, not a forty-four-year-old. We will have had numerous experiences over those twenty years. She will (as far as we know) have had none. She used to love listening to Mozart and going to the ballet; she will have enjoyed none of these activities since the age of twenty-four. In ten years' time her parents, if still alive, may or may not feel the same as they do today. But even if they do, Miriam knows nothing of their devotion. She will never again experience anything that amazes, thrills, and challenges human beings.

Miriam is maintained in the PVS because of the quality of the technology, nursing, and physiotherapy available. Were these not available, she would have succumbed shortly after the accident. Even without reference to the resources being devoted to her care, the question of whether she is still alive in a meaningful way cannot be avoided. Different people will come to different conclusions, but the ethical issues cannot be bypassed by reference to euthanasia or murder. PVS introduces novel dimensions to our decision-making, at once fascinating and almost grotesque in their ramifications.

15.3 Ethical issues in PVS

There is a profound ambiguity about PVS. Clinically, their lives are stable. But are they worth living? Would we want to be in a PVS for five, ten, or fifteen years. If we put ourselves in Miriam's position, what would we think? Of course, there lies the crux of the whole issue: we would be incapable of thinking. A further paradox is that PVS patients are not in a terminal state, since the damage to the higher centres of their brains will not kill them. They have to be nursed and fed, but if these are provided, their life spans may be long. But they cannot respond in any way that most people interpret as having meaning. If Miriam is not aware of anything, who is being nursed: is it the Miriam who was known to her family and friends, or is it their memories of Miriam? The contradictions are difficult to handle, and for this reason it has been described as either the lowest-functioning phase of life or the highest functioning phase of death. It is difficult to know which it is.

There is no getting away from the deepest of all dilemmas. Are PVS patients alive or are they dead? This in turn gets us to the heart of the dilemma presented by the definition of death. If they are alive, they demonstrate few (if any) of the characteristic features of human personhood. On the other hand, if they are dead, they still display some of the features of those who are alive. And so, if we return to one of the classic cases of someone in a PVS, Terry Schiavo, it is legitimate to ask: When did Terri Schiavo 'die'? Was it as a result of the withdrawal of food and fluids, or was it fifteen or so years earlier when she first went into the PVS? We find the more recent date the more amenable, and yet we should not peremptorily dismiss that earlier date. We know that it was only recently that her body organs ceased to function, but did she cease to exist as a person all those years earlier when the cerebral hemispheres of her brain had ceased to function?

Once we accept a higher brain definition of death we will conclude that an individual dies when their higher brain centres are destroyed. Life-sustaining treatment in these PVS patients can then be stopped, because we are presuming that the patients are dead even though their bodies may still be alive. There is no longer congruence between death of the person in any meaningful sense and death of that person's body.

The cases I have referred to also direct our attention towards the role of families and next of kin. Their input becomes problematic if PVS patients were to be categorised as being dead. In what senses can a family 'care' for someone who is dead? The caring takes on significantly different dimensions from the caring of a living, responding patient. PVS patients are vulnerable, but in what sense? Possibly the ones who are most vulnerable are the living, the families and caregivers, with their continuing responsibilities and ongoing concern for the PVS patient. There is no escape from the perplexities raised by the PVS state.

Requests to continue treatment for a patient who has been in a PVS for some months raises issues of medical judgment and the futility of ongoing medical treatment. These have to be weighed against the autonomy of the family, with issues of cost and resource allocation lurking in the background. As part of any decision-making there is the need to weigh the burdens and benefits of the PVS patient, especially in relation to the withdrawal of artificial nutrition and hydration. Will the patient benefit by being relieved of the burden of the PVS? Is it correct to consider this condition burdensome, given that patients are wholly unaware of their predicament? Is non-existence preferable to existence in the PVS?

What advantage does the PVS patient derive from continued existence? Nutritional support can preserve the functioning of the organs in a PVS patient, but it cannot restore the person to a conscious, reflective life. There is no way in which it can restore the patient to any semblance of normal existence. There will be no improvement in the patient's prognosis. If these outcomes are unattainable, is there a sense in which it can be considered to represent care, by bringing comfort and support to the patient? Even this is doubtful, since the patient is unaware that they are being cared for. On the other hand, the family may feel that their loved one is being cared for, and for some families this may continue for a very long period of time.

As these options are played out, there is no escape from the ambivalence of this condition, presenting as it does decisions that have a different character from anything previously encountered. No matter what conclusions are reached regarding the appropriate treatment or when to withdraw treatment, the PVS condition is quite different from anything met in normal human existence. When confronted by a long-term PVS patient, it becomes difficult to work out what is the nature of the compassionate response, and this is where the ethical and theological challenge arises. While compassion may normally amount to saving an individual's life, prolonging it, or improving its quality, this does not seem to be the case with the PVS patient. The patient's life is not saved by treatment, while prolonging life amounts to prolonging a destructive illness. When there is no way in which the quality of life can be improved, what does compassion amount to?

15.4 What contribution can Christians make?

Christians are as bemused by these challenges as are all other groups of people. There are no theological directives that will provide sure guideposts as to what path to take. Nevertheless, one would hope that there are a number of helpful pointers.

The first is the Christian acceptance of the reality of death. We will all die; all our lives will come to an end. The notion of medical futility is based on this premise. If it is clear that continued treatment will accomplish no more than an extension of the dying process, it has no place in the clinical armamentarium. Obviously, this conclusion relies on clinical judgment, and clinical judgment can be wrong and even misguided. If treatment appears to be futile, it should not be persevered with. Christians do not need to approach life with a mentality that requires human beings to stay alive at any cost. A point will come when death is to be welcomed as a necessary part of life.

Second, for members of the Christian community there is also recognition that the promise of a new heaven and a new earth takes away the fear in death. While society as a whole strives to live longer untouched by pain and suffering, the Christian response must be different. The promise and hope of ongoing life with Christ takes away the fear and uncertainty of death. Furthermore, not only have Christians been promised eternal life, they also have a forerunner, Jesus, who has tasted and conquered death. Thus the Christian approach must be one that does not consider the striving for length of days as essential. In fact the Christian may view such a striving as unhelpful and wrong; for it focuses on the here and now, placing the utmost importance on physical life on earth. While these are exceedingly general pointers that apply across the whole face of medicine, they come to a head with PVS, where the life in question is exceedingly debilitated biological life lacking any awareness (not simply a limited awareness) of personal life. Theologically, one has to ask what is the rationale for maintaining such an existence for Christians who look forward to a resurrected body (and one imagines a resurrected brain) after death.

Third, Christians frequently refer to humans as embodied individuals or embodied beings, in this way stressing the importance of our bodies to what we are as human beings, as being made in the image of God. From this it follows that our brains are integral to all we are as personal beings. From this discussion of the PVS it has become clear that the brainstem alone is an insufficient basis for personal life. Functioning cerebral hemispheres are also required, and hence appear to be essential for our lives as embodied individuals. The ethical implications of this are far-reaching, and will prove disconcerting to some. However, any response to long-term PVS patients has to take at least some account of it.

Fourth, for some Christians, a pro-life stance drives them to conclude that continuation of the existence of PVS patients is mandatory; under no circumstances should feeding and hydration be withdrawn. As I have indicated previously, the point that has to be determined is whether these actions constitute maintenance of life in a full human sense, or whether they are more akin to a prolongation of dying. Regardless of the conclusions we reach, life and death have assumed new connotations in this situation, ones that we have to grapple with using new thought forms.

16

Care of Older People

We live in societies dominated by youth and the interests of the young. This comes out particularly in the manner in which the media direct their attention far more at the young than at the old. It is the young who are prepared to spend money on consumables; hence, it is they who are targeted. So often we don't know what to make of the old. Ageism is unacceptable and retirement at sixty-five has disappeared from many societies, suggesting that there is a definite place for the old. And yet we are ambivalent. Do we really want older people hanging around taking the jobs that could go to those who are younger? Do we really think that older people are wiser or at least have a wisdom born of experience that might benefit the whole of society? Even churches are diffident, especially large ones with their emphasis on young people. While this is a welcome emphasis, one sometimes gets the impression that it is in part at the expense of the grey-haired members of the congregation who are largely taken for granted.

A complicating factor in societies' attitudes towards older people is that many of them are healthy and vigorous. They are far better equipped to contribute positively to society today than would have been the case fifty or one hundred years ago. This is why many can continue in full-time employment well beyond the age of sixty-five. While this is becoming increasingly widely accepted, it exists in tandem with advertisements galore aimed at the over-sixties, and sometimes the over-fifties, that now is the time to enjoy life and reap the reward of all those years of hard work. Once more, there is a place for such activities, as long as they don't carry the subtle message that there is no place for these age groups also to make a contribution to others within the community.

Old age isn't merely a transitional stage between life and death. Those who are older are one with everyone else making up humanity. Each individual older person is important, and societies should aim to bestow upon each older person honour and respect.

But this is no easy task in societies dominated by the allure to be healthy, fit, and young.

Beyond this, a Christian approach also stresses the whole person, so that older people are seen not just as individuals, but as sets of relationships. Unfortunately, it is these that are so rapidly broken down in old age, as friends and relations die, and as physical weakness limits the range of contacts the person would once have enjoyed. A further problem is that with changes in society and within the church, the older person may come to feel more and more estranged from once familiar landmarks and institutions. All too readily, the older person may become a stranger, physically, socially, and spiritually, as even the most basic of relationships with family, and with one's own past, break down. This estrangement is markedly accentuated if dementia sets in.

16.1 Confronting mortality

The biblical writers had no illusions about old age. They recognised its positive features and also its negative ones. Old age is a blessing from God. In Proverbs, grey hair is seen as a crown of splendour that is attained by a righteous life (Proverbs 16:31). In Ruth, God is viewed as renewing life and sustaining people in old age (Ruth 4:15). One even has to wonder whether the extremely long lives lived by the patriarchs, whatever they precisely signify, were symbolic of the blessing of old age. Over against these positive elements there are the negative ones. In 2 Samuel 19:35 Barzillai is recognised as showing declining discernment, taste, and hearing, while the preacher in Ecclesiastes 12:3 graphically describes losses of sight, teeth, and physical strength. Along similar lines, the psalmist viewed our span of years as nothing but trouble and sorrow (Psalm 90:10).

And then there is recognition of the wisdom of older people. In the Old Testament, wisdom and old age appear to have a special relationship. In this way, a corporate tradition was established and was brought to life for succeeding generations, who were to remember the days of old. This would be explained to them by older people, who had a special role to play in maintaining the nation's faith by recalling God's activity in the past. The patriarchs were regarded as the epitome of wisdom in old age. We should also note that it was the ageing Simeon and Anna who greeted and proclaimed the Saviour.

Respect for older people appeared to be one mark of a well-ordered society. In Israelite law, special provision was made for widows, while even adults were to honour their parents. Against this, disrespect for older people was a sign of chaos within society.

Coming through these and other instances is the centrality of hope no matter what changes occur throughout life. There is a continuity of identity regardless of what happens to an individual's body. This continuity of identity emphasises a broader continuity, from the past, through the present, and into the future. The 'real me' has been created by God and that relationship with God continues, no matter how frail or limited we may become.

Another central theme is that of weakness. Our temptation is to value most those who appear to be powerful and capable, the successful in society. And yet the heart of the Christian gospel is the very opposite, characterised as it is by God's self-emptying and by the way in which he became vulnerable and weak in Jesus. Within a Christian framework, weakness becomes acceptable, becoming the norm and even the new way. The result is that the weak, including the ageing, are to be highly valued within society. A related theme is that of equality. A Christian perspective recognises that all people of faith are members of Christ's body, regardless of age or ability. All are inextricably part of a whole and are united in a network of faith.

Foundational to these considerations is the limited life span of human beings; their mortality is central to numerous ethical considerations. In the context of ageing, it reminds us that we are dust, and to dust we shall return (Genesis 3:19–20). Once we come to terms with the fact that our days are numbered, we have an important starting-point for aspiring to wisdom (Psalm 90:12). A life of three score years and ten is not a totally misleading guide when confronted by the ethical, social, and spiritual dilemmas of ageing. It forces us to face up to the reality of our mortality, and we cast aside the illusion that we will go on living endlessly, more-or-less unchanged. An illness-free, trouble-free existence is, for most of human kind, an illusion, that should have no place in ethical decision-making.

Once we accept that our days are limited, we can begin to take life seriously. We can begin to appreciate what life is for, and how we can make the most of it in the limited time available. This fits in with Christian aspirations, with their drive to redeem the time, to be holy, to devote oneself to the service of others, and to live as though we will meet Christ today.

Mortality and ageing are inseparable. Acceptance of mortality leads to acceptance of one of its consequences for an increasing number of people, namely, ageing. From this there is no escape, either for ourselves as individuals or for our communities. This does not lead to opposition to improvements in modern medicine, but to a recognition that these are therapeutic initiatives and not a means of defeating death and of achieving immortality.

How are these general principles put into practice? Difficult choices frequently have to be made, due to limited resources or the lack of support provided to younger family members having to look after older people with long-term illness. Even more demanding are the added challenges posed by caring for those with dementia.

16.2 Making choices

Consider the following:

> Charles is thirty, Greg is seventy, and Jim is eighty. All are in hospital for the same reason, they have appendicitis. All are operated on, and all leave hospital fitter than when they came in. Apart from the appendicitis, Charles is in very good health and this is an aberration. Greg is in reasonably good health, apart from what he describes as the usual aches and pains of a seventy-year-old. Jim has Alzheimer's disease, and while his appendicitis has been sorted out, his dementia is as bad as ever—in fact, it may be a little worse after the general anaesthetic.

Surgery for appendicitis is usually an uneventful operation that has to be carried out. If it is not, the patient may end up with a serious and even life-threatening condition. It is as essential to carry it out on an eighty-year-old as on a thirty-year-old. If society decided that it was not worth carrying it out on eighty-year-olds, it would be treating them very differently from the way it treats thirty-year-olds. On some occasions it would be condemning these eighty-year-olds to death.

Now consider the following (case 3, chapter 1):

> Patricia is thirty and is on renal dialysis; she needs a kidney transplant and is on a waiting list. Apart from her kidney problems she has no other major health problems. She is married with a young son. Mary is seventy and is also on dialysis. She too is reasonably healthy apart from her kidney problems, and she too would like a kidney transplant. Discussion is taking place about the justification of this and whether she should be put on a waiting list, the doubt surrounding this stems from her age. Katherine is eighty and is in similar circumstances, suffering from kidney failure. She has just been put on dialysis but there is considerable discussion about whether this is justified, since she has moderate dementia and various heart problems, and she also finds it difficult to understand what is going on. No one would contemplate a kidney transplant.

These three patients are suffering from a medical condition that requires demanding, expensive and scarce treatment. Do their ages make any difference in this instance? There is competition for resources, and the procedures themselves are complex and make considerable demands on the patients and their caregivers. The age of the patients is beginning to be relevant, although the decisions taken will not be based solely on age. Probably the most difficult decision concerns Mary, the seventy-year-old, since she will be in direct competition for a scarce kidney transplant with younger patients who could benefit from them for a much longer period of time. Nevertheless, Mary must be given the best treatment possible for someone in her medical state.

The relevance of age for medical decision-making needs to be looked at a little more closely, since it is so easily misunderstood by those who would emphasise it too much, as well as by those who think it is completely irrelevant. It is a truism to state that for older people much of their finite life has already been lived; they have had their opportunities to experience what human life means, and to participate in the human community and in the relationships that make up that community. Older people are still an integral part of the human community, and they continue to be images of the God who made them. The younger members of this community continue to have responsibilities for them, but does the mere fact that they have had opportunities that younger people have not had, have any ethical ramifications? Additionally, as people age they become more dependent on others within the human community, placing on others the moral obligation to care and protect them in ways not required since their childhood.

There are two apparently conflicting pressures at work here. The one is in the direction of less protection for older people (as they have already had their opportunities), whereas the other is towards increased protection (due to their increased vulnerability). Of these two pressures, it is the second that accords more readily with the Christian emphasis on care for the weak and disadvantaged. And yet the conflict is more apparent than real. There is no question that older people are to be valued as all others in the human community are (or should be) valued. However, when there is competition for resources, choices have to be made, and this is why ethical decision-making is needed. Under these circumstances, the first pressure suggests that resources should be directed towards the young rather than the old, all other things being equal. However, the second pressure contends that care and the provision of the basic necessities of existence must be provided regardless of age. This is a fundamental prerequisite of ethical practice.

These principles are complementary, and both are important. To ignore the one or the other will result either in an unwillingness to make rigorously thought-out tough decisions, or in an uncaring harsh regime this devalues older people. Placing the needs of the younger patients first in a resource poor, and therefore competitive, environment will generally have little repercussion for most clinical procedures. What it is prepared to do is come to terms with our mortality and with the fact that our lives as earthly beings will one day cease. This is a deeply Christian emphasis, with its many overtones of our createdness and fall, and its reminder of the need of redemption and rebirth. After all, Christians look forward to a new body, a new heaven and a new earth.

Ageing is a part of life, rather than another medical obstacle to be overcome. We should also find a meaningful place for suffering and decline in life, and should not pretend that old age can be turned into some form of endless middle age. And so, while the ageing have a substantial claim upon public funds for health care, this is not an unlimited claim.

The interests and claims of elderly individuals are to be protected, but this in itself does not entail measures such as directing unlimited resources in their direction, pursuing unlimited life extension, or failing to balance the needs of different age groups. Society has an obligation to help people make it from youth to old age, but by the same token it does not have an unlimited obligation to continue the extension of life in old age. This is a prelude to freeing older people from unnecessary burdens imposed by excessive life-sustaining treatment. Compare the following:

> Annette is a vigorous seventy-five-year-old, who requires a hip replacement. This is done, and within a short time she is on her feet with the help of crutches. She feels renewed, and as soon as she can, she is back tending her garden, showing hospitality at home, visiting the 'elderly' and leading her Bible study group. Joy is also a seventy-five-year-old, but she has been going downhill for the last ten years, and now has heart problems, high blood pressure and diabetes. She is confined to bed, and tends to be confused for much of the time. After a heart attack, there is discussion about whether she should have coronary bypass surgery since there is the possibility this will prolong her life for a few weeks or possibly months. Her family think this would simply prolong her dying.

Annette and Joy are the same age. There is little doubt that Annette should receive the operation she needs, but Joy's case is substantially different. The operation will enable Annette to return to meaningful life. Joy will not be able to return to anything resembling normality, suggesting that she will not benefit from the operation. Any limits being set stem from serious reflection on what is best for the individual patient, and as such are precisely what one would expect of a Christian assessment.

The ageing process reminds us that no human life has ultimate value, that belongs to God alone. Older people are to be highly valued, but there are limits to what we can do or what resources we can make available. The challenge is to do our best to prevent growing old becoming an inevitable downward spiral. Sometimes the battle will be a very uneven one, especially when chronic debilitating illness intervenes, and we will lose. This is when devoted loving care shines through, and emerges as being far more important than using high technology in an inappropriate manner to maintain life for a few more days or weeks.

16.3 From ageing to dementia

One of the tragedies of ageing is not the ageing process itself, but the accompanying loss of mental abilities, from simple memory loss to deterioration of the personality, and ultimately to a complete breakdown in all we hold dear as human beings. This is the world of dementia. Thankfully, all older people are not so afflicted, and one of the redeeming features of ageing is the picture of a ninety-year-old full of wisdom and verve, cognitively vigorous and able to enter into debate and contribute to intellectual discussion as he or she would have done forty or fifty years earlier. Alas, there are many for whom this is worlds removed from where they are at. Alzheimer's disease, with its many crippling ramifications of behavioural and personality changes, has intervened and they will never again be what they once were.

Alzheimer's disease prompts a litany of questions and concerns, from the philosophical to the intensely practical. How do people respond to personality and behavioural changes of which they are aware, and which they know are destroying all that they have ever stood for? How do they cope with the knowledge that they are changing for the worse, and are dying as the person they know themselves to be?

Does the loss of the personality traits that once characterised a person have consequences for the value a society ascribes to that person? Is the life of a person with severe dementia worth maintaining, let alone saving? How are caregivers to respond to the increasing dependence of the patient upon them, and how can this be coped with in the midst of the grief at the 'loss' of a loved one?

It is one thing to be aware that you have a terminal illness and that you have a very limited time left on this earth, but it is something quite different to know that you will, in all probability, continue to live for some years, but will no longer be 'me' and that you will make increasingly unreasonable demands on those very close to you. Instead of caring for others as you are used to doing, you will have to be cared for in a way that has not occurred since your early childhood. Instead of being a leader of others, you will have to be led and assisted in every aspect of your life.

A graphic and intensely personal account of Alzheimer's disease is provided by Robert Davis in his autobiography: *My Journey into Alzheimer's Disease*. Following a highly successful ministry in a large American church, at the age of fifty-three he was diagnosed as suffering from Alzheimer's disease. With assistance, he recorded his thoughts as the dementia progressed, as he retired from the ministry, and as he came to terms with what was happening to him.

It is worth quoting Davis, since it brings us face-to-face with elements of the tragedy and perversity of this terrible illness. The poignancy comes through with an eloquence hard to reconcile with his diminishing as a human and as a person. Davis did not drift into dementia, rather, he worked through it and strove to control it as his own brain mechanisms were failing. In doing this, his cries are the cries of all with dementia; he spoke for them as a protagonist and sage. With muted and tragic eloquence, he sums up the predicament of this condition:

> I am still human. I laugh at the ridiculous disease that steals the most obvious things from my thoughts and leaves me spouting some of the most obscure, irrelevant information when the right button is pushed. I want to participate in life to my utmost limit. The reduced capacity, however, leaves me barely able to take care of my basic living needs, and there is nothing left over for being a productive member of society. This leaves me in a

> terrible dilemma. When I go out into society I look whole. There is no wheelchair, no bandage, or missing part to remind people of my loss.
>
> In Alzheimer's disease there is the loss of the personality, a diminished sense of self-worth. A highly productive person has to wonder why he is still alive and what purpose the Lord has in keeping him on this earth. As I struggle with the indignities that accompany daily living, I am losing my sense of humanity and self-worth. Blessed is the person who can take the Alzheimer's patient back to that happier time when they were worthwhile and allow them to see the situation in which they were of some use.[1]

How did Davis handle the appalling losses of his present state, and the even more devastating destruction that he knew awaited him in the near future? In the early stages he did not come-to-terms with a daily experience of his own slow disintegration as a person. He raged against it, and this continued until he had a spiritual crisis, following which he came to the conclusion that:

> I have a life that can be either frustrating and frightening or peaceful and submissive. The choice is mine. I choose to take things moment by moment, thankful for everything that I have, instead of raging wildly at the things that I have lost. I must thank God for the ability to do this . . . In accepting this progressive handicap as from the Lord, I am coming to a fuller understanding of that phrase from the Lord's Prayer, 'Thy will be done'.[2]

In another place, Davis expresses the same sentiment in different words, as he recognised the two options confronting him. He writes:

---

1. Robert Davis, *My Journey into Alzheimer's Disease* (Wheaton, Illinois: Tyndale House, 1989), 114 and 117.
2. *Ibid,* 65–6.

> We can either be bitter and groan and be miserable and curse God, or else we can thank God for what he has done, especially for giving us his great healing power when it was so critical in our lives . . . In the most helpless, hopeless, and extreme part of my life, Christ is here comforting and giving life meaning, even when all I have to look forward to in this life is becoming a mindless vegetable. [3]

It was this acceptance that enabled Robert Davis to come to terms with his continued inability to preach or teach. He recognised that all he would be able to do in the future would be limited to listening and praying. We can admire Davis for arriving at a position where he could begin to accept these appalling limitations, but we have to admit that his triumph would have been tinged with brokenness. While we do not know the latter part of his story, we can surmise that his condition would have deteriorated and his limitations would have become ever more painful. The disastrous nature of this condition medically is its lack of redemptive elements. The challenge in Christian terms is to discover how such elements can be injected, and what is their nature in the face of the inexorable decline of a human personality.

16.4 'I am not the man I was'

A natural reaction when faced with a demented individual is to conclude that they are of less value than those of us who are not demented. This is akin to the 'yuk' response in other biomedical areas. Those with severe Alzheimer's have to be cared for, treated as infants, reproved, and looked after in every conceivable way. Their human dignity can be hidden and a time may come when it has to be fought for. As the disease progresses, far more dependence has to be placed on what they were, on our memories of that person and what they stood for. The present is deceptive and forlorn. As one father said to his son on realising a silly mistake he had made: 'I am not the man I once was'. But he was still a father, a husband, and a

---

3. *Ibid*, 77.

grandfather. He still fitted into family relationships and a community of faith.

Let's call this man TB. His body is still here, and yet he is hardly with us as TB; he would be unrecognisable to his old colleagues whom he once controlled and instructed. He makes inordinate demands on his wife, although he is completely unaware of these and is completely unaware that she is sacrificing her own life to care for him and do everything that her love drives her to do. This tragic state of affairs will continue for a number of years, until a fall and head injury brings his life to an end. He never knew how dementia had clouded every aspect of his last years, nor how his wife died shortly after him, probably worn out by the loving care she had so generously bestowed on him. Now that he has gone, we who are left behind remember him as the person he was prior to his Alzheimer's, and those last years live on only in our memories. They did not exist for him.

There are no ready-made answers to episodes like this. The sacrifice of TB's wife was a sacrifice Christians would want people to make, and it is sacrifices such as this one that we celebrate. We rejoice that they represent the very best in human life, representing in some small way the sacrifice made by Christ for all mankind. Perhaps we have found the redemption in Alzheimer's disease, redemption inherent within the sacrificial acts of other human beings as they support the demented. This is not medically-based redemption; it is not found in a cure or even in partial therapy, though those may come one day. It is a far deeper remedy based upon the way in which we value and care for and uphold those incapable of looking after themselves.

What is noteworthy is that TB's wife was concerned for him in the little things of his life. She wanted him to live as dignified an existence as possible even when the pressures to lose his dignity were extremely powerful. For her, his loss of dignity was a loss of something that was central to what he was as a human being. With progressive Alzheimer's disease it is a losing battle, but it is a battle worth fighting for as long as possible. The little things in life become central, and it is these that are crucial in ethical decision-making. This fits in with Christian concerns where what we are, and how we live, become more important than what we say. It was in this spirit that Paul repeatedly instructed the Christians in the early church to imitate him as he sought to imitate Christ.

Once emphasis is on care rather than cure, the patient is protected by the dimensions of caring medicine, including comfort and palliation. This is not a short cut or cheap option, but is appropriate for patients suffering in these ways. In no sense does this lessen the value placed on demented patients; they can still be treated with dignity, even while acknowledging that acute care with high technology is out of place. This it seems to me is an appropriate response to patients facing not only inevitable decline and death, but also a diminished sense of self, an inability to compare the present with the past, a lack of memory, and a failure to understand their predicament.

17

Living in Society

Popular accounts of bioethics concentrate on the controversial, the great debates at the beginning and end of life. Inevitably, I have spent many pages of this book in this territory, but in this last section we have also had to face up to the unexciting decision-making that lies at the heart of bioethics in practice. As we have done this there has been one particular pressure that has raised its ugly head from time to time, and that is inadequate resources. More could be done if only there was more money; lives could be saved; the quality of people's lives could be improved. While I do not intend to tackle these issues in depth, it is important to note that these are important bioethical quandaries. They should also be of concern from a Christian standpoint.

17.1 From neglect to excess

It takes little insight to recognise the gross disparity that exists within our world. On the one hand are the desperately poor, struggling to survive on what meagre food they can grow in drought stricken areas. There are the refugee camps full to overflowing with those who have lost everything. Beyond all these there are the child soldiers and the sex slaves sold into prostitution. In stark contrast there are the rich; those of us who have so much—with countless educational and recreational opportunities, tempted by consumer goods galore, impossible for those who have nothing to even begin to imagine. We all inhabit the same world, and we all are created equal by the one God.

Consider practically every area of medical care. While the West is full of hospitals, medical staff and health care professionals, many of the poorest in our world have exceedingly limited access to any medical care. Take the care of women during labour and childbirth. In sub-Saharan Africa one in every sixteen women dies in childbirth, in comparison to one in 2,800 in the industrialised nations of the West.

Every year six million children under the age of five years die from hunger-related causes in developing countries. At the same time, in developed countries around the world billions of dollars is spent every year in helping those with infertility problems, with up to four billion dollars per year being spent on ART in the US alone. This comparison is not meant as a condemnation of the ARTs; it is simply an illustration of the ways in which money can be spent by those with the necessary funds. More extreme is the weight loss industry in the US, which is worth more than forty billion dollars a year. Interestingly, some suggest that there are now more overweight and obese people in the world than there are those who are starving; not because the latter are decreasing but because the former are increasing.

This is at the global level. Similar, if less extreme contrasts, occur in developed countries, where the gap between the rich and the poor, the healthy and the ill, the privileged and the underprivileged, grows larger each year. The disparities in health status are alarming, their sources stemming from poor housing conditions for the underprivileged, limited employment opportunities and educational attainment, abusive family relationships, and inadequate access to appropriate health care. The result is transgenerational deprivation.

Some of the resource issues are subtle. Think of neonatal intensive care units. Research has found that infants admitted to a neonatal intensive care unit that is running at full capacity are fifty percent more likely to die than those admitted to units running at half capacity. From this the conclusion has been drawn that units should be kept between seventy-five and eighty-five percent capacity to balance the needs for efficiency and safety. However, this is often impractical in public health systems, where many units run on full capacity most of the time.

The balance between public and private health care within societies raises complex ethical and social issues. While details are beyond the scope of this book, it is pertinent to point out that societies have a duty to provide as best they can for the basic health needs of all their citizens. This leads to the dictum of adequate provision for all, rather than optimum provision for the wealthy but less than adequate provision for the remainder. Whether this is achieved via a public health system alone, or a public-private mix, is a political decision.

A confounding factor that is intruding increasingly into this debate is the burgeoning demand for access to unproven treatments. There are numerous groups who lobby government for a particular treatment that they think will cure them, but for which there is no scientific evidence demonstrating any real benefit. The cost of such experimental procedures is often enormous.

For example, in Beijing Dr Huang Hongyun has performed numerous transplants of embryonic stem cells into patients with spinal cord injuries and neurodegenerative disorders. He has been carrying out these procedures with the approval of his hospital's ethics committee. However, there has been essentially no peer review of the beneficial effects of this work at an international level. Consequently, while other experts in the field regard the work as of dubious long-term benefit, his claims and the effusive support by patients have resulted in considerable pressure for this approach to be adopted in other countries. The relevance of this for the present context is that a dubious procedure would be introduced at considerable cost, money that could have been directed into other far more justifiable procedures that would actually assist needy patients. The ethical implications of this are obvious.

Regardless of the specific issue, the guiding response of Christians should be to focus on what might be best for as many people as possible, locally and globally (see discussion in chapter 2). While many of the situations are dauntingly complex, the aim should be to see that people are treated fairly and justly, and that those who do not qualify for specific medical interventions or where such interventions are unavailable, are still provided with basic care. The goal should be to treat people, especially the most vulnerable, with dignity and respect. Such ideals sound unattainable, but in their absence the path ahead will be guided by nothing other than self-interest.

17.2 Coping with differences

For the remainder of this chapter I shall turn to a different set of issues: how those within the Christian community cope with others, also within that community, with a different approach to some of the ethical issues we have encountered in the previous pages. On many of the questions we have faced the conclusions may be mutually exclusive. Differences will be encountered within and between communities, including church communities. On some occasions the communities will have radically different philosophies, precluding even the possibility of agreement on some of the seminal issues facing us. Professional groupings will also adopt stances on procedures of interest to them, and these may have considerable influence on public opinion. And then on some of these matters, governments have to reach conclusions on those processes that will or will not be allowed within the society, or that will or will not be funded. There is no way out of this maelstrom. Consider the following groups within a Christian frame of thinking:

> *Group A* believes that liberal attitudes towards abortion are wrong: they demean prenatal human life. The members of this group may even go so far as to state that abortion is murder. For this group there is no question what approach they should take, and consequently they vigorously oppose any use of embryonic stem cells. Every effort should be made to ensure that legislation prevents this ever occurring within their country. They do their best to assist in this effort, including lobbying parliamentarians in favour of the use of adult stem cells and against any derivation of stem cells from embryos.
>
> Starting from a Christian perspective, the members of this group consider that society should not tolerate practices that threaten the life of the unborn. The destruction of human embryos is clearly unchristian, and should be a central plank of Christian ethics. To tolerate even the occasional destruction of an embryo for research or even therapy is viewed as an abrogation of a fundamental Christian stance. Moreover, this stance should be espoused by all within society, including those with no Christian basis to their thinking or ethical position. Hence, it is appropriate that legal safeguards should be put in place to effect this pro-life position.

Group B is a denomination that is doing its best to think through social issues, and that wants to take a lead on social ethical questions. When confronted by the issue of embryo destruction, it finds that there are differences of opinion among its members. While most adopt a strongly conservative stance, serious questions are raised whether this should be an absolute position. Many have a feeling that there may be some situations where the value of embryos should be weighed against the possible medical benefits that may ensue from some carefully scrutinised research work. This is far removed from a liberal attitude, but some regard it as a seriously compromised position.

After considerable debate, the social affairs committee knows that it has to emerge with a way forward, and that it should produce a statement. This could contain an overview of what are regarded as crucial ethical and spiritual principles that should always be taken into account in coming to a conclusion. However, some consider this too vague and argue for a succinct statement opposing destructive embryo research under all circumstances. The latter approach wins a vote on the day, since it is seen as more faithfully expressing the Christian position, with its desire to protect all human life. This leaves some members feeling out on a limb, and asking whether a vote actually establishes a particular stance as being inherently Christian.

Group C is not a group as such, but a collection of individual Christians, who live and work within society. Their own positions vary on embryonic stem cell research, but tend to be conservative rather than liberal. However, as professionals who have to relate to all sorts of people on a day-to-day basis, they come into contact with many who have no Christian aspirations of any description. Some of these Christians are general practitioners, some are counsellors, some belong to government committees dealing with health issues or legislation. They rub shoulders with those who are well outside the Christian community,

> and they feel they have to relate to them in a meaningful way.
>
> These individuals accept that they are not in a position to impose their own personal values on those with whom they come into contact or onto society as a whole. They do their best to make their views known in what they consider are appropriate ways. Nevertheless, they realise they may have to be involved in decisions or even procedures with which they personally disagree. While they may sometimes be uncomfortable with this, their basic premise is that their aim is to make a difference, perhaps a small one, but still a difference. The overriding factor for these individuals is their wish to maintain a Christian presence in very compromised situations. Of course, there are other Christians who will disagree, and argue that any form of compromise is indeed precisely that, a relinquishing of the basic tenets of one's position as a Christian.

In these illustrations I have used embryonic stem cell research as an example. I could have used many others—abortion, contraception, artificial reproductive procedures, divorce, *de facto* relationships, single sex unions, homosexuality, euthanasia, even global warming. All have strong ethical components and very often there are strong Christian viewpoints. However, the strength of these viewpoints does not of necessity equate with the extent or clarity of biblical emphases.

What then about the approaches we have encountered in these illustrations? Is any one of them more Christian than the others? Indeed, are some of these essentially Christian, whereas others are not? Perhaps some are shams and indeed are sub-Christian. In other words, are any of these more faithful to the Christian revelation than others? And can we know for sure? These are important considerations because they will determine how we act and respond within society. I can only respond from my own personal experience.

I spend my time in the midst of those with different perspectives from my own on many bioethical issues. I also move in territory where it is far from clear what a Christian perspective might amount to. For some Christians, no Christian should put themselves into the position I frequently do. Had I followed this advice, I would have kept out of biomedical science, and in particular developmental anatomy and embryology; and I would not have been prepared to become a member of government ethics committees. I would have kept well away from these highly problematic disciplines and institutions, because in the eyes of some it is well-nigh impossible to retain one's integrity as a Christian when indulging in these activities. This is because many Christians consider one should adopt black-and-white positions on everything from the status of the human embryo to eugenics and euthanasia. There are seen to be clear boundaries, which should under no circumstances be transgressed, regardless of what those around us think. In looking at this matter we have to dig a little deeper into the nature of our ethical systems. On what are they based and to whom do they speak?

17.3 Ethical and theological interfaces

Christians frequently look to *theological ethics*. This is ethical analysis within a specifically Christian context. The aim here is to emerge with theological principles that help to address contemporary ethical issues, with biblical and theological drivers as the main thrust. I have considerable sympathy with this approach, and yet if we are not very careful, it may have little to say to those who do not function within a Christian framework, and possibly with quite a different worldview. To base one's ethical stance on the character of God, the incarnation or the resurrection may be exceedingly fruitful in deriving principles of general relevance to the human condition, but how do you translate those principles into thought forms that will be understood by those outside the Christian community? One's values have to be translated into the language and concepts of those who lack a theological base.

It is at this point that I frequently feel that theological ethics, or at least its proponents, let us down. Having established what are regarded as Christian standards, these are then applied indiscriminately to the whole of society as though that society is Christian and accepts Christian presuppositions. The duty of Christians is to ensure that these standards and expectations are met by all, even by those who do not accept the presuppositions underlying the purportedly Christian position.

Over against theological ethics stands *philosophical ethics,* which may contain little with which Christians feel comfortable. This is because writers start from a wide variety of philosophical bases, some of which have little in common with anything Christian. Nevertheless, some of these perspectives may be useful for Christians, on account of their critical analyses. If philosophical approaches teach us nothing else, it is that we are to be open in our investigations and are never to be content with simplistic answers. These approaches can provide helpful, even if disconcerting, insights into complex and startlingly new questions. They can complement Christian thinking, and need not prove destructive if one's Christian foundation is a strong one. In my view we have much to learn from a wide variety of secular writers, because we are frequently dealing with issues where there is no agreed Christian viewpoint.

A further approach is that of *virtue ethics,* with its emphasis upon how we are to act in practice (see chapter 1). When confronted by bioethical dilemmas of staggering proportions, how do ordinary people act? After all, it is ordinary people who bear the brunt of decision-making, since invariably it is their families who are affected and will have to live with the consequences of their decision-making. This is where virtue ethics have a part to play, with their stress on the importance of personal character. In order to act morally, we are to be people of sensitivity and integrity. Virtues such as kindness, generosity, respect for others, honesty, and compassion constitute the model of moral conduct.

Virtue ethics sit comfortably alongside many Christian aspirations. They allow Christians to find those of like mind so that together they can tackle difficult and perplexing bioethical dilemmas. Virtue ethics complement and enhance the two previous approaches.

In the light of these considerations, what conclusions can we draw with regard to the approaches of the three groups we encountered in the previous section?

Group A depends upon the insights provided by theological ethics, paying little regard to either of the other two categories. In this we see both the strengths and the weaknesses of theological ethics. Members of this group find it difficult to move out of the territory in which they are comfortable and interact with those far removed from the Christian community. They are good at enunciating the positions they espouse and the positions they expect others to espouse alongside them. However, their attitudes towards those who come to different conclusions tend to be confrontational. A 'them' and 'us' mentality is set up. Whether or not this is the Christian way is a matter of debate, but I do not believe it is the only model of the Christian way.

Group B is aware of differences of opinion within its ranks, and yet concludes that one stance has to be adopted. It again errs on the side of theological ethics, added to which is the strange notion that democracy has some bearing on Christian values. It is this uneasy admixture that concerns me most, regardless of the ethical position adopted. Why should we think that majority opinion has anything whatsoever to do with the validity or otherwise of a Christian perspective? I very much doubt that it has. In my view a denomination, attempting to speak on behalf of a diversity of constituents, should seek to sketch out the far more assured underlying theological principles, leaving it to its adherents to apply them in real world situations. This allows for a diverse medley of responses, but within the bounds set by the general principles.

Group C, while borrowing from theological ethics, is prepared to look to philosophical ethics for guidance. The members here also place considerable store by virtue ethics. The heterogeneity of this group is both its strength and weakness. All will not come to the same conclusions; some may go tragically astray. The working out of basic principles within specific real life situations is a responsibility thrust upon all of us as those made in the image of God and especially for Christians who are being conformed to the likeness of Christ. We continually have to ask whether any purported solutions will improve the lives of ordinary people and enhance their dignity and standing as human beings. This is a deeply ethical approach, rather than a legislative one. It also places considerable demands upon us to demonstrate a better way, through the quality and integrity of our lives.

Inherent within everything I have said up to this point has been an underlying query, namely, which audience do we have in mind when stating how others should act in the bioethical realm? It seems to me there are three major ones to take into account.

The *first* is the one closest to me; this is the sphere that encompasses myself, my family and others very close to me. How would I act in a particular situation? What conclusions would I reach for myself, and those for whom I have direct responsibility? There is no question here of different perspectives or different worldviews. Solutions have to be mapped out starting from a Christian base, and interpreting that base in whatever ways seem best. This is what one might call the ideal sphere, no matter how difficult the issues may be.

The *second* audience is the wider Christian community, where one can expect some agreement on general approaches. This does not preclude differences of opinion, but at least one is talking much the same language. One can refer to theological principles and can debate the issues taking these into account. There is a freedom here to discuss and perhaps debate difficult issues from an agreed foundation. However, the situation in practice may be far removed for this, because Christians can fight vigorously over many questions, including bioethical ones. Problems arise when certain interpretations of Scripture are regarded as correct, resulting in the acceptance of certain practices and the rejection of others, even by Christians. My response is to say that Christians should be working together to seek the mind of Christ, especially when differences of opinion have major repercussions for the manner in which people are treated.

If there are problems within the Christian community, there will probably be infinitely greater ones when confronted by the *third* audience, namely, wider society. Here there may be little in the way of any agreement on fundamental principles or on how ethical issues should be approached. This is where many Christians feel threatened by the foreign nature of this environment and by what may be little sympathy for Christian aspirations. However, it is here that Christians are to demonstrate the relevance and worth of their values. They will only influence others by the quality of their arguments and by the integrity of what they are as people. In order to act like this, there has to be openness in attitudes and a thorough understanding of the culture within which we are operating.

Underlying my stance throughout this book there has been a presupposition that there will never be a Christian consensus on specific matters within bioethics. This does not mean that Christians will always take diametrically opposing views on fundamental issues, such as the dignity of every individual. Additionally, Christians on the whole will tend to take more conservative positions on a range of bioethical issues than do many others. But this is far removed from some doctrinaire stance that all have to sign up to. What is of crucial importance is to know why we move in one direction rather than another, and what is the theological basis for this. We will have to work hard to ensure that our fundamental stance is informed by what is possible medically, by the very demanding realities of some people's situations, and by always asking what might be in the best interests of those most affected. It is also important to ask what our stance tells us about our own hopes and fears, and why we move in one direction rather than another.

17.4 Preventing the future?

The very idea that we can prevent the future is not merely strange; it is impossible. We cannot prevent the future, which will arrive unheralded, wanted or unwanted, on our doorsteps. But can we prevent one kind of future while encouraging another kind of future? This is what bioethicists are attempting to do, to close one door and open another. In acting like this they are aiming to control future directions and future developments. The question is whether they can do this, or does it lie solely in the hands of the scientists and clinicians? Who are the policy makers and who is actually determining the future? No wonder there is so much angst among groups like theologians and social scientists, as they picture the human race going down paths mapped out by reductionistic scientists.

To look into the future is a hazardous, and some might say extremely unwise, pastime. Our chances of being appallingly wrong are very high indeed. But there may be a few things worth saying. At the level of detailed analysis we do not know with any accuracy what questions will arise before they have arisen at a scientific level. The direction that scientists take is so often determined by the in-built rationale of the science itself, and not by the pronouncements of ethicists or theologians. We are notoriously poor at predicting exactly what will turn out to be of scientific value. This poses many difficulties for ethicists and theologians, who feel they are being left behind and have no role in determining what should and should not be done. I see no way around this.

Imagine a world many years in the future, 2080 in fact. There is nothing special about this particular year, any more than 1984 or 2001 were special. In fact, as we look back on those other two years, we probably think of them as fairly ordinary. And yet, when those novels (*1984*, and *2001: A Space Odyssey*) were written, each in their very different ways looked forward to a future time when life had taken on totally different dimensions, unknown, unparalleled, and grimly strange. These were indeed 'brave new worlds'. 2080 will be no different and yet it is difficult to believe that it will not be a world of biotechnological control and biomedical manipulation.

There will be few books since everything will be available on-line. Information will be nearly instant, although the problems with this will be considerable. A new industry will have started up to assist in sorting out useful from useless information. The information overload will be immense. No one will wear spectacles since all forms of eye defects will be treated via laser surgery. In the same way there will be no surgery in the old fashioned sense, since laser and remote controlled surgery will have taken over. Even hospitals will almost have ceased to exist; day surgeries will serve almost every need in the community. Alzheimer's disease will be a phenomenon of the past, with people living to 130 years as a rule and without the threat of dementia hanging over their heads. Infertility will have been conquered and few people will have babies naturally. Why should they, when what we know as IVF and PGD will be so routine and easy to administer? Clones will exist and will be treated as perfectly ordinary members of society. Most are anonymous, just as those conceived by IVF are anonymous. Over thirty per cent of the population will have artificial parts of some sort—for example, brain implants, with large tracts of the frontal lobes of their brains having been replaced by artificial devices, to make them more loving and considerate.

Of course, there are problems. It is difficult to know what is real, and the idea of the natural seems to have disappeared almost entirely. Most people at some stage of their lives have organs like the heart and kidneys replaced by small artificial devices that fit neatly inside their bodies. They don't have to wait for these organs to malfunction to have them replaced; the implants are said to function better than the natural ones. Legs and joints are routinely replaced by prostheses, and few people over the age of forty-five have any of their own natural joints. There are no individuals with Down syndrome or any other genetic condition, since only healthy babies are born. However, people still die, even if many are centenarians when they do.

I am not for one moment suggesting that these pictures will bear any resemblance to what will exist in 2080, but that is not important. The world of 2080 will be dramatically different from the one of 2007 or thereabouts. Two points are significant. The first is that the origins of all the possibilities are already with us. The second is that human beings, no matter how changed in some respects, will be substantially similar to today's people.

It is significant that the world I have just envisaged has become totally dependent upon technological 'fixes' to almost everything. And yet, the future for them will be as uncertain as it ever was, and the technology can let them down. Sometimes there are even tragedies. And in the end, everyone withers and dies, although some of them rebel against death far more than they would have done seventy years or so previously. Death is far more of an ugly intrusion than it used to be.

Between our world and that of 2080 is a continuum. There will be no sudden point when our world becomes that far-off world. There is continuity between the two. The world of 2080 is already with us to some extent. Nothing I have included in it is a surprise, since everything there is here already. If one wants to describe the world of 2080 as a nightmare, that nightmare is a present reality. It will not depend upon a wayward group of scientists getting out of control. All of us going about our day-to-day business are already partaking in this transition.

The sort of biological and medical developments I have been dealing with are everyday developments. They are part of the warp and woof of daily existence. There is one small change here and another small change there, most of the changes being welcome ones—at least for some sections of the population. We are not surrounded by Frankenstein-like scientists in white coats working to an agenda aimed at conquering the world. They are ordinary people doing ordinary jobs. Their normality is their most striking feature. But how do we cope with the changes being wrought by them?

Christians tend to have been reared on Armageddon-like visions, and hence find these small but cumulatively massive changes difficult to come to terms with. The result I believe is that we cling to the maleficence of science and scientists, at least in selected areas. In this way we have something to combat and argue against. The trouble is that all too often this approach forces us to exaggerate the issues in order to provide us with big picture developments to combat, whether cloning, embryonic stem cells, designer babies, or euthanasia. Far too often we condemn these procedures by comparing them with Nazi-like atrocities.

The trouble is that while we are concentrating on these issues we are missing the tenor of the actual debates that are going on. We are also missing the Bible's consistent emphasis on careful stewardship. People of faith are to *be* Christ's people in the consulting room, in the laboratory, on the committees. They are to think through every issue that comes their way and are to be one with those struggling to come to some resolution of what for them are taxing matters.

Everything we touch is eschatological; it's future-oriented. The future can be a future of hope even as we face incredible unknowns. But we are to face it head on; we are to be realistic, accepting that many aspects of the future will not be the same as the present, let alone the past.

Glossary

Adult stem cells: stem cells derived from tissues other than the early embryo, such as fetal or adult organs and tissue. Blood and bone marrow are the best known examples.

Allotransplantation: the transfer of tissues or whole organs from one individual to another within the same species.

Alzheimer's disease (AD): the most common cause of dementia, a neurodegenerative disorder characterised initially by disturbances of memory, and eventually by severe changes in personality.

Altered nuclear transfer (ANT): a procedure that involves altering a gene essential to development before performing cell nuclear transfer, creating an impaired 'embryo' that could never develop; may be considered to provide a less ethically problematic source of embryonic stem cells.

Amniocentesis: a test in which some of the amniotic fluid surrounding the foetus is withdrawn from the amniotic sac and analysed for abnormal genes or chromosomes; carried out at around fourteen to eighteen weeks' gestation; frequently conducted to test for chromosomal abnormalities such as Down syndrome.

Anencephaly: a severe congenital abnormality in which the vault of the skull is absent, with the cerebral hemispheres of the brain completely missing, or reduced to small masses attached to the base of the skull.

Aneuploidy: the condition of having an abnormal number of chromosomes; an example is Down syndrome, where there are three, rather than two, copies of chromosome 21.

Artificial insemination: the introduction of semen into the vagina or cervix by artificial means.

Artificial reproductive technologies (ARTs): medical treatments designed to help couples with fertility problems achieve pregnancy; involves the manipulation of both eggs and sperm; IVF is the best-known example.

AZT: azidothymidine (also called Zidovudine or Retrovir); an antiretroviral drug that inhibits the human immunodeficiency virus (HIV) that causes AIDS.

Blastocyst: an early embryo at five to seven days' gestation, after it reaches the cavity of the uterus; consists of a sphere of cells, with a fluid-filled cavity; the cells of the inner cell mass give rise to the future individual; the outer trophectoderm develops into the placenta.

Blastomere: one cell of a blastocyst.

Brainstem: the lower portion of the brain which connects with the spinal cord and controls automatic functions such as breathing and swallowing.

Cerebral hemispheres: the largest parts of the brain in humans; control higher functions of thought, memory, language, sensation and voluntary movements.

Cloning: asexual reproduction; the nucleus (and chromosomes) of an egg is replaced with the nucleus of a body cell of an adult, causing the egg to develop as if it had been fertilised without the involvement of sperm; there are two types of cloning: therapeutic (research) cloning and reproductive cloning.

Chimeric embryo: an embryo composed of a mixture of cells from different sources or species.

Chromosomes: long thread-like associations of genes found in the nucleus of a cell; consist of DNA and protein.

Consequentialism: the philosophical viewpoint which judges the rightness or wrongness of proposed courses of action on the basis of the goodness or badness of their likely outcomes.

Cystic fibrosis: a genetic disorder resulting from a single gene defect in which the sufferer's lungs, intestines and pancreas become clogged with thick mucus.

Dementia: irreversible and progressive impairment of mental functions; including intellectual deterioration, disordered personality and an inability to carry out the tasks of daily living.

Dialysis: common treatment for kidney failure, involving the use of a machine to cleanse the blood of waste products, a function usually performed by the kidney.

DNA (deoxyribose nucleic acid): a double-stranded, helical molecule found in the nucleus of a cell; carries the genetic information necessary for the organisation and functioning of most living cells and controls the inheritance of characteristics.

Donor insemination (DI): artificial insemination with the sperm from a donor.

Down Syndrome: a genetic disorder characterised by symptoms of mental retardation and possibly a variety of defects of the gut, lungs and heart; results from an extra copy of chromosome 21.

Ectopic pregnancy: development of the embryo outside the uterus.

Egg: the female gamete, also referred to as an oocyte or ovum, from a woman's ovary.

Electric shock therapy (ECT): a type of psychiatric therapy in which an electric current is briefly applied to produce a seizure; used to treat severe depression that is not responding well to other forms of treatment.

Embryo: the stage of development from fertilisation up to eight weeks' gestation in humans, by which point all the major organs have been laid down; the first two weeks after fertilisation are variously referred to as pre-embryo or preimplantation embryo.

Embryonic stem (ES) cells: stem cells derived from the inner cell mass of early embryos (blastocysts).

Enucleated egg: an egg that has had its nucleus removed.

Epididymis: Portion of the male genital tract where sperm collect after leaving the testis and sperm maturation is partially accomplished.

Fertilisation: the act of rendering gametes capable of further development; begins with contact between sperm and egg, leading to their fusion, which stimulates the completion of egg maturation.

Foetus: the developing human being from the end of the eighth week of gestation until birth.

Gamete: the mature male or female sex cell.

Gene: a unit of DNA in a chromosome; the biological unit of heredity.

Gene therapy: the replacement of a gene responsible for a disease such as cystic fibrosis by a (normal) gene in an attempt to remove that disease from the individual; this can be carried out in the embryo or in the individual after birth.

Genetic engineering: the manipulation of genetic information in an embryo in order to control the characteristics of the future individual; the term is frequently used in a negative, critical sense.

Genetic testing: a test to determine whether a person has certain gene changes (mutations) or chromosome changes which are known to cause or increase the risk for certain diseases.

Gestation: the period of development from the time of fertilisation of the egg until birth.

Higher brain death: death of the cerebral hemispheres (responsible for thinking and emotion) while the brainstem (responsible for basic functions such as breathing) is unaffected; personalistic definition of death.

Human leukocyte antigen (HLA) tissue typing: an additional step to PGD to determine whether an embryo could result in a child suitable for providing a tissue match for transplantation to an ill sibling.

Hybrid embryo: an embryo composed of a mixture of genes from different sources or species.

Immunosuppression: inhibition of the body's immune system; may be deliberately induced with drugs in preparation for organ transplantation to prevent rejection of the donor tissue.

Implantation: the embedding of the early embryo (between six and fourteen days' gestation) in the lining of the uterus (womb), so that further development of the embryo can take place.

Infertility: inability of a couple to conceive after twelve months of normal sexual practice without contraception.

Inner cell mass (ICM): the cluster of cells in a blastocyst which protrude into the fluid-filled cavity, and subsequently develop into the embryo proper; appears at five to seven days' gestation.

Intracytoplasmic sperm injection (ICSI): an artificial reproductive technique used in some cases of male infertility; involves the injection of a single sperm directly into the egg.

Intrauterine device (IUD): method of contraception in which a plastic or metal device is inserted in a woman's uterus to prevent pregnancy.

***In vitro* fertilisation (IVF):** the process of fertilising a (human) egg with a (human) sperm *in vitro* in the laboratory and therefore outside the body of the woman; embryo transfer may follow, and the term 'IVF' is used to cover both the fertilisation and the embryo transfer.

Natural family planning: method of contraception based on determination of the fertile and infertile days in a menstrual cycle by observation of the naturally occurring signs and abstinence from sexual intercourse on fertile days.

Oesophageal atresia: a condition in which the oesophagus (the muscular tube that carries food from the mouth to the stomach) fails to form properly during development.

Parkinson's disease: a progressive neurodegenerative disease characterised by motor disorders, in particular tremor and a general decrease in normal movements.

Persistent vegetative state (PVS): a condition resulting from severe damage to the higher centres of the brain; after a few months most authorities consider the condition to be permanent; the patient is unable to engage in any mental activity but retains the ability to swallow, breathe and blink, and can absorb nutrients supplied through a nasogastric tube.

Person: sometimes used as a synonym for 'human being', but increasingly used to mean a sentient being that has a concept of itself, and is (potentially) capable of reflective, rational thought.

Pre-implantation genetic diagnosis (PGD): a procedure devised to test early human embryos for serious inherited genetic conditions, with the subsequent transfer of only unaffected embryos to a woman's uterus.

Pregnancy wastage: loss of an embryo or foetus during the period of gestation; it is the failure of a fertilised egg to result in the birth of a living newborn (excluding factors such as induced abortion or use of contraception).

Prenatal diagnosis: medical tests intended to detect a disorder in the foetus during pregnancy, includes amniocentesis, ultrasound and chorionic villus sampling.

Primitive streak: a thickening of the ectoderm which appears in the human embryo at fourteen to fifteen days' gestation; often considered to represent the transition from a non-organised to an organised state during embryonic development; its appearance marks the end of the time during which research can be undertaken on embryos.

Raelians: a religious organisation which believes that scientifically advanced extraterrestrials created life on Earth through genetic engineering, and that a combination of human cloning and 'mind transfer' can provide eternal life.

Reproductive cloning: the use of somatic cell nuclear transfer (SCNT) to produce genetically identical human beings.

Research cloning: the use of somatic cell nuclear transfer (SCNT) to produce tissues for research purposes rather than complete human beings.

Rhythm method: see natural family planning.

Severe combined immune deficiency (SCID): a congenital immune disorder disease in which the body does not produce the immune cells that resist infection; children with it are susceptible to infectious disease and if untreated it is lethal within the first year or two of life.

Somatic cell nuclear transfer (SCNT): the transfer of the nucleus of a somatic (body) cell of an adult into an egg which has had its nucleus removed; also known as cloning.

Somatic cells: the ordinary cells in an organism (that is, not the reproductive cells).

Spina bifida: a congenital defect in which the spinal column fails to fuse properly during foetal development; often resulting in hydrocephalus and other neurological disorders.

Stem cells: undifferentiated cells which can divide indefinitely, and in some cases are capable of forming any cell type in the body.

Surplus embryos: embryos created as a part of fertility treatment that are left over once the treatment has finished; they are capable of development but were not implanted because more embryos were created than were ultimately required.

Surrogacy: one woman bearing a child for another woman, where the surrogate carries the embryo of the intending parents, or is artificially inseminated with sperm from the partner of the second woman; it may involve IVF.

Tay-Sachs disease: a genetic disorder resulting from a single gene defect in which lipids accumulate in the nervous tissue, resulting in death in early childhood.

Therapeutic cloning: the use of somatic cell nuclear transfer (SCNT) to produce tissues for medical purposes rather than complete human beings.

Trophectoderm: the outer cell layer of the blastocyst and the precursor of the placenta.

Uterus: hollow muscular organ in the female body, in which the fertilised egg normally becomes embedded, and in which the developing embryo and foetus is nourished.

Whole brain death: death of all of the brain, including both the cerebral hemispheres (responsible for thinking and emotion) and the brainstem; biological definition of death.

Zygote: the product of the union of the male and female gametes at fertilisation; a fertilised egg.

Further Reading

Australian Institute of Health and Welfare National Perinatal Statistics Unit and Fertility Society of Australia, *Assisted Reproduction Technology in Australia and New Zealand 2004* (Sydney: AIHW National Perinatal Statistics Unit, 2006). Available at: <www.npsu.unsw.edu.au/NPSUweb.nsf/page/art10high.htm> Accessed on 14 May 2007.

Beauchamp, T and Childress, J, *Principles of Biomedical Ethics,* fifth edition (New York: Oxford University Press, 2001).

Bergersen, F, Clarke J, Ewing P, Garrett G, and White J, *The Cloning of Human Cells: a Response to the Scientific Issues from an Ethical and Theological Perspective for the Anglican Synod of Canberra and Goulburn by a Committee*, (2002). Available at: <www.canberragoulburn.anglican.org/HTML/publications/CLONING.PDF> Accessed on 19 February 2007.

Bouma, H, Diekema, D, Langerak, E, Rottman, T, and Verhey, A, *Christian Faith, Health and Medical Practice* (Grand Rapids, Michigan: Eerdmans, 1989).

Bryant, J and Searle, J, *Life in our Hands: A Christian Perspective on Genetics and Cloning* (Leicester: Inter-Varsity Press, 2004).

Campbell, A, Gillett, G, and Jones, G, *Medical Ethics, fourth edition* (Melbourne: Oxford University Press, 2005).

Centers for Disease Control and Prevention, *2004 Assisted Reproductive Technology Success Rates: National Summary and Fertility Clinic Reports*, (Atlanta: US Department of Health and Human Services, 2006). Available at: <www.cdc.gov/ART/ART2004/index.htm> Accessed on 19 February 2007.

Church of Scotland, Church and Society Council, *Report of the Working Group on Embryo Research, Human Stem Cells and Cloned Embryos* (2006). Available at: www.srtp.org.uk/cloning.shtml Accessed on 19 February 2007.

Davies, G, *Genius, Grief and Grace: A Doctor Looks at Suffering and Success* (Fearn, Scotland: Christian Focus Publications, 2001).

Davis, R, *My Journey into Alzheimer's Disease* (Wheaton, Illinois: Tyndale House, 1989).

Deane-Drummond, C and Scott, PM (editors), *Future Perfect?* (London: T&T Clark International, 2006).

Deane-Drummond, C, *Genetics and Christian Ethics* (Cambridge: Cambridge University Press, 2006).

Guillebaud, J, *Contraception: Your Questions Answered,* third edition (London: Churchill Livingstone, 1999).

Hatcher, RA, Trussell, J, Stewart, F, Cates, W Jr, Stewart GK, Guest, F, and Kowal, D (editors), *Contraceptive Technology,* seventeenth edition (New York: Ardent Media, 1998).

Hui, EC, *At the Beginning of Life: Dilemmas in Theological Bioethics* (Downers Grove, Illinois: Inter-Varsity Press, 2002).

Human Fertilisation and Embryology Authority, *Facts and Figures* (London: HFEA, 2007). Available at: <www.hfea.gov.uk/cps/rde/xchg/SID-3F57D79B-BF1FB0FD/hfea/hs.xsl/406.html> Accessed on 19 February 2007.

Human Fertilisation and Embryology Authority, *The HFEA Guide to Infertility 2006/07* (London: HFEA, 2007). Available at: <www.hfea.gov.uk/cps/rde/xchg/SID-3F57D79B-1802BEFA/hfea/hs.xsl/1131.html> Accessed on 19 February 2007.

Jones, DG, 'The human embryo: From oblivion to meaningful life', *Science and Christian Belief* 6 (1994): 3–19.

Jones, DG, *Valuing People: Human Value in a World of Medical Technology* (Carlisle: Paternoster Press, 1999).

Jones, DG, *Clones: The Clowns of Technology?* (Carlisle: Paternoster Press, 2001).

Jones, DG, *Designers of the Future: Who Should Make the Decisions?* (Oxford: Monarch Books, 2005).

Jones, DG, 'Responses to the human embryo and embryonic stem cells: Scientific and theological assessments', *Science and Christian Belief* 17 (2005): 199–222.

Jones, DG, 'Enhancement: are ethicists excessively influenced by baseless speculations?', *Medical Humanities* 32 (2006): 77–81.

Jones, DG and Towns, CR, 'Navigating the quagmire: the regulation of human embryonic stem cell research', *Human Reproduction* 21 (2005): 1113–6.

King, J, *William Cowper: A Biography* (Durham: Duke University Press, 1986).

Lammers, SE and Verhey, A (editors), *On Moral Medicine* (Grand Rapids, Michigan: Eerdmans, 1987).

McCullagh, P, *Brain Dead, Brain Absent, Brain Donors: Human Subjects or Human Objects?* (Chichester: John Wiley & Sons, 1993).

Miller, R, *Straight Talking about Mental Illness,* second edition (Christchurch: Schizophrenia Fellowship of New Zealand, 2000).

Mitchell, CB, 'The president should have consulted Solomon', The Center for Bioethics and Human Dignity, posted 11 August 2001.

Available at: <www.cbhd.org/resources/stemcells/mitchell_2001-08-11.htm> Accessed on 19 February 2007.

Nuffield Council on Bioethics, *Critical Care Decisions in Fetal and Neonatal Medicine: Ethical Issues* (London: Nuffield Council on Bioethics, 2006). Available at: <www.nuffieldbioethics.org/go/ourwork/prolonginglife/publication_406.html> Accessed on 19 February 2007.

Peterson, JC, *Genetic Turning Points* (Grand Rapids, Michigan: Eerdmans, 2001).

Smedes, L, *Mere Morality* (Tring: Lion, 1983).

Waters, B and Cole-Turner, R (editors), *God and the Embryo* (Washington DC: Georgetown University Press, 2003).

Wield, C, *Life After Darkness: A Doctor's Journey through Severe Depression* (Oxford: Radcliffe, 2006).

Wyatt, J, *Matters of Life and Death* (Leicester: Inter-Varsity Press, 1998).

Wyatt, J, 'Neonatal ethics', *CMF Files* 27 (2004). Available at: <www.cmf.org.uk/literature/content.asp?context=article&id=143> Accessed on 19 February 2007.

Index

CPSIA information can be obtained
at www.ICGtesting.com
Printed in the USA
LVHW03s0138160618
580660LV00002B/33/P

9 781920 691752